Mark S Williams

F/V Black Sheep

MARK S. WILLIAMS

F/V Black Sheep

FISHING VESSEL BLACK SHEEP
Sometimes it's easier to die than to live.

Gloucester, Massachusetts
2006

"Pirates of the Maine Coast" was previously printed as "Imprisoned in Maine" in **Windchill: Crime Stories by New England Writers,** published by Level Best Books, www.LevelBestBooks.com.

This book was printed in the United States of America.

To order additional copies of this book visit fvBlackSheep.com or write to:
Silver Perch Press
136 Bass Avenue
Gloucester, Massachusetts 01930
Email: msblacksheep@adelphia.net

Author's web site: www.fvBlackSheep.com
Author's web site designed and sponsored by Parlez-Moi Press

Book design and typography: Valentine-Design.com of Gloucester
Cover design: Kathleen Valentine
Front cover photograph of f/v Black Sheep by Jay Albert
Back cover author's photograph and Man at the Wheel by Kathleen Valentine

Dedicated to the more than five thousand Gloucester fishermen, who sailed out of Gloucester Harbor since the beginning, to make a living for their families, and never came back. Sail on, guys.

Died while this book was being written:
Steve Waldron, fisherman, friend, and one crackerjack marine mechanic
Christopher Varchos, decorated hero of World War II
Gerald Vahe, friend
Geoffrey Thomas, captain of the Blivyfish—may you have five keepers in every trap from now on.

TABLE OF CONTENTS

THE AFTERNOON OF THE DOLPHIN

Storms in the Northern Hemisphere rotate counter-clockwise. A northeast wind denotes a passing low, a storm if you will, a rough ocean and a day off for a thirty-six foot lobster boat. A "blow day" fishermen call it. On this day, however, the storm was mostly over and I had been hauling lobster gear by myself for the last seven hours. I ran my boat, Black Sheep, in from my outermost trawls at the range. The two lighthouses that stand on Thacher Island a few hundred yards apart north and south, are aligned roughly east and west at the range—exactly five and a quarter miles from the beach.

A light rain falls and the day is gray. It's a day that accentuates the colors that would be unpretentious on a sunny day. I'm wet but warm. I call that "acceptable wet". I wear only the bottom of a Farmer John Rubber Grundy, the rubber suit that all fishermen wear. To wear the top, or rain coat, would be far too hot—hauling lobster traps is too labor intensive to be done while covered in rubber. I have always preferred wet to hot.

Even in the rain the view is enough to make you believe in God. Good Harbor Beach is about a mile off my starboard. The building we have always called the Hess House sits high on the rocks at the mouth of the tidal river known as the Creek. The wooden footbridge that crosses it from the road to the beach, supported by two piles of rip-rap, has people on it headed for a walk on the beach in the rain. A hundred yards or so up the road is a large white stucco-sided building. It's the last house on Bass Avenue. The Williams Guest House sits shimmering in a light coat of rain. The area I view now is where I have spent most of my life and learned many of the lessons that will serve me well on this day of days.

The marsh grass in the tidal basin behind it is bent to the west by the northeast breeze. It is brown but appears golden at this distance.

The tidal water that covered it a short time before has succumbed to the force of the moon's gravity and recedes, draining back to the ocean from which it came—as it has in cycles, called tides, for millions of years. The creek drains away from the swimming hole known as The Warm Pot, scoured out where two small creeks intersect and continue on to the sea.

Behind the marsh sits a complex of condominiums. They sit on a former pig farm that small boys, armed with BB guns, traversed in search of game and high adventure not so long ago. Behind it, and to the right, is a grave—my father. Before this day is done, he will save my life, as he has before. He lies near his new friend, Sergeant Dana, a veteran of World War II.

As the blue-gray water meets the beach, it rises up metamorphosing, turning white, and smashing with a gentle roar. The sound reaches me in seconds. A large black dog runs left to right forcing the gulls that all face the same way into the northeast wind. Up into the wind they fly e-e-e-e-e'ing as only seagulls can. A large V of Canada Geese glides down into the marsh smashing into the water and honking.

During the summer thousands of people bask in the sun and frolic in the surf. Half naked females walk the water's edge. Children run to and fro and try to capture any living thing in the creek when the tide is out. With but a few people walking on it this day, the beach has the ambiance of an empty football stadium.

The rock that hides just beneath the water a few hundred yards behind Salt Island forces the water over it to turn white every few seconds. The "red nun" buoy behind it disappears in every wave and pops up like the nose of an emerging Polaris missile in the trough between each wave. It warns the unwary of the rock and Salt Island beyond. Cormorants sit on the west end of Salt Island, the dark rock stained white by them, contrasting sharply with their black feathers.

When you spend a lot of time on the water something that doesn't belong stands out. Something doesn't fit. From three hundred yards I close on a UFO—Unidentified Floating Object. At fifty it makes sense—a baby dolphin tangled in a floating net. Draggers. It's bad enough that they kill too many little fish compared to the number of legal sized ones that they catch, but they treat the ocean like their own private trash dump.

I lean over with the gaff and, as I pull the net clear, I see many other dolphins surround the little one. When I pull the net off of the baby, it squeaks and four adult dolphins simultaneously leap into the air and splash down, showering the boat and me. One swims right up to the baby and, turning on its side, looks at me with big soft eyes. The mother, I guess. She and the others form around the baby and swim off. That doesn't happen every day.

I head off toward my next trawl.

I circle the upwind, the double-buoyed, east end buoy of my trawl. I use the wind to stop the boat saving wear and tear on my transmission. I prepare to haul the best trawl of the day which is, of course, the last trawl of the day.

The Black Sheep is rigged right. That means the davit off of which the speed block—or pulley—hangs is on the right side. The buoy is hauled out of the water via a gaff, usually a hockey stick with a hook duct-taped to its end (unless you are a lobsterman in a Peter Benchley novel where a boat hook was used—trust me, hockey sticks are the norm.) Wise lobstermen always have two on-board. There are enough ways to cut short a day of lobster fishing, lack of a gaff isn't a very bright one. Sorry, Peter, no self-respecting lobster man would use a boat hook.

The buoy line underneath the buoy is gaffed and the buoy is pulled aboard and the boat continues on by the pick-up spot and leaves enough slack in the buoy line so that it is easy to pull the buoy onboard. A handle on the dash is twisted and the hypso-lytic hauler is engaged. Two steel disks, twelve inches in diameter, are screwed together as one. Both plates have lips all around the periphery like two coffee saucers back-to-back forming a groove that the rope will stick in. It spins counterclockwise. The buoy line is inserted in the groove at about nine o'clock and it stays engaged until about three o'clock where an obstruction in the groove, called a "knife", pops it out. The rope piles on the deck directly below the hauler. Smart fishermen kick it behind them toward the stern. Dumb, lazy lobstermen stand on it and work off of it. In short, the hydro-slave, as we call it, is an automatic rope-hauler. By picking up the upwind buoy, you let the forces that be work with you. Drift-ing down the trawl from trap to trap, you let the wind move your boat instead of the engine. Novi style boats are tailor made for this. The high bow acts like a sail in the wind. When you lobster alone, you quickly discover that there is enough to do without putting the boat in and out of gear, powering into the wind, and jacking it up the trawl line, instead of merely drifting free of charge and hauling as you go.

The first lobster trap (or "pot") announces its arrival by smacking into the side of your boat. You flip the hauler on, brace your knees against the boat, and lean out (not a good idea to lean too far), grabbing the bridle, a section of rope tied cross-wise on the trap. The bridle is tied to the gangeon, a short rope that connects the trap that you are hauling to the ground line, the line that all the traps are connected to . As you haul the trap aboard, you spin it to the left. The door on the top of the trap is rigged to open away from you for easy access. Next, you simultaneously take up the strain on the gangeon and flick the hauler back on, while you guide the knot into the hauler spinning it until the knife knocks it out. The hauler can't haul knots and will spit them out unless you grab the hauling gangeon and put a strain on it.

As the door to the trap is opened the hauler is left on at a speed learned by years of experience and continues to haul traps onto the boat. The first priority is to quickly remove the large, or legal-sized, lobsters before they bust each other up. I put them on a table with many separate compartments called a "culling table". I put them all the same way and the dividers keep the lobsters from crunching each other up on the way to the cooking pot. Next, I remove the lobsters that require measuring—most will be "shorts". They get flicked back over the side—at least on most boats. Next any collateral fish that I am not going to eat get thrown back. Finally, a mesh bag filled with herring is placed on the bait hook and the trap is closed. Oily fish with loads of Omega oil is better for bait than white fish. Lobsters have very healthy hearts. The bait hangs between the two openings to the trap called kitchen heads. A lobster will usually enter, eat, and then exit the same way. Sometimes another lobster will enter the trap and lobster number one will flip backwards, up and into the parlor head, or rear part of the trap. Ninety-nine percent of the time, this is how lobsters get caught. Trust me. I burnt hundreds of tanks of air trying to get an edge on my fellow lobstermen by diving and observing. I never did.

The lobster traps I fish are essentially the same as they were a hundred years ago. They are not very efficient. If they were, given the number of traps in the water, the lobster would have gone extinct years ago. Trust me, folks, on an average day I throw back twenty times the amount of poundage that ends up in the trap compared to what I sell.

By now the hauler has hauled enough ground line so that the first trap in can be taken across the boat to the port side where it is placed on the trap table and be the last trap off. The rest of the traps in this ten pot trawl will be placed behind it down to the stern across from it and up the starboard side. The last trap in will be on the boat under the davit. It will be the first to go back into the water taking the rest, one at a time (usually). It is called "setting back". As I arrive back at the davit, the next trap bangs into the boat. For reasons soon to be apparent, I remember this particular trawl in detail.

A northeast wind creates such shitty sea conditions, it is usually a day off when it bangs. It never blows ten to twenty, as predicted. It is fifteen to twenty-five, with gusts to thirty-five. Because I always pick up the upwind buoy, my east-end buoy line is seldom pulled through the hauler and cleaned off. It's loaded with all kinds of sea life—sea weed and assorted shit that gets thrown all over the place, but mostly splashes on my face. Besides good luck, this is the reason I wear a baseball cap backwards. If you wear it the right way the visor continually hits the speedblock as you work which is very aggravating. Also, it really sucks when you get back shore-side and, while engaging a honey in a little conversation, a little crab falls out of your hair. Most don't wait for an explanation.

About halfway through the trawl a herring gull appears out of nowhere and lands gracefully on my deck near the bow. He keeps his footing precariously on the moving deck. Gracefully, he turns his rear to me and squirts a great, big, runny, white dump all over my nice clean foredeck. It runs down the slope to the cabin like a rapid, frothy white river. It's such a pleasant thing to watch. He looks at me stupidly and emits that dumb e-e-e-e-e-e that only seagulls can generate. It has the same effect on me as fingernails on a chalkboard. Spencer Tracey hit it right on the head in Captains

Courageous when he made fun of John Barrymore's laugh—"E-e-e-e-e—you laugh like a seagull." Kipling must have spent time on a fishing boat or around fishermen. Over the years my mild dislike of seagulls has developed into intense hatred. I abhor the things.

Once, while in my truck on a shore run, a seagull with a broken wing appeared in the road—not an uncommon sight around Gloucester. The things are so stupid they fly into the ground on a regular basis. A little girl, with her mom and dad on the sidewalk, was trying to lure the poor, injured bird out of the road and out of harm's way. Fount of human kindness that I am, I decided to forego my usual course of action—honest. I cut hard to the right and, of course, so did the bird. It popped under my right front tire like a basketball. Poor little girl and mom and dad were upset, to say the least. The little girl fell to her knees in tears and her Dad comforted her while making hand gestures at me. I felt bad, really. Of course, I was laughing so hard I almost drove the truck onto the rocks three times in the next few minutes.

My next trap has two large females in it. I grab them in my rubber-gloved hands. The size of rubber gloves is critical—too big and they can catch in the hauler breaking fingers, which makes slow going for the rest of the day. Gloves that are too tight make it tough to work. Sorel #6 is my size.

Before I flip the lobsters over to check for eggs I know they are females. The female is inherently more violent than the males and needs to be separated before they can smash up the other lobsters.

"E-e-e-e-e-e-e," comes blasting at me from the feathered rat on my bow. I launch a very hard-shelled, short lobster from the hauling station. It flies across the deck, through the cabin and out its window across the deck and smashes with a resounding crunch into the bird's head. He takes to the air in a flurry. In thirty minutes he will return—that is the memory span of a seagull. The next trap has two cod in it. I have no market for a few cod and drop them overboard. After all, I'm not a dragger, why kill everything?

To this day, I wonder why I took off my Grundys. I never do that. I always wait until the last trawl has been set. I'm a creature of habit except when someone, usually a brother lobsterman, threatens to kill me. Then I vary my habits a little. But this day something makes me take off my rubbers. I swear to God there was a faint whiff of whiting in the air.

The last trap sits baited on the trap table. Nine others are around the boat behind it. The buoy line to it runs to the single west end buoy, still in the water to save time—there is no need to haul it. I head due east. The last trap out will be the first trap in. The buoy line attached to the last trap in/first trap out draws tight and drags behind the boat. Hard-bottom (meaning, rocks) is where the lobsters are currently residing and up they loom on the sounder—four to six footers. I pass Donny Kangas's west buoy and continue on to his east. He runs five pot trawls. His double east pops up. He doesn't use two buoys, he merely sticks a piece of Styrofoam on the stick which saves the frugal Finn a little money. It's as good as a buoy. Anything added to a buoy differentiates it as the east end, an old rubber glove, a plastic bleach bottle, a plastic oil container. Hell, one guy uses condoms stuck on the top of the stick which passes through the buoy. Unused I trust.

I pass his east end and give him about a first down (that's ten yards for you foreigners) and push the trap on the table over the side. I go forward into the cabin and steam my boat due east. Something pulls on my right foot but I dismiss it because I'm busy looking for other trawls. I'm trying not to set on anybody. As the eighth trap slides down the table and into the water, I lean forward to write down the loran coordinates. I've done this a thousand times....BANG!

An invisible monster grabs my right leg just above the ankle. Like a bear trap it smashes into me, knocking me off my feet, hurling me to the deck, sucking all of my breath out. I shoot the length of the deck exploding into the stern, blasted into a state of semi-consciousness. Lobstermen call this a "Gloucester sleigh ride". The monster, with every ounce of it's existence, tries to pull me up over the stern and give me an express ride to the bottom, twenty fathoms below. Dazed, I manage to brace my butt against the stern and grab onto the protruding lip. It takes all my strength to keep from being pulled up and over.

Imagine you are standing on the sidewalk and a car with a rope tied to its bumper and attached to your lower leg takes off and drags you twenty feet, smashes you into a four foot high brick wall, and continues dragging you against it. You know that if you go over that wall you will drown in 120 feet of water. Slowly my head stops spinning and little by little things come into focus. I look down at my right leg and what happened is only too obvious. I had stepped on the pile of rope under the hauler as I set back, just as I had a million times before. A half loop of rope had somehow gotten on top of another half loop and I had stepped right through both. The traps in the water, exerting thousands of pounds of pressure, had pulled it taut and cinched it around my calf. It was a book-perfect example of a clove hitch knot. The clove hitch is a slip knot, this means it doesn't tighten down on itself. Instead it cinches down on whatever object is between both loops—a horse post, a railing, my leg. Fishermen call it a "knife knot" and the only way to undo it is with a rope wrench, a knife. The dragging traps exert thousands of pounds of pressure on my leg and I almost pass out from the pain as the boat chugs on at four or five knots.

If I go over the side, I'm dead. My breath comes in gasps.

Control your breathing, I remind myself, you've been here before. Think! Reason your way out of this situation. Breathe slow and deep and you'll live. Breathe quickly and shallow and you'll hyper-ventilate—which leads to panic and death.

At any moment I can be ripped up over the stern and take an express ride to hell—to the cold and the dark, to drown in the blackness. I face the four greatest fears of all men—being underwater, in the dark, unable to breathe and face to face with the unknown.

Knife, idiot. In your right rear pocket. I'd forgotten I have a knife in my right pants pocket. That's what panic does, it makes you stupid. I release my grip on the lip of the boat and reach back. Bad idea. As I reach back I am jerked up on the stern and almost out of the boat. The heels of my feet catch on the lip saving me from going over. I battle my way back and down inside. It takes a full five minutes to get back where I was and I am exhausted. Panting I hold on for my life. I can't feel my right foot. Why? I look down and my vision narrows to a tunnel. All I can see is the clove hitch above my right ankle. Where did that come from? That must be the problem—what's all that red stuff? It's blood ... it's my blood. I continue the battle to control my breathing. It's weird, I can feel every part of my body magnified to the tenth power. I can feel my heart banging, my blood pumping through me. I grab the lip as hard as I can with my left hand and snake my right hand back to my rear pocket. It's empty. It's a worse feeling than finding your wallet missing, trust me. My senses are all magnified intensely. The knife is on the deck, a yard in front of me. Seconds pass like hours. My leg is swollen and bloody. The nylon is stretched as hard as wire cable. It has eaten through my pants and there is much blood, my foot is twice its normal size and feels like it is about to explode. The blood, mixed with the saltwater on the deck, expands in an ever-growing pool around me. The pain is agonizing....

Did you ever think you were going to die? I don't mean the nano second before a car wreck, have you ever had fifteen or twenty minutes thinking every second is going to be your last one in life as we know it. What's it like? What do you think about? Would your whole life pass in front of you? Mine did. Deep in my brain parts of it begin to burn as if coming to life for the first time. Somewhere in the two-thirds of my previously unknown and unused brain, the sights and sounds, and even smells, of my whole life begin to shoot by at light speed and yet I remember them in detail. Just that fast the pain stops. It turns right off. I feel high, oh, so much higher than I've ever felt artificially. I am flying, brother, soaring with the clouds underneath me. And a smell—it's the damndest thing—what is that smell? It descends on me like a thick cloud. What the hell? Where have I smelled that before? It's over-powering—nice, sweet, intoxicating. It is so permeating it becomes difficult to breathe through my nose and I open my mouth to inhale through both. My God. It smells like the essence of female, just washed and standing in the shower. Am I losing my mind? Here you are in a world of shit and what's on your mind?

What the..... He stands in front of me in blue corduroy work clothes. "Ted" is written over his left breast pocket. My father. And it comes to me, the smell is fish—whiting. Whiting doesn't smell like fish, I swear to God. It smells exactly like what I thought it was. He lowers his glasses. If he had been any closer I would have, from experience, ducked.

"Ma-ah-k," he says pointing at me with his right index finger, "I have a task for you." He gives me a look that would make a man with a gun go for it.

Suddenly, it's the early Sixties. I am thirteen years old working for the first time at the Empire Fish Company at Harbor Loop in Gloucester, Massachusetts.

I was the youngest teenager you can be and was in my rebellious stage—a real pain in the ass to my parents. To be in one's rebellious stage in the Williams house was to be in a very precarious stage to be sure. I was a "D" student and when it came to school, I just didn't give a shit. My father had decided to put me to work for the summer despite the fact that I was considerably underage which was against the law. In and around the Empire Fish Company, my father was the law. He was the law and that meant wise-assed thirteen year olds could shovel shit, which is just about what my first day on the job would entail. The lessons I learned that summer were to keep me alive again and again through this day and throughout my life.

PART ONE
GROWING UP IN GLOUCESTER

BLANK

CHAPTER 1 - EMPIRE FISH, EARLY 1960S

"This is what I want you to do. I have a job that will require keen wit, intellectual stamina but, most of all, a strong back." He motioned to a pile of fish "gurry", a putrid mixture of fish heads, eyes, guts, smashed fish bodies, and, of course, grey-brownish fish shit.

"I want this pile—to make it as perspicuous as possible we will call it Pile A—moved in its entirety to here." He walked twenty feet across the wharf and, pulling a six-inch filleting knife out of a vertical wood beam, flicked it into the wharf where it stuck straight up vibrating. "We will now designate this Point B. Do you understand so far?"

I mumbled something.

"Speak up. Separate your teeth and speak clearly."

"Yeah," I replied.

"No, no, no. It is 'yes, sir' or 'yes, father', not 'yeah'." He gave me one of those melt-the-paint-off-a-house looks.

"Yes, sir," I replied out of fear. "Except what does 'perspicuous' mean?"

"Very good. 'Perspicuous' means simple. If you don't understand a word or what I want, ask. That's how you learn." He picked up a fish shovel and held it out. "Your tool for completion of this most important task, is this shovel."

"Why does this pile need to be moved?" I asked innocently.

He lowered his glasses again. Oh shit, I thought.

"I am a man. I do not ordinarily explain myself to children. However, I will make an exception just this once." He looked me up and down, studying me. "I am the big dog, your boss. YOU are the little dog, the puppy, my employee. Your place in the big plan as my son or employee is to do what I say, when I say it, and in a manner in which I tell you to or you will suffer a world of hurt. Is that real fucking clear?"

When he used the f-word the situation was even more serious

than when he lowered his glasses.

"Congratulations, you are an S.O.B."

"What?"

"A Son Of the Boss." He laughed. "Do you understand EXACTLY what I want done?"

"Yes, sir," I replied.

"Begin."

I shoved the shovel into the smelly pile and dragged it across the wharf near the knife and dumped it. As I dragged the shovel back toward the pile he passed me.

"This isn't so hard," I murmured over my shoulder. Even as I was speaking a battle raged inside me. My brain battled with my mouth to stay still. Unfortunately, my mouth won—which it does to this day.

He stopped. Shit, I thought, I did it again.

"Oh my, I am so happy that you find this task to your liking and are so sure of its simplicity and are so certain of its completion considering that you have never shoveled gurry before in your entire short life." He could go from speaking like the educated man he was to an ignorant wharf worker and back in a nanosecond.

"I certainly hope you find your job here at Empire Fish to be rewarding and intellectually stimulating."

I buried the shovel in the pile.

"You can work at your own speed."

"That sounds good," I said.

"Why, I'm just tickled pink that this job pleases you," he said. "Oh, gosh, there is one minor detail I left out. How remiss of me. It is now 1:30 in the afternoon. My job is done at 5:00 sharp. If yours is not done by then, you can walk home. This will no doubt result in me receiving a severe chastisement from your mother. This will not please me, do you understand?"

"Yeah."

He just looked at me harder.

"Yes, sir. I'll be done by five."

"Talk is cheap, actions are what count. Do remove the knife from the floor and return it to its proper place." He motioned for me to come closer. "Shoveling gurry is a ball-breaker. Pace yourself. It's better to pace yourself and work continuously than to burn yourself out and have to stop and rest. Figure out what pace you can work at and keep moving. The water fountain is over there." He pointed. "You can dehydrate long before your body tells you. If you get dehydrated you will not be able to work and this will not please me so drink more water than you want. That way you won't have to play catch-up, a game you will loose."

"What does dehydrate mean?"

"Excellent. It means a lack of water." He looked at me. "Now explain to me exactly what you are to do."

"I am to move Pile A to where it becomes Pile B by 5 pm."

"Correct. Now I've given you hints but it is up to you to determine exactly how you accomplish this task. It's your—key word coming up—responsibility. Proceed." And he walked off.

He would explain exactly what he wanted from a worker. As soon as he got a "yes, I understand" he would leave. If it wasn't done correctly on his return, you got yelled at. On occasion, if he failed to explain himself and the worker screwed up he would stop whatever he was doing, take the blame and work alongside the person until he was caught up. He didn't care if the worker was male, female, white, pink, or a left-handed hermaphrodite. In his domain at Empire Fish he was King. You understood your job, you did your job, or you got the fuck out of HIS plant. It was just that simple.

Gurry could best be described as the Material from Hell when it comes to shoveling it, particularly twenty feet from Point A to Point B. First it is very heavy, like very wet snow. Second, it won't stay on the shovel. I tried carrying it a few feet in the air—no good. Most of a shovelful would end up as a trail from A to B. Next I tried dragging a shovelful. No good. Easier—but, again, half the gurry would slide off. Next I tried pushing the shovel. Bingo! As long as I kept a certain amount of headway up ninety percent stayed on the shovel. In fifteen minutes my clothes were soaked through and I was half-blind from sweat in my eyes. As I moved the gurry I began to think of an easier way to move this shit. I kept knocking my baseball cap off. I turned it around, a habit of mine until the present day. When I wear a baseball cap backwards, no harm can befall me. And I can get the job done no matter what it is. Lots of people ask me why I always have a baseball cap on backwards. It comes from almost dying and not—it's a good luck charm.

Like I said, no harm can befall me when my cap is on backwards. I don't give ten fucks how dumb it looks, it's a fisherman thing.

You need to raise your voice to be heard over the machinery on the wharf of Empire Fish Company. The two electric winches hummed as they pulled the rope attached to large canvas barrels that would disappear into a large hatch passing into the bowels of the fishing boat tied at the dock. The squeaking of the winch, the humming of the rope, and the winding through the pulley was musical. The barrels would reappear in a short time brimming with whiting some falling off on the trip back to the dock. A lumper, whose job was to move fish from boat to wharf, on an elevated platform would wind the rope three times clockwise around the spinning drum called, very politically incorrectly, a "nigger head".

In a mild attempt to explain this slight, the wharf words did change with the times. The winch evolved over time to an "African-American head", to a "head of color", to a "black head", and finally, joining the twenty-first century, just plain old "head". Well, at least the wharf workers didn't bring the heads from Africa as slaves, as my country did—they just used politically incorrect terms for a winch. Men everywhere shout at one another, some in English and Italian, others in Portuguese and some in the language of the wharf.

"Hohay" from the hold of a boat means the canvas barrel is full. The lumper in the hold had filled it. Now the lumper above takes up slack and hauls it out. It will fly up and swing to the wharf where it is dumped onto a conveyor belt that is lined with men separating ice from fish as it races into Empire to be processed. This procedure will be repeated non-stop until the boat is empty. It is hard physical work and all the lumpers have bulging muscles and sweat profusely. Most have a cigarette clenched between their lips as they work. The wooden floor of the Plant, as the old man called Empire, was wet. Ice chunks were tossed all over by the apron-clad men who stood along the conveyor, picking them out and tossing them to where they crunched underfoot. The ice, combined with the fish guts, gurry, and small whiting, made the footing treacherous and only an idiot would traverse it with his hands in his pockets. Even now, when I find myself walking on ice with my hands in my pockets, I can hear my father scream, "Get your hands out of your pockets before you fall and break your arm."

"Alright, for Christ's sake," I always reply, which is fine until people nearby look at me like I'm crazy and then quickly look the other way.

The mildly sweet smell of whiting is, to this day, my favorite fragrance. It isn't a "fishy" smell but is oceanic, erotic, and very feminine—though I'm not dumb enough to blurt that out in romantic moments.

All over the plant men move things on forklifts which dart to and fro balancing their loads on two iron tongs elevated a few feet in front of them. Large dump trucks move backwards and forwards, air brakes hissing loudly, crunching pieces of ice. At a quick glance it appears to be total confusion. Yelling and hand signals seem to be the only means of communication. As I dragged shovelfuls of gurry across the dock, it all began to make sense.

Many apron-clad men, and a few women, stand on an elevated platform where a conveyor whizzes past in front of them full of whiting which they pluck off and place in another slotted conveyor moving faster just behind it. For diversion, small, flat fish are tossed like Frisbees at the flat metal wall in such a way that they stick. He who sticks the most, wins. This conveyor carries the fish into a machine which cuts off their heads and eviscerates each fish. The fish then fall into a large vat filled with brine which cleans them. A man with large biceps using a big dip net takes them from that vat and deposits them on another conveyor which moves them to the next room. Many females wearing hair-nets place them in individual boxes and move them to another conveyor where they are run through a machine which wraps them in brightly colored paper with the Empire logo. Ka-chink, ka-chink, it sings. From there they are stacked in metal trays on wooden pallets. When the pallets are full a forklift appears. If the forklift doesn't show up right on cue, the driver gets on my father's shit list. This was not a good list to be on. They were taken to the freezer, frozen and then trucked all over the country.

On one of my water breaks I noticed a man surrounded by all the girls packing fish into boxes. He had a white girl's apron on and a hair net. His back was to me but he was mimicking their limp hand movements. Hell, he even packed fish like the girls.

What a pussy, I thought, who the hell would work a girl's job?

He was laughing and joking and talking with the girls who all laughed and joked back. He was just one of the girls, the veritable center of attention. Then he turned around and I was shocked. There stood my father the boss of Empire Fish company, former football all-state twice in High School, star running back at Boston College and in the National Football League—the toughest man on the waterfront. He wore bright red lipstick (I hoped he borrowed it), white makeup powder (I hoped he borrowed it), a hair net, and had two towels stuffed down the front of his shirt forming two large breasts. With respect to all women present, he was hands-down, the ugliest female there—or on the face of the planet, for that matter.

All the girls were laughing uproariously and yet every hand visible had a fish or two in it. The line was boxing fish at Warp Factor Nine. He winked at me and went back to joking and packing fish with that limp wrist motion. Every now and then he'd throw his head back like he was fixing his hair. He could do any job in the whole place and do it better than anyone else. Packing fish was a girl's job in the early Sixties—men did not do girl's jobs. But he did it for the girls's morale at the worst time of the day, the last two hours when everyone was beat. He didn't care one bit. I'd venture to say no one laughed at him in his lipstick and hairnet—at least not twice.

"Every job in this plant is as important as any other," he used to say. If he wasn't doing his foreman's job you could find him somewhere in the plant working with the troops. The effect on morale was staggering, particularly from three to quitting time when everyone was far to right of a little tired. If dressing and acting like a woman made things a little easier on the girls during the last two grueling hours of the day, he looked on it as part of his job.

To a thirteen year old boy, the workings of the Plant were fascinating.

By this time I was dying. I was soaked with sweat, my underwear had chaffed my groin which burnt from the salt. It stung like bees with each movement. I drank as much water as I could and was still thirsty. He did warn me.

A dump truck backed up to Pile B and stopped, it's air brakes hissing. I was moving the gurry to where it could be reached by a small conveyor into the truck. Gee, and all this while I thought the old man was having me move it for shits and giggles. I had purpose. I had reason. But most importantly, I had only an hour left until five and fully half of the pile is still in Pile A status.

The driver of the truck jumped out. "Low man on the totem pole?" he shouted.

I shrugged.

"He usually puts two men on a pile this big."

Somehow this did not surprise me.

"Hi. I'm Larry Fields," he said extending his hand which I shook.

"Mark Williams," I said.

"Aren't you a little young to work here?"

"Four years."

"Are you his son?"

"Yes."

"Well, that explains it," he said. "You got a long way to go before five."

"Yep."

"Sorry, kid, better you than me. Your first day and you got the worst job in the plant. Why does that not surprise me?" He laughed. "I have to make a run." He jumped back in his truck and, with a slushing of air brakes, he drove off. The wharf shook as he pulled away.

I took a break, propped up by the shovel. I was soaked in sweat and breathing as fast as I could. He appeared out of nowhere. I really hated it when he did that. It was kind of startling, especially when he had boobs and makeup on, ensuring that everyone on the entire wharf was watching him and, of course, me.

"You are aware that you have a snowball's chance in hell of finishing on time, don't you?"

"The truck driver said you usually put two men on a pile this big."

"He did, did he? How unfortunate for you. I am just so frightfully sorry." He talked loud enough for everyone on the wharf to hear, of course. "Do you feel unduly picked on? Persecuted? How unfortunate for you. Poor little Markey, my gosh, I am driven to tears. Boo-hoo-hoo." He had the whole wharf laughing.

Prick, I thought. I had a very pleasant fleeting vision flash through my head. It consisted of the shovel I was holding smashing into the back of his head and him falling forward into the fish shit. God, it was pleasurable, orgasmic even—albeit quick.

"Come here," he commanded pointing to the wharf in front of him. He pulled his paper boobs out dropping them on the wharf, threw the hairnet down and wiped the makeup off on his sleeve. I stood in front of him. He took a knee so his face was level with mine. He looked at me hard with a look that penetrated straight through me. He moved his glasses forward on his nose.

Oh, fuck, I thought, why did I drop my shovel?

"Were you thinking of whacking your poor old father with that shovel?"

Double fuck. He's a goddamn mind-reader.

"No," I said meekly.

"Liar," he shot back. "Well, there ain't one goddamn man and probably a few women what haven't wanted to go upside my head with a shovel at one time or other and deservedly so. Why should you be any different?" He laughed. "One guy even succeeded."

"What happened?" I blurted.

"He made the fatal mistake of not killing me."

"What happened to him?"

"At present, you have no need to know the particulars. Listen and listen close. Life is far from fair and the sooner you figure that out the better and it's my job to help you. You got a bad deal today. Tough. Boys pussy out, men do their best—they deal with it." He looked at me. "Work sucks but we all have to do it. What you want to do is find something you don't mind doing, or even like to do, that you can make a living at. This would be lucky and rare. If you can do this you will be better off than ninety percent of the people in the world."

I looked at my father and nodded.

"Look around you," he said. "Do you want to do shit like this for the rest of your life?"

"Nope," I said.

"You mean you don't want to work for the rest of your life like you have today?"

"Nope."

"What?"

"No, sir."

"Excuse me, I can't quite hear you." He cupped his ear.

"No, sir!" I yelled.

"I want to see you apply yourself in school a lot harder next fall or you will be doing shit like this for the rest of your life. Now enough lessons for one day. I have a Plant to run and you have a pile to move."

He stood and, as he turned to leave he tapped his forehead.

"Think," he said.

Think? What the hell does he mean?

Halfway between Pile A and Pile B a little bomb exploded in my mind. Doing really back breaking manual labor is very conducive to creative thinking about how to get the job done more easily. On the other side of the wharf a man with a hose was moving a pile of ice across the floor and down a hole into the harbor. There was another hose right next to me. By twisting the nozzle, the velocity of the water coming out could increase to the point where it would push me right back on my butt—it was that powerful. In minutes I was moving Pile A in a veritable river into Pile B!

Another dull light on the tree came on and I put three wooden racks down around Pile B in a crude semi-circle. When a few feet of gurry piled up in front of it I shoveled it up and onto the pile. It was five times as fast as dragging one shovelful at a time. Lifting a shovelful of gurry is a bitch because you have to move fast or lose half of it back onto the wharf. I started to get dizzy and weak in the knees. I started giggling.

A dark-skinned man with bulging muscles appeared in front of me.

"What's so funny?" he asked.

"If I fall down and die, my mother will kill him," I said.

He relayed this to the men putting whiting on the conveyor and they all laughed. Something about Ted fearing the wrath of his wife must have struck them funny. Big Muscles returned to the large vat of whiting. I noticed he started bailing them onto the conveyor twice as fast as before. He returned a short time later.

"My name is Manning Silvera. My fellow workers have

appropriately named me The Portagee."

"Mark," I said.

"Okay, kid, why don't you get on that hose and blow that fish over here just like you were doing."

I did. This guy was a machine. He shoveled about ten times as fast as me and he was so strong that one hundred percent of his shovelful made it to the top of the pile. Pile A became Pile B in no time. I was done. I said thanks to The Portagee and he returned to his job at the vat. He was a little behind because he had stopped to help me. I was physically destroyed.

As I stood leaning on the shovel one of the rules that I was to live by became forever imprinted on my being. I will not instigate a fight, verbal or physical, for little or no reason. But under no circumstances will I stand by while someone, anyone, who is incapable of defending himself or herself is abused. My father reinforced this later in the day. If you do me good, I will do you better. If you hurt me or do me bad, I will fucking nuke you into non-existence. I went over to the vat, grabbed a dip net and helped Manning catch up.

Lifting a dip net full of whiting out of the vat and up onto the conveyor was done totally with the arms. No wonder Manny had such massive biceps—it wasn't from doing curls for the girls. He didn't say anything, he just nodded. The table in the next room was full of whiting in no time. We stood resting on the dip nets. The vat was empty.

"Gentlemen." Once again my father had appeared out of nowhere. "Nothing to do?"

"Worked ourselves out of a job, boss," Manning said motioning to the full table.

"So it would seem," he said lighting two Kents and handing one to Manning. They both inhaled deeply. "Mark, don't you ever start smoking these things."

I looked at him with a 'yeah, right' look.

"This is what I am going to call a 'reverse lesson'—do as I say, not as I do."

Manning laughed. They say when my father was younger he was on his second day without a smoke and a very large and quarrelsome individual who was on Pop's shit list displeased him in some manner. He rendered the man unconscious with one hard left.

"You seem to have turned Pile A into Pile B in the allotted time."

"He helped," I said pointing to my partner in shit moving.

"Did you have to ask him to help bailing," he asked Manning.

"Nope, came over on his own."

The old man's eyes lit up.

"Outstanding. I see a small ray of sunlight in the darkness. A very small tree begins to grow. A long and very bumpy road ahead, I am sure, but nonetheless, I am a very good driver."

I was far from the first wise-assed punk he had shaped up. He and Manning had a good laugh. At the time I had no idea what he was talking about but what I learned working for him at Empire Fish that summer was to save my life over and over. To this day I am approached by men I don't know, all with the same story, "My father worked for your father and so did I for one summer. I have been thanking him on a regular basis for the rest of my life." At his wake and funeral, men from all over the country—doctors, successful businessmen, career soldiers, lawyers (so he made a few mistakes)—told me the same story.

Suddenly, in a very loud voice for all to hear, he said, "Mark, there is one small problem. There has been a minor change of plans. I want you to move Pile B back to its original spot."

I cocked the dip net like a baseball bat to hit him.

"Just kidding," he yelled.

"He seems to have quite a temper," Manning said.

"He gets it from his mother."

The entire wharf had a good laugh—at my expense, of course.

"Give me that weapon," he said to me.

I gave it to him and he started bailing, as more whiting began pouring into the vat.

"Your son have a game today?" he asked Manning.

"Yes, at five o'clock."

"Take off. I'll punch your time card."

"Thanks, Ted," Manning said. "But you know that pisses Mario off." Mario was the owner of Empire Fish.

"You deal with me and I'll deal with Mario. That's the way

it works around here. Boot."

Manning shook my hand. "It was a pleasure to work with you, Mark," he said. "I look forward to doing it again."

He left. My father nodded approvingly.

"Ya know, if you were dogging it, he never would have said that. He suffers from terminal honesty and would never suck up to the boss." He looked at me. "Now you have earned yourself a choice for the rest of the day. Would you rather help your poor, decrepit old man bail or would you rather wash down the deck?"

I don't know where it came from but I spoke in tongues. "With all due respect, sir, I would prefer to be as far from you as fucking possible for the rest of the day, sir," I said without hesitation.

"As long as you work like a man, you are allowed to speak like one. If you drop that word at home your mother is going to know where you learned it. This will cause me a significant amount of rebuke from your mother. Can you guess what my response to this will be?"

"Yes, sir," I replied.

"Well, I guess I rated that retort," he said. "Proceed."

Before I could leave, Mario, the plant owner, showed up wearing his black, full-brimmed hat and smoking a big old stogie.

"Teddy, why you let Manning go early?"

"His son has a baseball game."

"He punch out?"

"Told him not to, I'll punch him out at five."

"So I'm paying him for NOT doing his job?"

"No, you're paying me to do his job. And not as much as I deserve."

"You don't have enough to do running this place that you do his job, too?"

"I can do my job and his job at the same time. I can do any job in this plant and my job. I can even do my big, fat owner's job and mine."

He dropped the dip net and moved cat-fast to Mario, grabbing his hat with one hand and his cigar with the other. Putting on the hat, which was way big for him, and puffing on the cigar, he began dancing around the astonished Mario. "Now let me see, it is the crack of ten in the morning and I am just getting to Empire Fish and the first thing I am gonna do is sit at my desk and figure out how much money my foreman has made for me since he started work at five this morning." There was much laughter among those within earshot. He continued to dance around and puff on the cigar.

"Oh, look. It's lunch time. I wonder how much more money my foreman has made for me since ten a.m. Boy, am I hungry! I'm going over to The Gloucester House and get a little something to eat. I'm back at my desk at two p.m. and feel much better. It might be because I ate enough to feed a good-sized country and drank two bottles of wine." Mario stood still, taking the abuse. "Oh, I wonder how much money my handsome foreman has made for me in two hours. Let me see, two trailer trucks full and on the highway! Why I could have paid for fifty of my lunches with the profit from just half of one of those trucks. Boy, am I so lucky to have such a great foreman to make all my money for me." He continued dancing. "Oh, look it's five—time to call my bookie and bet a few thou that my foreman made for me today on the Sox tonight. I am just so tired. It was such a hard day.

"Oh! I know what I am going to do! I'm going to give my foreman who makes me so much money a big, fat raise because he deserves it and because he has ten offers to coach high school football if I don't make him the best paid foreman on the waterfront."

Mario turned to me. "You know, Mark, I hope you are not a wise guy like your father is."

The two men were eye-to-eye. The laughter from those listening was loud.

"Hat." Mario said. My father placed it gingerly on his head.

"Stogie." My father placed it in Mario's mouth.

"You a real wise guy, you know that?"

They were silent for what seemed like hours.

"Fifty a week," Mario finally said.

"C-note."

"That's a hell of a raise."

"I am a hell of a boss and I have always wanted to coach football."

Mario stared at him. "I'll tell you what, wise guy, I'll give you a buck and a half if you don't talk to me for a month."

"Deal."

Mario turned to walk away then turned back to my father. "Would you explain to me how I can be the one giving you shit and end up giving you a raise?"

"Money, money, money," my father said and dropped a dip net full of whiting on the conveyor. "I make you a lot of money. You pay me a lot of money to make you a lot of money."

A short time later as I washed down the deck, the lumper standing on the elevated platform emptied the last canvas bucket of whiting from the boat.

"Hey you," he yelled at me, "spray some water up here and wash some of this fish shit off my rubbers."

I was young and dumb but by no means stupid. I ventured an observation, "It will nail you in the face."

"Wise fucking kid, just do what I tell you."

This guy was old, I mean he had to be in his twenties. Barrel-chested with bulging muscles, he was quite intimidating.

"Spray some water up here, you little shit, before I come down there and slap you around."

"But..." I started.

"Don't talk, dimwit, just do it."

I twisted the nozzle to a narrower setting and blasted the guy right in the chest. Sure enough it blew up right into his face, knocking his smoke out and blowing his hair straight up. He lost his footing and fell to the wharf, face down, landing in fish gurry. The entire wharf had witnessed this and the laughter roared. The lumper, stood up with fish shit matting his hair and fish intestines sliding down his face. Some of the guts must have worked their way inside his rubbers and down his back because he rotated both shoulders in circles as if he was attempting to scratch his back. The laughter grew louder but the lumper failed to join in. Young men make fools of themselves on a regular basis with little help from anyone else. In his case, he held me responsible for his own stupidity and lack of knowledge of the basic laws of physics. He glared at me with blazing, red eyes, his chest heaving. The men and women on the wharf hooted but he failed to find any jocularity in the situation.

He picked up an enormous, oh, my Jesus, magnum five-pronged, elephant-killing pitchfork and started toward me with a look of pure rage on his face. The onlookers, realizing the gravity of the situation, went very quiet. The five points of the prongs were worn shiny silver and gleamed and sparkled in the bright overhead lights. That was all I could see—everything else disappeared. My breathing came in gasps and I was as frightened as a boy could be, more scared than I'd ever been in my life. The wharf was covered in gurry and pieces of ice. He slipped and stumbled but continued to bear down on me. As the distance between us shortened his expression was one of pure insanity. I was sure he was going to stick that pitchfork right through me and hurl me across the wharf. My breath was coming so rapidly it made me dizzy. I was completely paralyzed.

From nowhere he appeared, the man in a blue work uniform with "Ted" written on his shirt. Standing in the shadows, just out of the lumper's view where only I could see him, he stared at me. He tapped his forehead and mouthed the word, "Think."

What? I thought. What's he waiting for? Why doesn't he help me? I had tunnel vision and all I could see was that pitchfork coming at me. That maniac was almost on me and he was trying to tell me something?

My father moved closer still out of the lumper's vision. "Think your way out of it." He yelled again, tapping his forehead.

Suddenly I realized I was still holding the hose. With a quick twist of my wrist I raised the nozzle and blasted the guy right in the face. He staggered backward blinded.

"Outstanding!" My old man yelled and loud applause broke out all over the wharf.

Pitchfork Man struggled to his feet looking totally berserk. He moved with catlike speed right at me. I had stopped being afraid. I turned, twisting the nozzle to its narrowest setting, I blew him off his feet again. The old man swiped his hand across his throat and I cut the water off. The audience was still applauding.

But Pitchfork Man hadn't had enough. He lunged forward and grabbed me with both hands pressing his thumbs into my throat. I was paralyzed. I could smell perspiration and stale cigarette smoke. Strangely I went from feeling numb to a weird high. I was no longer afraid and the sweet smell of whiting became overpowering. The lumper's mouth was moving and he sprayed spit in my face. It was only a split second but seemed like an hour. The pressure on my throat increased and sound seemed to return in a very loud hiss-s-s-s-S-S-S. As his face contorted in murderous rage it suddenly exploded in a red spray, white teeth flying everywhere. One even landed in my shirt pocket. The pressure on my throat disappeared as a left fist followed by a blue shirt sleeve smashed the man's face while at the same time I was pulled gently backwards by his right hand.

The punch had literally crushed the face into a featureless ball. Knocked as far to the left as it could go his head snapped back as blood cascaded from his nose and gushed from his toothless mouth all over his chest and onto me. Still standing he rapidly blinked unfocused eyes. His head rolled back and forth as though he just couldn't comprehend what had just happened. Then he collapsed straight down like he was deflated, landing on both knees and pitching forward face down on the deck. He rolled onto his side, drawing up his knees in classic fetal position, both hands covering his groin. The blood sprayed from his mouth as he struggled to breathe. It mixed with the water on the deck and spread pooling outward.

I was born on the right side of the tracks but managed to spend most of my life on the wrong side, where all the fun is. I've watched more than a few people get punched. I spent five years in three different martial arts. And I never saw a reaction to one punch like I saw that day. Holy shit, did that guy get clobbered.

My father picked me up off the deck.

"Are you alright?" he asked smiling.

"Better than him," I said pointing to the prostrate man spraying blood and clutching his groin.

"Well, that's the way I planned it." He shrugged. "Correct me if I'm wrong but did you not say a short time ago that you preferred to be someplace other than where I was?"

"Well, yeah, but that was before that asshole tried to stick a pitchfork in me and choke me to death."

"A valid point to be sure, nonetheless I think a 'thank you' is in order."

The whole wharf was listening.

"A simple 'thank you, father' or 'thank you, boss' will suffice."

"Thanks, boss."

"I'm sorry I didn't quite hear that."

"THANKS, BOSS!" I screamed.

"Very good. That was sufficient sucking up—not obscene sucking up, but sufficient."

Everyone within earshot was laughing.

At that moment, the freezer boss of Empire Fish showed up—my father's brother, my Uncle Bill.

"Trouble, Ted?" he asked, nodding toward the prostrate lumper clutching his groin.

"A minor problem but I'm sure there will be ramifications," he said as he lit two smokes and handed one to my uncle.

Uncle Bill's face lit up. "Oh, this is just too good. I haven't dropped anyone in a dog's age."

They were joined by another man, Bill Walima, the plant's mechanic, a long-time friend of my father and uncle. A group of the beaten lumper's friends, also lumpers, approached the three. Uncle Bill motioned me to the rear and the three men formed a line in front of the lumpers. I counted seven lumpers. The lumpers stopped a few feet in front to the three and simultaneously dropped their aprons on the deck.

An unseen line, a DMZ, was drawn between the men. Any encroachment and hostilities would ensue. Both sides sized up the opposition as the machinery on the dock was shut off. Workers from the front of the plant arrived—the word had spread and those who had witnessed the incident whispered to those who had not. Smokes were fired up and no one spoke above a whisper.

An occasional whisper, running water, seagull cries, and the moaning of the fallen lumper were the only sounds. The tension was palpable.

"You hit him when he wasn't looking," one lumper yelled at my father.

"Yeah, you sucker punched him," another lumper hollered.

"Yes. I did."

"Why did you fuck him up like that?" a third lumper demanded.

"To, as you have so tersely put it, 'fuck him up' implies that I beat him for a period of time while, in point of fact, I only hit him twice. Now, understand this, I don't normally explain what I, as foreman of Empire Fish, do, but in this case I'll make an exception for you. The reason your friend is lying in fish shit trying to breathe is quite perspicuous."

A look of confusion came over most of the lumpers.

"What do you mean 'perspicuous'?"

"Mark!" my father yelled as loud as possible. "Please explain, with as many of the adjectives that your mother had better never hear, what 'perspicuous' means."

I stepped forward into the DMZ in front of my father and let fly. "Assholes, it means simple, as simple as possible, you fucking morons!"

As I backed past my father he stared at me wide-eyed. "Where the hell did you learn to swear like that?"

"Listening to you when you were working on the house and didn't think anybody could hear you," I shot back. My father was an excellent football player and foreman, but he was the world's worst carpenter.

Uncle Bill and Bill Walima were both chuckling.

"Okay, big man, why did you hit him?" one of the lumpers hollered.

My father turned to him. "He displeased me."

The three men faced seven, better than two-to-one odds. Bill Walima had worked for my father for years but he called my father a friend and would stand with him for this, if for no other, reason. My Uncle Bill would stand shoulder to shoulder with his brother against superior odds as he had since they were little boys growing up on Portagee Hill overlooking Gloucester Harbor. They were new to this country from Baybull, Newfoundland. "Newfies" the other boys taunted them. My father was small in stature grow-ing up and was picked on by the other boys. Uncle Bill protected him. If my father told me once, he told me a thousand times, "Don't you never watch anyone get bullied. You step in, you hear?" Uncle Bill stood with his brother against superior odds with no questions asked. Retreat or surrender were not options.

"You think because you used to be a big football player you

can just go around hitting people?" a lumper asked.

"Assholes are assholes. I pretty much hit them at will."

"You think because you are the boss here you can do what you want?" another lumper hollered. "You ain't our boss."

"If I was your boss, dimwit, you would be engaged in some constructive manual labor instead of standing here talking yourself into some serious shit. Right, Billy?"

"Aw, I don't know, brother Ted. I'm kind of looking forward to the entertainment."

Uncle Bill whispered something to my father and Bill Wilema and they all giggled pointing at the lumpers' feet.

"What makes you old guys think you stand a chance against all of us?" said another motioning to the group of them.

"You don't like the odds, shithead?" Uncle Bill quipped. "There's a phone right over there, call for reinforcements."

The three older men laughed as did most of the onlookers.

"You guys are beginning to bore me," said the foreman of Empire Fish. "And I hate to be bored. Why don't you fucking little dogs sashay on over here and see what you can do to the big dogs."

What happened next could best be described as a very loud silence. A perceived wrong had been committed and one group of men intended to exact retribution from the other. The two groups were at war. No diplomatic solution was possible. One side was not about to call the other side to have lunch and discuss it. Hostilities were eminent. The problem would be solved as these kind of problems have been solved between men from the beginning of time—through force and violence.

The three Empire warriors would face seven. The average age of the three was forty-five, of the opposition twenty-five. Weapons of the day, hands and feet. Rules of engagement—none.

Uncle Bill turned away from the lumpers as though dismissing them. Boy, I thought, that was dumb.

One man leaped toward him. Right into a tremendous right handed punch that smashed him off his feet and onto the deck unmoving with his face a bloody mess.

"Gentlemen, it is now only two to one," Uncle Bill beamed, stepping back across the DMZ.

"Come on, puppies, yip, yip, yip," Uncle Bill taunted.

The three older men did the last thing the younger men expected. They attacked. The opposition made a fatal mistake in hand-to-hand combat, to a man, they hesitated. Surprised, some tried to retreat from the charge.

The football player drew first blood. Sidestepping to the right he smashed his left forearm into his opponent's throat and smashed him to the deck with a thud. Momentum carried him into his next opponent, legs pumping as though going for extra yardage, he smashed head-first into him driving him into the side of a dump truck. He lay motionless on the wharf. Uncle Bill had two lumpers tied up in a wrestling match. Bill Walima was boxing—dancing, weaving, twisting, never getting hit and punching his opponent at will. What a show! I thought, this is better than TV!

As the one my father knocked to the deck struggled to his feet, swearing, Pop yelled, "Set. Hike." He took two steps forward like a field goal kicker and smashed a right foot into his opponent's face, standing him straight up and back-pedaling him for twenty feet.

"Up, up. Stay up. Left, left," he yelled as the guy passed me. I turned in time to see the guy's head crash into a conveyor passing about five feet above the deck. He crumpled, face first, onto the wharf.

I whirled back to see my father holding his hands out, questioning. "Well? Was the kick good?"

I shot my arms straight up. "Three points," I hollered.

"Sometimes I just kill myself," he said.

He leaned close. "Now, Mark, we don't need to tell your mother about the day's festivities, do we?"

"Nope." I shook my head.

"Did you learn anything from all this unpleasantness?"

The answer hit me like a ton of bricks. "Their boots. They couldn't move in those big boots."

"Excellent." He gave me a big smile and tapped his right temple, then headed toward his brother.

Uncle Bill hit one of his opponents with two quick lefts and a tremendous right splattering blood and what looked like white Chicklets all over the place. The guy flopped to the deck like a thrown blanket. At the same time Bill Walima dropped a guy to his knees. He fell forward and lay there. Uncle Bill turned into a smashing fist that spun him one hundred eighty degrees. He slumped to the deck balancing on his right hand. Just as suddenly he launched forward like a missile cocking his left hand back as he moved. With his full weight he threw an upper cut that caught the guy under his chin and literally knocked him into the air. The guy staggered forward with that dumb, questioning look on his face.

He crumpled to the deck, extremely unconscious.

"Get hit, Billy?" My father said as he fired up two smokes.

"Ech." Uncle Bill snatched up a piece of ice from the deck and held it to his cheek. They stood smoking as they watched Bill Walima dance and weave and hit the last conscious lumper at will.

My father and Uncle Bill both held Black Belts in the fighting art of the American street, the best hand-to-hand fighting in the world. I know what a Black Belt in Martial Arts can do, I am one. But we have nothing on a good old American street fighter.

Bill Walima, to the lumpers detriment, was a professional boxer in his younger years. He had adapted to street fighting by standing sideways to his opponent, avoiding a fight-ending groin shot. Other than that he moved like a ballet dancer.

Twenty years later as Bill and my father stood at a bar, a younger and much larger man approached them. He said he had heard that Bill used to be a boxer and he wanted to see proof. As the man cocked his hand back he was stunned by two lefts and a right that dropped him to his knees. He was carried out.

"Another drink, Ted?" Bill asked.

My father called his style, "Just elegant."

He danced around his opponent easily dodging punches, never throwing one punch but combinations that only a professional boxer would use. One punch led to another and he always kept his two feet under him. Every time the lumper threw a punch he would easily avoid it and answer it with two or three—pow, pow, pow. Move, hit, move, move, hit, hit, move. Never off balance. He wasn't even breathing hard. I stood with my uncle and father. No one spoke a word, we all knew we were in the presence of greatness.

The guy was cut over each eye, both bleeding and blinding him. The guy was getting murdered. Bill Walima stepped back from his hapless opponent.

"Son, you're all done. I can keep this up all day. Why don't you just give in?"

The man was much younger than Bill and straightened to his full height.

"Ain't quitting," he said, his jaw jutting out.

My father stepped in front of Bill Walima as they exchanged glances.

He looked the lumper up and down. "Highly commendable." He took a drag on his smoke. "Son, there is nobody in this plant, or in this city for that matter, who can stand in front of this man if he doesn't want him to." He pointed at Bill Walima.

The lumper was continually wiping blood from his eyes. His obviously broken nose was pushed far to one side and on every labored breath blood pumped out of his face. Tears began rolling down his cheeks leaving streaks through the blood. He tried to hold his arms out but they fell uselessly at his sides. His head moved up and down finally then fell to the side resting on his shoulder. His knees began to shake and he collapsed forward. Pop grabbed his shirt and gently lowered him to the deck. As he lay bleeding on the deck the three older men surrounded him.

"Not much of a fighter," my father said. "But certainly no quitter."

All the spectators, mostly my father's workers, began to applaud and whistle. All and all it had been a good show, a pleasant break from the backbreaking work of processing fresh fish.

"Back to work," my father hollered over the noise. One by one the machines came noisily to life. A short time later I looked up as two more lumpers pounced on my father from behind a dump truck. One held him from behind with both arms under his shoulders and his hands pushed against the back of his neck. He looked helpless.

Uncle Bill appeared and knelt down beside me taking out more smokes.

"Aren't you going to help him?" I asked.

"Watch your father and you remember," he said lighting the smokes. My father was being held in a classic Full Nelson. He proceeded to demonstrate how to classically get out of it. As one lumper approached him from the front cocking his head back, my father kicked up with both feet, snapping his right foot straight out. The heel caught the man under his chin snapping his head back as far as it would go. He fell forward to his knees and rolled onto his side, blood pouring from his mouth. Pop then back-pedaled like the defensive back he once was, forcing the lumper behind him into the side of a dump truck with a thud. Raising his right foot as high as possible, he brought it down as hard as he could, smashing into the man's instep with a crunch. Even through the heavy rubber boot, the lumper reacted with a scream and gave up his grasp. He began hopping helplessly on one foot. The old man grabbed him by the apron straps and pulled him toward a conveyor belt carrying gurry up and into a dump truck. In one fluid movement he twisted the man's arm down, threw his leg under and behind his crotch, then jerked it up somersaulting him up onto his ass where he sat on the conveyor belt dazed. Pop flipped the conveyor belt switch to full blast and he shot up screaming, only stopping when he landed head down in the truck full of fish gurry, his legs waving wildly.

Uncle Bill was laughing so hard he burnt himself with one cigarette and dropped the other.

The slots on the fish-heading machine were filled for the last time and one by one the men backed away removing their gloves, most lighting up butts.

The end of the day of repetitive labor is conducive to good humor. Most people were laughing and making jokes. Manning's replacement dumped his last net full of whiting on the conveyor, waved to me and made a big bicep muscle. Smiling he yelled loud enough for all to hear, "On the table!"

That told the girls that all they needed to do was clear the table and it's quitting time. The packing table was full. The prospect of going home was enough to produce a fresh spurt of energy even when they were bone tired from doing the same thing for over eight hours. The waxed boxes passed through a machine that wrapped them in Empire wrapping paper and dated them. Placed in metal trays and piled on a pallet, they were fork-lifted to Uncle Bill's freezer, frozen and trucked all over the country. Many people would eat what was processed at Empire Fish that day.

As the last of the fish was packed, cheering and applause

broke out among the women. As they filed out of the packing room, talking and gesturing to one another with their hands their day was far from over. Most would go home to cook dinner and care for children. With the last of the machines turned off the silence was sensuous, as if you could feel it. As if it was an entity. Even with the hose splashing and the occasional yell from the lumper in the dump truck, it could be described as a very noisy quiet.

"TedEEEEE!" pierced the quiet like a speeding bullet. Mario had arrived. "How you expect em to get my boats unloaded if you beat up my lumpers?"

Bill Walima showed back up.

"We were attacked and forced to defend ourselves," my father said motioning to the two Bills. "Besides, the day's over."

Lumpers lay twisted and bloodied on the deck. One was kneeling, sobbing, his chin bobbing up and down. Another attempted to struggle to his feet and collapsed back to his knees, blood from his nose leaving a red streak all the way to his belt. He mumbled unintelligibly to no one in particular.

Mario started counting the lumpers, pointing with his index finger. "...six, seven, eight."

A muffled scream from the dump truck indicated the whereabouts of the last lumper.

"Don't forget the one Ted threw in the dump truck," Uncle Bill laughed.

"You went eight to three?" ventured the owner. "What the fuck are you guys? The freaking Three Musketeers or something? You turn my wharf into a goddamned battle field, you guys."

He stood shaking his head. Another wail came from the truck. The poor man covered in fish shit was just too spent to crawl out.

"Get up there and pull him out!" Mario gave them a pater- nal look.

My father and his brother stood by drawing on their coffin nails. "When we finish our smokes."

"He could drown in that shit," said Mario sternly.

"A better than good possibility," said the foreman of Empire Fish to his boss.

"Tedeeeeeee!" the owner of Empire Fish bellowed.

The two men dropped their smokes and jumped up on the tailgate of the truck. They reached as far down as they could to grab him by the shoulders and haul him over the side dripping fish intestines. As they pulled him up, the lumper began screaming a tirade of obscenities with his considerably profane vocabulary. Even I could see what was about to happen. They pushed him back into the fish gurry, headfirst. His legs flailed back and forth as he tried to extricate himself.

As they jumped back down to the deck it was apparent that Mario was struggling to look stern and not show that he was laughing.

"Tedeee, you the boss a this whole place. How many times I got ta tell ya not to fight? We call the police. We call my people (Mario's people could best be described as being like Tony Soprano's, nuff said?) Tedeee, I don't pay you to fight."

"I look upon fighting as part of the entertainment value that makes my employment at Empire Fish so rewarding, my fat boss."

"You a wise guy, you know that?"

"I prefer to think of it as part of my charming ways," he shot back.

"You gotta get more control over yourself!" Mario's hands were flailing madly as he spoke. There is a saying in Gloucester that if you hold an Italian's hands while he is talking he'll explode.

Uncle Bill was chuckling.

Mario turned on him. "I expect this from Billy, he always in trouble. But, Tedeeee, you the big boss here. I expect some kind of example from you. And you, Bill Walima, you the calm one! I expect a certain amount of trouble from these two Black Irish Newfie Micks from Portagee Hill. I never hear you so much as raise your voice or swear. Why can't you two be more passive like Bill Walima?"

Bill Walima stood by looking like a portrait of innocence.

My father and Uncle Bill gave him a terrible look.

"Keep it up, Bill, and we'll rat you out," Pop said.

"You guys," Mario blurted shaking his head. "Suppose you get hurt and can't work? Huh? Suppose you cripple someone. Who's gonna pay the medical bills? How about you kill one and go to jail? Who's gonna support your family? Huh? Me? I'm not made of money! You got to start acting like responsible family men, not children. You too old for this kind of shit, you not kids anymore."

I sat back and absorbed every word. It was seldom, if ever, that I got to see my father admonished. Except for my mother, there was no one on this planet that could talk to him like this.

"What would Betty say if she knew you did stuff like this in front of the boy?"

Pop shook his head a little, acknowledging the reprimand.

"You guys gotta stop this violence, it just leads to more trouble. Now what the hell happened that left my lumpers laying all fucked up all over my wharf like a big bunch of bloody codfish, for Christ's sake?"

The three men just shook their heads lamely.

Mario stepped over to me and patted me on the shoulder. "That a good boy, Mark. Now tell old Mario what this is all about."

Mario was a good sized man. 100% Sicilian, he always wore a black, broad-brimmed hat, black pants and shirt and thick-heeled pointy boots. I was still a little shaken. As I told the story, my little chin started bouncing and big, old crocodile tears ran down my face which had someone else's blood on it.

"HE DID WHAT???" Mario screamed when I got to the part about the pitchfork. "Which one?"

I pointed.

Mario's eyes went to full open and then glazed over. Pitchfork Boy was on all fours trying to get to his feet. Mario took three steps and kicked him flush in the ribs with a sickening thud. It sounded like he kicked an old couch. Hapless Pitchfork Boy landed about ten feet away sitting up, back to a metal tub. Mario moved like a flash. Grabbing the guy's shirt collar with his left hand, he threw a right hand smack into an already bloody nose. Blood splashed everywhere. He shifted his weight to his rear foot and smashed the man's head with his fist against the tub—wack, wack. Blood spilling in all directions with each punch. Even at that young age I knew the difference between fighting someone and killing him. Mario was killing him.

Pop grabbed his right hand in mid punch with both his arms.

Uncle Bill and Bill Walima grabbed his left arm. It took all three men to pull him away from the obviously unconscious man who slid over, gurgling blood and trying to breathe. The three men struggled to hold Mario who continued trying to kick the prone man.

"Mario, it's me. It's me," my father screamed at him.

Finally his eyes came back into some kind of focus and he looked at the men clutching him as if awaking from a trance. He quit struggling.

Since then I've heard it called "going Italian", but also "going Irish" and "being Indian mad". It's all the same. There are some people you just don't want to piss off. Nationality has nothing to do with it. The three men turned Mario loose.

"Get that piece of shit out of my plant. I don't ever want to see him again here ... EVER!"

"Well, boss, if he lives I'll see to it," my father said soberly.

The three men stared at Mario, all straight-faced. It was worse than laughing.

"If I can't pound a piece of shit in my own fish plant what the hell is the point of owning it in the first place?"

The silence continued.

"Where in the hell does it say I am the one to set examples around here? Do as I say, not as I do," Mario turned toward me and waved. I waved back and he headed to his office, muttering to himself in Italian. The very silent group of onlookers made a generous path for him. The lumpers, bloodied and prone on the deck, began coming to their senses and stumbling to their feet, helping each other.

"Well, that was quite stimulating," said the foreman. "Gentlemen." He addressed his two cohorts. "There is nothing like beating up a bunch of young, dumb, full-of-cummers, half your age to make you feel young, now is there?"

"We managed to muddle through, considering our advanced age, now didn't we?" said Uncle Bill. "I think we should retire to one of Duncan Street's seedier gin mills across the street for a beer."

"When have we ever had just one beer?"

"Perhaps today will be a first." My uncle said not smiling. Ted and Bill Walima laughed.

"Enough of this frivolous banter," Bill Walima said, "I suggest we saunter over to that den of iniquity whose only redeeming value is that it has the coldest beer in town. Come, gentlemen! Enough of this gab. I vote we turn the demon alcohol loose and the devil be damned."

The other two stared at him, stunned by his eloquence and the fact that he was a man of few words.

"Come, musketeers! Onward and upward," my father added. "Come on, kid and fellow combatants." He waved me over.

We crossed through the Empire yard toward Duncan Street. The boss looked at his watch and let out a scream.

"FIVE O'CLOCK!"

Workers fifty yards away getting into their cars and starting them, stuck their heads out to wave to us. Heads and arms popped out of the Ladies Room nodding and waving. Mario waved from his office window. The seagulls and pigeons as high as three stories up, jumped into flight. Women walking up Duncan Street all turned and waved, smiling. Drunks outside the bar we were headed toward yelled back. Compared to my father's scream, they were whispering.

The signal to begin work, for "mug up" (or "coffee break"), lunch, and the end of the day at Empire Fish was not a horn or a bell or anything else artificial, it was my father's vocal chords. But it was far more than a signal or reaffirmation of tomorrow's starting time, the yell was a loud, but respectful, way of saying good-night to all who had worked at Empire that day. To the lumpers it was a reminder of who made and enforced the law at Empire Fish.

"Is your face okay?" I asked my uncle.

"He hit like a little girl," he shrugged.

"I don't know, Billy," said his brother, "Kids today have no respect for their elders."

"Perhaps sometime during our rather violent encounter they did manage to gain a little respect for their betters," said Bill Walima.

"Very well put, as usual, Bill," said my father.

We crossed Duncan Street and arrived at the bar's entrance. I had butterflies as big as B-52s circling in my stomach. Imagine, for the first time in my life (and, believe me, not the last)

I would be privy to all the sordid things that transpire in a bar. I could just imagine all the decadent activities inside. I was drooling with anticipation.

"You can't come in," the old man said. I was blasted in the belly with both barrels of a .12 gauge shotgun. MY guts were falling to the sidewalk and I fought with my whole existence not to cry.

"I'll bring you a Coke."

"Why the hell can't he come in?" Uncle Bill demanded.

Go, Uncle Bill, I thought, loud enough to be heard.

"First and foremost, Betty would kill me, for Christ's sake. I'll be sleeping in Mario's office for a week. Secondly, and to a much lesser degree, it's illegal. He's only thirteen years old and if I am correctly apprised of the situation the legal drinking age is twenty-one which makes him just a tad young to be drinking."

"He shoveled shit for eight hours with the big dogs, why the hell can't he drink like a big dog? Christ's sake, Teddy, he's already seen way more than he should have. Besides they tell me he dropped that dipshit with the hose as cool as a cucumber. He may be a little dog but he acts like a big one."

"Bravely spoken, Billy. You don't have to deal with Betty."

"Shit, Ted, don't you wear the pants in your house?"

"Nope," Pop replied without hesitation, "not in ethical matters like this."

"Ted, you're covered in blood. Mark has it splattered all over himself. You're already busted big time."

"A very valid point, brother Bill." He turned to Bill Walima, "Well, chatterbox, what do you think?"

"As previously stated and with all due respect, my friend," Bill Walima drawled, "you talk too goddamned much. I think we three men and this budding young man should cease all superficial banter, enter this den of iniquity, and partake of its only redeeming attributes, the coldest beer and best bourbon in town."

He was a man of few words, but when it was important he could be eloquent.

"Damn, Bill, that was alright!"

Uncle Bill nodded agreement.

Turning to me the boss said, "If I let you come in this shithole can you keep your mouth shut at home?"

"Yes, sir!"

"Oh, it's 'sir' again, is it? I have it on good authority that you referred to me in less than favorable terms earlier today."

Drat. He had eyes and ears everywhere.

"Hell. That don't distinguish him in these parts," Uncle Bill said.

Pop nodded. "I guess he earned the right. Gentlemen, shall we?"

Behind my father, I then entered a foreign and unknown world—the forbidden and erotic world of the Silver Perch. I was thirteen.

CHAPTER 2 - THE PERCH

The cigarette smoke was thick. Fortunately I was half the height of everyone around me so it was mostly above me, like a solid cloud layer. The smell of cigarettes, cigars, beer, fish, perspiration, and, surprisingly, perfume permeated the room. Cigarette butts and shiny fish scales littered the sawdust covered floor. It was really filthy. I had never seen such a revolting floor. I absolutely loved it. I was in Shangra-la, walking on clouds.

The stools at the bar were occupied by men in work clothes tipping frosty mugs to their mouths and drinking greedily. They nodded and gestured at each other with their index fingers, some laughing loudly.

Standing behind those seated at the bar was another row of men taking pulls on frosty mugs, arguing, shaking heads in agreement or disagreement. Most of them alternated taking a slug of beer with a drag on their cigarettes. The click of Zippo lighters being snapped open and closed echoed through the bar like crickets.

We were halfway to the bar and heads turned, all eyes on the three men and the boy. Eye contact was made, nods and greetings were exchanged. The buzz rose and then fell back to where it was as conversations continued.

Mixed in among the men at the tables were many gaily dressed women with large red lips and low-cut dresses revealing incredible boobs. A hand grabbed my right arm and guided me gently but firmly to one of them.

"My! What a handsome young man," she cooed. "Are you Teddy's little boy?"

I found myself sitting on her lap looking right at two of the nicest boobs I had ever seen. At that age I had little basis for comparison but they looked great. It was the beginning of a lifelong appreciation. Plus she smelled so nice.

"You're the guy who decked Peter out on the dock with the water hose." News travels fast on the waterfront.

"Yes, ma'am," I said.

"And he calls me 'ma'am', how cute!" She gave me a big kiss on the cheek and smushed my face into her nice, pillowy boobs. God, she smelled good.

Who said sexual ability begins at puberty? I had a semi and I was still a baby.

"I can't leave you alone for a minute." My father once again appeared out of nowhere and helped me off her lap.

Shithead, I remember thinking.

"But, Teddy, he's so cute. I wasn't going to hurt him."

"Young lady, I am quite sure you meant him no harm. I was thinking of myself. My wife is sure enough going to figure out he has seen way more than he should thus far today. If she were to find out I let him sit on a girl of, shall we say, your charms, it would be very bad for me."

"I really didn't mind," I chipped in.

"I'm just quite sure of that," he said guiding me away.

Asshole, I thought.

Uncle Bill was laughing and Bill Walima was smiling as we approached the bar. Men stepped aside as we passed. One of the seated men stood.

"Here, Ted, take this one."

The boss put a hand on his shoulder and pushed him back down.

"No, Ted, I've had my two. Three leads to four and so on and so forth and I'll wind up wearing my dinner instead of eating it."

My father laughed, "I am acutely aware of that situation."

As he stood to leave he noticed me. "Nice job with the hose, kid." He smiled and walked off.

Three other men downed their beers and stood to leave. "Here you go, guys," one said.

We all sat down. My head was about level with the bar. Everyone towered over me.

"Barkeep, three boiler-makers, if you will," my father said to what had to be the most surly bartender I have ever seen (except for Jack Muniz at Halibut Point who is by far the most surly on the east coast) and I have seen a few. He was large, gap-toothed, hairy, scar-faced and greasy.

"And what would the little boy like?" he asked sarcastically.

"A beer," I said without hesitation.

The boss stared at me, the bartender made no move.

"Christ's sake, Ted, a beer ain't gonna kill him," Uncle Bill said.

"No. But it might get me killed when we get home."

"Oh, for God's sake, Ted, show a little backbone."

"She's gonna fucking kill me," he said shaking his head. "Barkeep, give him a beer."

"I don't serve rug rats," he snorted.

"I said, give him a beer, ugly."

Great, I thought, now I'll get a beer for sure. The ugly bastard has the old man pissed.

"Look, mister big football hero, you ain't the boss in here."

I don't know how many teeth my father displaced from people calling him a 'big football hero'. But his nickname should have been The Dentist. Oh boy, I thought, here we go again.

Bill Walima got up and, moving over, cut in front of my father.

"Excuse me, sir, you do own this shithole, don't you? Could I have a brief word with you while you're still conscious?"

"So, who's stopping you, you Rockport fag?"

"Very funny but quite incorrect. Allow me to point out a few facts that I am sure an individual as stupid, and I must say, butt-ugly, as you, will be capable of digesting. One, half the individuals in this place are under age. Two, there are twice as many people in here as the fire code will allow. Three, you serve illegally after one and on Sundays. Four, those three young ladies at that table over there are not selling Girl Scout cookies. Five, the beer cans here have no tax stamps on them and finally, six, I take offense at you calling this fine young man a rug rat. So, in conclusion, if you don't want this Rockport faggot to stroll around this bar and make an even greasier spot out of you than you already are—if that is possible—I want to see three boilermakers and one beer appear on this bar no sooner than yesterday."

It was a standoff. One of the bartender's friends appeared

and whispered something in his ear—no doubt about Bill Walima's boxing abilities. The bartender's eye's went wide and three boiler-makers appeared on the bar just that fast.

"Eloquent as usual," my father said. Uncle Bill nodded. Bill Walima winked at me and downed his shot, followed by a long pull on his beer.

"And what did the little boy want?" the bartender asked sarcastically.

"A beer," I ordered for the first time in my life. Now, one hundred thousand times later, I still say the same ambiguous thing—which usually gets the same response though with much less sarcasm.

"Which brand?"

"Budweiser," I said sounding as much like an adult as I could manage.

He reached behind him into a galvanized tub with a block of ice and cans of beer floating in it. A dripping can of Bud appeared in front of me. He slid the church key toward me. It hit the can and bounced onto the floor.

"Oops, excuse me, little man, I'm just so sorry," he scowled at me.

My father started to stand but I put my hand on his belt and he sat back down.

"I'd like a glass," I said to Mr. Surly.

"All out," he said.

I had noticed that before I asked. I was an observant and devious little troublemaker even at that age. Trust me, I got worse with age.

"What type of glass, little boy?"

"Hopefully, one that is cleaner than you and the rest of this shithole."

Uncle Bill spit beer laughing and the other men just stared at me with a didn't-think-you-had-it-in-you look.

"I'll be right back," he snarled.

As soon as he was out of sight I grabbed the beer and shook it for all it was worth. The three men chuckled in anticipation. I pushed it back as far as I could reach.

Ugly returned. "I couldn't find one with little bears on it so this will have to do." He shoved it toward me.

"Thank you so much." I just sat there.

"Well?" He glared at me.

"You opened theirs. You can open mine," I said.

"You little bas-....," he looked at my father and his voice trailed off.

"This is how you pop a can," he said to me as he punched a triangular hole into the top of the can. Beer squirted up hitting him smack in the face, blasting his hair back, foaming up his nostrils and soaking his whole head. He hopped back snorting beer out his nose. The entire bar erupted with laughter. The bartender dropped the empty can and glared at me as foam ran down his face and dripped onto the bar. I picked the can up and shook it.

"I'd like a different can please, this one seems a bit used."

He reached back and grabbed another one, popped it and set it down in front of me with a look of sheer mayhem in his eyes.

I lifted the icy cold can and took a few sips. The fact that it tasted excellent has, since that day thirty odd years ago, cost me a considerable amount of money and worlds of trouble on more than one occasion. And I wouldn't trade all the trouble I've gotten into thanks to beer for anything.

I sat in a waterfront bar, drinking a man's drink, on Duncan Street, in the Sixties. In all my thirteen years I never had it so good and rarely have since. A pat on my arm announced the arrival of Mario.

"Gentlemen," my father said. "We are now graced with the presence of our esteemed owner, Mr. Mario Lamony, who, as we all know, is well-respected on the water front for his calm disposition and non-violent ways."

Mario just shook his head. A glass of Italian Red appeared in front of him.

"A veritable fount of human kindness and pacifist supreme," my father continued.

"Mark, your father is a real wise guy, you know that?" Mario said to me. "I hope you don't grow up to be a wise guy like him."

"Actually, Mario old dog, he's quite the wise ass already. The only problem I see will be keeping him in one piece long enough to grow up."

All the men at the bar chuckled.

Mario tossed back the whole glass of wine and placed it on the bar where it was replaced by Mr. Surly.

"Listen up, Mr. Wise Guy, the cops called me and are coming down here to talk to you."

"Concerning what?" Pop said innocently.

"You remember that lumper you deposited in the dump truck?"

"Vaguely. Billy did we throw someone in a dump truck today?"

"What truck?" asked Uncle Bill.

"You two are a pair, I gotta say. I seen you throw him back with my own eyes."

"Oh, that guy," said Pop. "Billy, was the guy we threw in that truck the same one that passed by us in the truck screaming before we came in here?"

"I guess," he shrugged.

"Well, listen up, three fucking Musketeers," said Mario. "He was still in the truck when it dumped its load on the conveyor leading to the grinder at Gorton Pew—you know? The big corkscrew crusher that turns everything into chicken feed? He must have fallen and knocked himself out cause when he wakes up he's still too weak to move and he starts screaming. Before anyone can do anything he gets dumped on the screw with all the gurry and the screw started to suck him down. He was screaming for God and his mother and crying. Just about the time he is gonna be crunched up into little pieces to feed to the fucking chickens, some genius figures it might be a good idea to turn the goddamn thing off. It took them ten minutes to haul the guy out because he fainted."

The three men seated at the bar were portraits of empathy for the poor man. They broke into uproarious laughter so loud Mario had to stop talking three times.

Finally, Ted spoke up. "Is the kid alright?"

"Well, the cops say mostly the kid just sits on a stool and can't speak," Mario said.

"Can't speak or won't speak?" Uncle Bill asked.

"Can't. They said he was psychologically mute or some such shit like that."

"Too many people babbling too much shit in the world anyway," Uncle Bill said.

"Yeah, well, the sergeant is on his way down here to talk to you all."

This day was getting better all the time. With a little luck I might get to see the old man arrested and thrown in jail. How much cooler could it get than that? Wicked awesome!

"Did they say which sergeant is coming down?" Pop asked Mario.

"Yeah, the one I was talking to—a Sergeant Duke Ryan."

To this day I remember the shit-eating grin my father flashed.

I learned from a very early age not to screw with the police. Even today I don't disrespect them. This lesson has kept me out of jail in four different states and any country that borders on the North Sea.

A deadly silence fell on the bar as the law entered.

A sergeant about my father's age arrived followed by a young cop. Their eyes bounced up and down, right and left, taking in everything as they crossed the room to the bar. Any place where alcohol is served is a hazardous environment for a uniformed cop. They walked up to Mario.

"Good afternoon, sir," Mario nodded.

"I'm interested in talking to the three individuals who are alleged to have been involved with some type of unpleasantness at Empire this afternoon," the sergeant said.

Mario shrugged his shoulders.

Ted stood and approached the sergeant. "Excuse me." He lowered his glasses and squinted as though he really needed to read the nametag of his good friend.

"Ah, yes, Officer Ryan, is it?"

"And you are?"

"Ted Williams."

"The baseball player?"

"No. I am the foreman of Empire Fish. I did play a small amount of football in my youth. What can I do for you officer?"

The two continued to act as if they had just met.

"Ah, yes, Mr. Williams. We have a report of a disturbance

at Empire this afternoon."

"Disturbance?" He raised both hands, palms up and turned to his fellow conspirators and me. "Did you guys notice any disturbance this afternoon?"

I shook my head from side to side.

"Are you letting him have a beer?" Duke said under his breath. "Jesus, Ted, she's gonna kill you."

Pop nodded.

Both Bills turned to Duke shaking their heads from side to side. Both were spattered in blood and had their hands wrapped in handkerchiefs that were stained where blood had soaked through at the knuckle. Mario stifled a laugh by downing his glass of wine.

"Aha," said Duke turning to my father who was equally blood-splattered and white-knuckled. "Excuse me, sir, but why are you covered in blood and with skinned knuckles."

My father shrugged. "Fish blood."

"Red paint." My uncle said simultaneously.

Pop rolled his eyes while the two Bills kept their eyes on their drinks.

"So you are telling me, Mr. Williams, that all those red spots are fish blood and red paint?"

"Why that's absolutely correct, Officer."

"And your knuckles?"

My father frowned, thinking intently. "Gloves."

"Gloves?"

"Yeah. We ran out of work gloves. Wharf work is really hard on the knuckles."

Duke nodded. "I bet it is."

The young cop stared back and forth between them flabbergasted. "This is a bunch of bull!" He studied them. "Three older guys in their forties—one in tan, one in green and one in blue—and one old guy dressed in black with a black-brimmed hat! For Christ's sake, this is them!!!"

Duke turned to him. "Did you say 'old guys'?"

"Well, yeah! And an under-age kid who, as we speak, sits at the bar drinking beer, for Christ's sake! They beat the shit out of eight guys, one of whom is still in the hospital, and another one ended up at the dehydration plant where he almost got ground up into chicken food. He lost his ability to speak—he may never be right in the head again." He stared at his superior officer. "We were sent down here to pick them up on charges of assault. Assault and battery and mayhem. Why, they could be guilty of assault with intent to kill!"

Duke turned to the Empire contingent. "Did you gentlemen see any group of individuals who fit that description?"

They all silently shook their heads.

The rookie was furious. "We have a statement that at the end of the fight an older Italian-type of man came along, dressed in black with a black, full-rimmed hat on and pounded one of those guys until the others pulled him off. Said individual is still in the hospital and will be for quite some time."

Mario took off his black, full-rimmed hat and said, "I'm not Italian. I'm Sicilian. Everybody knows that's much better. Where you from, boy, the moon? Everybody in Gloucester knows Italian from Sicilian."

"There you have it. He's Sicilian not guinea," Duke said. "Can't be the same guy, let's go."

The young cop stared at him shell shocked, eyes and mouth wide open.

"While we waste our time here bothering these innocent, hard-working men, the perpetrators of this heinous crime are getting away."

"B-but... what about the kid? He's under-aged to be sitting in a shithole drinking beer?"

Duke turned to me. "How old are you, son?"

"Twenty-six," I blurted, dribbling beer down my chin.

My father covered his face with his hand. The two Bills chuckled into their beers.

"There you have it," said Officer Ryan, "he's five years legal."

"But he doesn't look sixteen, let alone twenty-six!" The rookie was dumbfounded.

"He's always been small for his age," my father said.

"Really, Officer Patrick, if that's the best power of observation you can muster, perhaps you should consider a transfer to the fire department," Duke chastised.

"At least ask to see his I.D." the rookie stammered.

"So now you want to insinuate that this fine young man is a liar? You seem bound and determined to mess with this group of hard-working men. What is your problem, rookie?"

"But, but..."

"Oh, alright. If you insist. Show him your driver's license, son."

I swallowed hard. "I don't have it with me. It's home in my car."

"There you have it," Duke said triumphantly.

The poor rookie just rolled his head back in disbelief and surrender.

"Come on, son, we're out of here. We have bothered these upstanding pillars of the community enough for one day. We have other fish to fry." Duke shook hands with Uncle Bill and Bill Walima.

When they were out of earshot my father leaned over to me. "Where the hell did you learn to prevaricate like that?"

"What does 'prevaricate' mean?"

"Lie."

"I listen to you explain to Mother about why you're two hours late every Friday night."

All the men laughed.

When it quieted back down he leaned back to me. "Mark, lying is wrong and sometimes you should do as I say and not as I do."

"How am I supposed to know one from the other?"

"I'm working on it, I'm working on it," he muttered. "You know, being a father is very difficult at times. I never said I was perfect, you know."

Duke finished his good-byes and turned to the stupefied rookie. "Come on, son. We need to get out of here and look for the four men whom these gentlemen so closely resemble and hold them to accounts. Call me crazy but somehow I don't think we will but... it's our job to try our best. We'll leave these gentlemen to have a quiet beer at the end of a hard day without police interference."

The rookie looked like he had finally caught on.

"Wait for me in the car," Duke told him.

The old man told Duke to take a box of haddock from the

front seat of his car. There would be only one ten-pound box of haddock headed for the Williams house that night.

"Thank you, Mr. Williams for your time and I apologize for any inconvenience."

"Quite alright, Officer Ryan, and a good day to you."

He nodded and patted me on the shoulder. "Quite a rowdy bunch of individuals you choose to drink with young man."

I shrugged and he smiled and pointed to Uncle Bill. "Watch out for that one there. He can be a most disagreeable individual."

Uncle Bill chuckled and Duke turned to leave.

"FUCKING COPS!"

I spun around. A very large and inordinately scruffy looking individual was blocking the young cop's way as he attempted to leave the bar.

As always seems to happen when cops enter a bar, there is one asshole with a beef fueled by alcohol. I remember thinking, even at that young age, what kind of a freaking moron would start shit with a man who wears a gun? He looked to be about two heads taller than the rookie and twice his size overall.

"Excuse me, sir," the young cop said calmly. "You seem to be in our way. Would you please move?"

Duke watched the scene with a look of utter disdain.

The young cop was clean-shaven. His uniform was pressed and his shoes were glossed black, standing out in the yellowish sawdust covering the floor. His antagonist had scraggly hair all over his face, slicked down and greasy on his head, and had brown teeth.

"I don't like cops," he announced. Every eye in the place was on them.

"Yes, sir," the rookie said, "I believe we have already established that."

"Are you getting smart with me?"

"Why, no, sir. I apologize if I gave that impression. That was not my intention. However, it would seem appearing smart with such a dumb, ignorant cocksucker as yourself could hardly be avoided by anyone of even moderate intelligence."

Watching them, Duke smiled a wide, face-splitting smile. My father started to rise but Duke put a hand on his shoulder and he sat back down.

The man's eyes narrowed to slits and he hissed, "I hate cops but you're so pretty I don't know whether I want to fight you or fuck you."

With the exception of the Empire crew, the entire bar erupted in cat-calls and wolf-whistles.

"So, honey-pie, are you gonna try and pull that club on me, fight me like a man, or just drop your pants and bend over for me."

Duke looked like a cat ready to pounce but he just stood there, taking in every word.

In polite company, it would be said that the cop's nemesis 'dressed to the right'. However, where I spend most of my day, we'd just say he had his dick down his right pant leg. It was exactly there that the rookie pointed his revolver when it appeared, seemingly out of thin air. The bar went totally silent.

"How about a third option?" he said his eyes never leaving the man's face.

"You wouldn't dare shoot me." He broke out in a heavy sweat.

The click of the hammer locking back on the revolver echoed through the bar like a cannon shot. The rookie pressed the barrel firmly against the protuberance running down the inner thigh of the now heavily sweating man.

"You fucking cops think you can do anything." The bartender bellowed.

Duke sneered and tapped the bar with his forefinger.

"Bourbon," he said icily.

The bartender, continuing his surly behavior, suddenly slammed the shot glass down to the bar, spilling most of it.

"You're a very funny man, Mister Bartender," Duke hissed.

"Well, we aim to entertain."

"Yes, sir, barkeep, you're a real howl." The attention of the crowd shifted from the stand-off near the door to Duke who put a finger in the shot glass and picked a squished cockroach out of it. He held it out and examined it.

Most of the bar laughed at the latest slight against the police—all except the profusely sweating man with the .38 pressed against his penis. Duke laughed along with the bar patrons, good-naturedly.

"Yes, nothing like freshly squeezed cockroach to flavor your bourbon, I always say."

The bartender glared at him. "I guess it takes a lot to rile some cops."

"Is that so?" Duke said.

Then the bartender said the phrase that has started more trouble than the Germans this century...

"Maybe you're just yellow," he snarled.

Duke flicked the cockroach onto the floor. "Pick it up and eat it." Everyone turned toward the bar. All heads swivelled back and forth between the two. They didn't know which action to watch, Duke and the bartender or the rookie and the ugly but terrified loud-mouth.

"Get your ugly ass out from behind that bar and eat it."

I knew some more serious shit was about to happen.

"What are you going to do, cop? Arrest me?"

"Not exactly."

"You gonna pull your gun on me, too, cop?"

"Wouldn't waste the bullet."

The bartender walked up to Duke and they stood the proverbial toe-to-toe. The bartender looked down at the smaller cop and sneered.

"Fuck you and your motherfucking badge."

Duke stood on the balls of his feet. He wore his revolver on his right side and on his left was a sinister-looking and well-scratched black club through a lanyard.

"Come on, cop. What rules do you want to go by?"

"Cop's rules," he hissed. Cat-fast his left foot moved back as his hand snaked across his body for the club, he shifted his full weight back to the right and swung straight up in an arc smashing the guy's face. It sounded like a baseball connecting with a bat. The bartender's face exploded, blood splashing across the mirror in back of the bar, across the line of liquor bottles, across the bar, across me. I had a ringside seat.

The stick was back in Duke's belt so fast it seemed never to have moved. The bartender stood swaying back and forth, his eyes unfocused. Blood gushed from his flattened nose to his mouth in two streams that merged into one and then out of the corners of his mouth where it flowed to the floor like water running from a faucet, not dripping, but fast enough to make an uninterrupted hum as it strikes the tub. He labored to breathe and every time he exhaled blood covered teeth clicked to the floor and skidded through the sawdust that stuck to them like a snowball rolling down a snowy hill. He wavered for a minute then collapsed, jelly-like, to the floor. He lay face down and blood pooled near his mouth then made its way toward the center of the floor, marking the low point of the low establishment.

Duke bent over the man and, using his club as a pry-bar, flipped him onto his back.

"Hold this a minute, young man," he said handing me his club. "I seem to have broken the lanyard on that last draw."

It seemed an inordinately heavy piece of wood to me and had a dome of shiny metal protruding from the bottom of the shaft.

Using his thumb and forefinger, Duke picked up the cockroach and placed it in what was left of the barkeep's mouth.

"It would have been easier if you'd done this yourself, asshole," he said loud enough for all to hear.

"FREEZE!"

All heads in the bar snapped back to the rookie who pushed his pistol harder against the penis of the quivering man who had just tried to move away.

"Take a good look at my trigger finger," he said in a low, dangerous voice. "That's right, shit-for-brains. The trigger is pulled. Only my thumb on the hammer is stopping you from sitting down to pee for the rest of your life."

The man, displaying commendable common sense, became a statue once again.

Still holding his pistol at its very precarious position he raised his voice so everyone in the bar could hear.

"Does anyone see anything?"

All the heads in the bar moved from side to side.

The rookie turned toward the bar. "Are you guys seeing anything?"

The Empire workers, all of whom wore glasses, removed

them and placed them on the bar. The symbolism was blatant.

"How about you, Mr. Twenty-six? You see anything?"

I looked at my father who nodded. I put one hand over my eyes and waved the other back and forth in front of them like a blind man. Duke nodded to me, as did my father. The rookie winked. The man with the endangered penis continued to tremble.

"The way he's shaking, that gun could go off at any time, rook," Duke said.

"That's a fact, Officer Ryan." The rookie kept his eyes on the quivering man in front of him.

"I mean one little move and..."

BANG! Heads snapped up, every butt in the bar puckered and pee ran down the man's pant leg and pooled in the sawdust.

Uncle Bill, always a wicked kidder, grinned, the remains of a smashed beer bottle in hand. The broken shards glittered on the bar as everyone in the bar howled with laughter.

"Aw, now that's disgusting." The rookie's nose wrinkled. "Well, at least you got to pee standing up because if I move my thumb you'll be sitting down to pee forevermore."

Another round of hoots filled the bar.

"Aw, come on, let me go," Pee-Boy pleaded.

"You don't look so tough in front of your friends now, do you, tough guy?"

"You suck, cop."

"What did you say?" He pressed the gun harder forcing the man to his tip toes.

Duke smiled with admiration and amusement.

"Repeat after me, asshole," the rookie snarled. "Duke Ryan is the best police officer in this city."

"DUKE RYAN IS THE BEST POLICE OFFICER IN THIS CITY!"

As the crowd laughed a police lieutenant appeared as if out of nowhere. He walked up to the rookie who nodded to him maintaining his thumb firmly on the weapon's hammer. The Lieutenant studied the situation and then addressed the man on tiptoes.

"Sir, I hope for your sake that young man has a very strong thumb."

"How do you uncock this thing?" the young cop asked.

It was all the man could take. His legs buckled and he plopped down abruptly, sliding over onto his side where he lay not moving.

The Lieutenant crossed to Duke nodding at the Empire contingent.

"Gentlemen."

They nodded back.

He stopped in front of me and picked up my beer. He glanced over at the rookie.

"Twenty-six," the rookie said shrugging his shoulders.

"That so?" He tapped his forehead pensively. He looked at me. "So that would mean you were born in 19--?"

"Thirty-seven!" I chirped just that fast. To this day I have no idea how I did the math that quickly.

"Correct," he said raising an eyebrow.

My father and his friends nodded their heads in agreement.

"This your father?" the Lieutenant asked.

"Yes."

He turned to my father. "Mr. Williams."

"Yes?"

"I expect I'm going to have to roll a squad car over to 136 Bass Avenue a bit later."

My father took a quick gulp of his beer.

"I expect your wife is going to kill you."

My father nodded agreement.

The Lieutenant turned to Duke. "Good afternoon, sergeant."

"Sir."

"That individual over there lying on the floor seemed to hold a rather high opinion of your law enforcement capabilities."

"Yes, sir, he did. It would seem that he is an insightful and perceptive individual."

The Lieutenant looked him up and down. "Without insinuating in any way that you are anything but a most capable and excellent officer of the law, I might venture forth the fact that said individual had a cocked .38, trigger pulled and thumb on the hammer, pointed at his penis by one of your brother officers who seems to be in a somewhat foul mood. Would you agree that this could be construed—not by me, you understand—but perhaps by a judge as maybe some small amount of duress. Perhaps even some type of wrong-doing. Maybe—and I realize this is probably a reach—some type of crime."

"That would depend on the judge, I would say, sir."

"Yes, I suppose it would." He lowered his eyes to the bar. "Is that whiskey you're drinking, sergeant?"

"Yes, sir. More specifically, bourbon."

"Are you sure, sergeant? It doesn't look dark enough to be of very high quality. What bottle did it come out of?"

Duke poured him a shot. The Lieutenant held it out in front of his face, swirling the liquid around and examining it closely. He took a sip, smiled, and downed the shot.

"I bet that bourbon is the best thing in this armpit of a bar."

"Very astute, Lieutenant."

"Thank you, sergeant. Moving right along, would you care to explain to me why that rather understandably apprehensive man had an officer of the law pointing a cocked .38 at, shall we say, a rather sensitive part of his anatomy?"

"Certainly, sir. He displayed a complete and utter lack of respect for me and my young partner. In a rather loud voice he disrespected the badge and furthermore, sir, I believe him to be a Democrat."

The Lieutenant drummed his fingers on the bar. "You say he's a Democrat?"

"Yes, sir, my wife works at the polls."

Nodding the Lieutenant said, "Well, then, I'd have to call that sufficient cause to threaten to blow his dick off."

"Yes, sir."

The Lieutenant turned to the Empire contingent. "Gentlemen, is that the skinny of it?"

They all nodded as my father stood up. "Yes, sir, Lieutenant, sir, these two fine officers were verbally assaulted and displayed commendable restraint. Only when they were physically assaulted did they resort to what myself and my son and three friends found a very shocking and distasteful but, nonetheless necessary, avenue of behavior including the threat of, or use of, violence."

Everyone kept a straight face.

"Officer Ryan," he turned back to Duke. "I don't seem to see a bartender. If it wouldn't be breaking union rules, could I impose upon you to perhaps pour a round of drinks for these gentlemen."

Duke looked at the rookie and before he could speak, the young cop was behind the bar grabbing beers and pouring bourbon.

"Chain of command, sergeant?"

"Yes, sir."

The Lieutenant nodded. "I'm very sorry if this incident upset you and your friends. Would you testify in a court of law as to what transpired here today in, shall we say, a bit of an exaggerated version of the truth?"

My father stood and extended his hand. "You have all of our words on it."

The Lieutenant shook his hand. Everyone knew my father. His word was not only his bond, it was his life. All nodded.

"Well, sergeant, I think we are all covered here."

"Yes, sir, I believe so."

The Lieutenant turned to the sergeant. "Some rather creative writing in the reports tonight, I think."

"Yes, sir."

He concealed a faint smile. "I'll be looking forward to it."

"Thank you, sir."

"Carry on, sergeant."

"Yes, sir."

He started for the door but then stopped. "Sergeant, would I be correct in assuming the prostrate man behind the bar with his face smashed in a pool of blood and with what appears to be some type of squished bug protruding from his mouth in some way displeased you today?"

"That would be a very astute and correct observation, sir."

"Uh-huh." He turned to the Empire crew and nodded to them, to me, to each of the two police officers and then walked out of the bar.

"You know, that Lieutenant Marr is pretty smart for an officer," Sergeant Duke Leland Ryan said. "He might even make chief some day."

Everyone nodded.

The bar was as silent as if someone had thrown a switch. I

turned to see the biggest lumper from the earlier fight walk into the bar wearing a nasty scowl on his very battered face. He was joined by four others showing the unmistakable signs of the altercation on their faces. Each carried a shiny, five pronged pitchfork balanced on his shoulder. Impaled on each pitchfork was a monstrous, half-fathom long, snow white and silver lined haddock impaled through the mouth and out through the gills for ease of transport.

"Bill," my father said under his breath. "How many?"

"Five."

The lumper in the lead motioned to the others to stop and they stood halfway across the room as the big lumper approached my father. Pop stood but motioned his friends to remain seated.

"We didn't know Peter laid a hand on your boy," he said sticking out his hand. "We're sorry."

"Anyone can make a mistake," my father said, taking his hand. "Christ knows I've made my share."

The lumper turned to me. "Are you alright?"

"Peachy," I replied.

He nodded and then turned to leave.

My father looked at me. "Peachy?"

I shrugged.

"You watch too much TV."

The lumper rejoined his friends and the five walked out of the bar, the big old haddocks bouncing off their backs with every step.

Uncle Bill finished his beer and lit a smoke. "I thought we were going to have to kick their asses again." He winked at me. "We seem to have a serious problem, brother Ted."

"What's that, Billy?"

"I would like another beer and the barkeep seems somewhat less than capable of getting it."

My father stood scratching his chin. He addressed the entire bar. "Ladies, gentlemen, due to a rather bad case of diarrhea of the mouth, the bartender-slash-owner is incapable of serving any more drinks this evening and, in all probability, for many nights yet to come. We are all in a bad situation. However, I believe I have a solution, simple though it might be... for one drink, and one drink only,..." He yelled the sentence guaranteed to induce rioting in any bar, anywhere, since ever there were bars. "The bar is OPEN!"

Pandemonium ensued. Everyone rose and surged toward the bar in a frenzied wave. The wave rose to its peak and then crashed down over the bar as everyone hollered their drink of choice.

"Bud!"

"Schlitz!"

"Bourbon!"

"Vodka!"

Uncle Bill and Bill Walima ran behind the bar and began passing out drinks.

"You are all on the honor system to pay," yelled Uncle Bill. That brought a bunch of hoots.

Bill Walima rolled the bartender onto his stomach. When he saw me looking he said, "That's so he doesn't drown in his own blood."

I was learning all kinds of cool shit this day.

"Beer?" Uncle Bill asked the rookie.

He shook his head and Uncle Bill drew him a Coke.

"One of us should not have beer on his breath," he said to Duke.

"Right you are, lad, and since you are five hundred years my junior, you made the right choice."

"Did I go too far with that guy?"

"Hell, no. You were beautiful. A thing of joy to behold, you were. You didn't just represent yourself. He disrespected your badge—the law itself. You done real good. You're the law. You're a cop on duty and its your right and responsibility to exercise a competitive edge in any type of confrontation. And don't you forget it." Rising Duke slapped him on the back. "Did you see my boy in action, Ted? This is my boy here. I'll make a walking, flat-footed, waterfront cop out of him yet, you betcha." He grinned. "Sonny, you shut that sorry son of a bitch up big time. OUTSTANDING!"

By this time everyone had a drink and the bar had quieted down some. Bill Walima emptied his shot glass, placed it on the bar, and addressed us.

"I found that individual to be lewd and crude and his behavior was socially unacceptable and I sincerely doubt that his ability to verbally communicate for awhile will, in any way, shape, or form, have any effect on the overall evolution of mankind to a higher plane of consciousness."

The old man and Uncle Bill stared at him in awe. "Jesus, Bill, that was eloquent."

I, of course, was trying to make sense of what he had just said.

"Well, rook," Duke said as he pushed his stool away from the bar and stood, "it's about time we went somewhere else to protect and serve the public."

The cops and the Empire crew shook hands.

"Take it easy, Mr. Twenty-six," the young cop said shaking my hand. "I'm Aran Patrician, and you?"

"Mark," I replied. "Nice to make your acquaintance."

They walked across and out of the bar.

My father looked at me and lowered his glasses.

Oh, shit, I thought, here it comes.

"You saw a lot of shit today that you probably should not have. Did you learn anything?"

I sat silently thinking as hard as I could. He tapped his forehead with his finger.

It hit me. "To think?"

He grinned. "Bingo," he said loudly. "Exactly. You thought. You reasoned your way out of a bad situation. Ya hear that, Billy?"

"Yep. He was some cool under fire."

Bill Walima smiled at me also.

"That guy with the pitchfork really scared me."

"Yes, he did," Pop said. "I let him."

"Why?" I stuttered.

"I'm your father, not your babysitter. My job is to teach you."

"But why?"

"That's what fathers do. Sometimes the lessons are easy and clear cut, sometimes they're not. The hardest ones are the most important. I work too long and hard. Time is a luxury I do not have. An opportunity presented itself today to teach you the most important lesson of all, how to stay cool and think under pressure. That's how you stay alive when it's not that easy to. As you go through life, sooner or later you're going to find yourself in a bad situation. When all around you panic, call to God, or go into hysterics, you take a deep breath. The quick short ones are like putting one foot in the grave. You reason your way out of it no matter how bad it is. There are always options. Keep thinking and don't you never goddamn quit. That's your best chance to live, you hear me?"

"Yes, sir."

"As far as drinking is concerned, that one in front of you is your last for seven years. Are we clear?"

I nodded.

"As far as fighting is concerned I'll make it real simple. Don't you never let anyone be bullied—man or woman, verbally or physically. Don't you never start a fight but don't you never walk away from one, you hear me?"

"Yes, sir." To this day I have lived by his words and someday I'll die by them.

"If you have to fight, you win any goddamn way you can. You be vicious. So goddamn vicious that even if you lose the fight your opponent will never want a rematch. You understand?"

"Yes, sir."

"And that will be enough of life's lessons for one day. Gentlemen," he said standing, "I have enjoyed the pleasure of your company and the day's festivities but I fear it is time to call it a day. With that I wish you farewell as I am sure my wife has prepared a sumptuous dinner which, hopefully, I will be able to partake of before I am murdered." He put an arm around my shoulders. "Come, fellow combatant and boozer. We are gone."

Uncle Bill and Bill Walima waved good-bye and we started across the bar toward the door.

Halfway there our way was blocked by the very scantily-clad female with the very, very large boobs.

"Teddy, are you going home so soon and taking the cute little boy with you?" she said bending over and giving me a full view of those two perfect breasts. I would have stayed in a heartbeat.

I've always been such a slut. Give me a drink or two and include a pretty female and I am just so easy, easy, easy. Which, of course, makes me ... male.

"Yes," Pop said taking a firm hold of my shoulder, "I'm afraid so."

"Oh, Teddy, why don't you stay and have one last beer?"

"Young lady, there are many reasons why I must continue on and out of this establishment. First and foremost is fear for my life."

"Oh, Teddy, how much trouble can I get the both of you in?" She reached her hand out to me.

He had a tight grip on my shoulder restraining me.

Bastard. Given the choice between Mom's cooking, good as it was, or this girl's lap again, I knew what I would choose.

"Mark, remember when I said the lessons were over for the day? I was a bit premature."

I was still staring at those boobs. He turned me to face him. "Look at me. What is the most dangerous thing you have seen today?"

"The pitchfork?" I asked sneaking another look at the girl's assets.

"Wrong," he snapped. "It's right in front of you!"

"Her?" I stammered.

"Yes. To a man, in your case, a boy, there is nothing more dangerous on this planet than a pretty female and a glass of whis-key—a woman's ass and the whiskey glass. And don't you never forget it. Pretty women and liquor have done in more men than both World Wars."

Now I can tell you that I have disregarded this advice over and over but it was still the best advice I was ever given. However I sure have had a lot of fun disregarding it. And, you know, correct me if I'm wrong, but we do only get to live once and it is woefully short.

"Teddy," she said feigning crying. "You're terrible."

"You'll handle it," he said.

I, under considerable duress—mostly physical, continued toward the door. When we got there, my father turned around and made an announcement, "Ladies and gentlemen, the bar is again open."

Once again pandemonium ensued and a wave descended on the bar.

"Sometimes I'm just too good," he said laughing. "You see that?"

I nodded.

"What kind of alcohol do you think is the most dangerous?"

"The hard stuff?" I snapped back.

"Nope," he said. "The free stuff. And don't you never forget it. I've watched free alcohol cause trouble and deaths over and over again."

Christ, was he right.

We exited the waterfront haunt known as The Silver Perch and all of its glorious, forbidden iniquities, and got into the car.

"When we get home, you have to go upstairs and clean up before your mother sees you or it's gonna be bad."

I nodded.

"And, for Christ's sake, let me do the talking."

"Are you going to lie?" It was beautiful. I had him cold.

"Perhaps. But mostly by omission."

"That means you're just not going to tell her."

"And perhaps exaggerate the truth a bit."

"You're gonna lie."

He sighed. "Mark, I hope that if you ever find yourself in my position right now, you can explain to your son about lying to your wife better than I just did. I'm not the perfect father, you know."

"I've noticed," I shot back. God, that felt good!!

We drove the rest of the way in silence.

We made it through the door of the house and halfway up the stairs.

Unfortunately I was not very experienced at ascending stairs intoxicated (I've since mastered it). I fell ass over elbows. It was far from the last time I was to fall down the stairs drunk, but it was the first—and the timing could not have been worse.

"Freeze like a statue NOW!" She was standing there pointing at the floor in front of my father. My mother, all five feet of her, wore a less than happy face.

Pop grabbed me by the arm and stood me up before I smashed into the radiator.

"Are you alright?" he asked.

"Yes."

"Smooth." He let go of me. "Way to go."

"Are you sure he's alright?" my mother said. "He's covered in blood."

My father's eyes went wide and his mind sprang into action. "He must have had a bloody nose and it splashed all over him. Right, Mark?"

I was concentrating on trying not to sway.

"Right? Mark?" He repeated.

"Yea. Bloody nose."

"His nose doesn't seem to bleeding now, does it, Mr. Ted Williams, Mr. Big Football Star? Why is my son covered in blood?"

"Blood?" He looked me over. "Where? Oh, that's just fish blood."

"And you're covered in blood, too."

"Well, it's not mine. And I'm fine—thanks for asking."

She glared at him. "Fish blood," she said disgusted. "How did you manage to skin every one of your knuckles?"

"Well.... I just tripped and fell."

"Do you see d-u-m-b written on my forehead?" She clamped her fists on her hips. "Did I just fall off the turnip truck?"

"No, dear."

"Oh, don't you 'dear' me! You fell? Malarkey. In twenty years I have never seen you 'just fall'. Even with eleven guys trying to knock you down, you managed to stay on your feet. You might maybe want to try another explanation."

He started to talk but she held up her hand and cut him short. "Enough. You!" She pointed at me. "Bath!" She pointed the way.

I took two steps.

"Freeze right there. I smell beer."

Pop shrugged. "I stopped for one with the boys. I got a hundred and fifty dollar a week raise today, dear."

"Just knock it off with the 'dear'! One hundred fifty dollars a week won't help you now. The two words 'one beer' are not in your vocabulary. You expect me to believe you stopped for a beer with your brother and Bill Walima and had one? It would be the first time in your lives that you entered a bar and had just one. Don't insult my intelligence." She leaned closer to me. "I smell beer on him."

"Well," Pop was struggling. "Maybe some got spilled on him."

"You took him into that dive?!"

"I'll have you know The Silver Perch is a fine establishment."

"Oh, please." She looked at me again. "I smell perfume on him. Tell me I don't smell perfume on him!"

We are like so-o-o busted, I thought.

"You don't smell perfume on him," Pop agreed.

"Hilarious," she shot back. "Cheap perfume at that. What has he been into today?"

I just tried really hard to stand as still as possible.

"Did you let him drink beer today?"

With all his options exhausted my father did a terrible thing—the only dishonorable thing I've ever seen him do. He threw me to the wolves. He pushed me under the bus. It was painful.

"Mark, did you sneak a beer?"

I stood silently. He had betrayed me. "Yes," I mumbled.

"Oh, bullshit," she said. Mother never swore. When she did it was serious. "Drinking beer in the company of floozies? Just what are you trying to teach him?"

"Actually, I was trying to teach him to use his brain to stay alive in situations that aren't all that easy to live through."

"By giving him beer and having him consort with tramps at the ripe old age of thirteen?"

"I will teach him with whatever I am given and do whatever it takes."

"What's a floozie?" I asked innocently.

Pop had all he could do not to laugh out loud.

"Never you mind," Mother said. "What exactly did you do today?"

"I worked."

She frowned at me. "You're not going to rat him out, are you?"

"He hits a lot harder than you do."

Now Mother had all she could do to remain stern. "Both of you. Up those stairs. Bath. Dinner is in fifteen minutes. MOVE!"

We had one type of fish or another at the Williams household about five out of seven days. There were times when I wished my father ran a meat plant but the fish was always just hours old.

We had white haddock baked just long enough with cheese and bread crumbs on top; mackerel, dark and moist, right off the grill, so rich that to put butter on it would be overkill; two inch thick pieces of halibut, and swordfish cooked just right. You don't cook fish, you heat it. Sometimes there were long, thin pieces of grey sole rolled around a shrimp stuffing; lobsters boiled and baked; scallops so huge they had to be cut in half to cook correctly—wrapped in bacon they're a treat; butterfish whose name explains texture and taste; little smelts with the heads still on. The heads are delicious. Picking a smelt up and crunching the heads off in my mouth drove my sisters and mother nuts which was reason enough to do it. It once sent a date running for the little girls room years later but they were so tasty.... as was she.

This night at the Williams house it was thick slabs of virgin white meat cut from fathom-long haddock, covered with Italian bread crumbs and Parmesan cheese. It broke into large flaky pieces at the first touch of a fork—no knife was needed—and would melt in your mouth before you could chew it.

The last fish onto the boat is, of course, the freshest. The lumpers would take them for themselves and hide them in secret places all around Empire. My father knew all the hiding places. There were also scallops as big as tennis balls, as well as fresh native corn, so sweet and tender a toothless man could eat it right off the cob. Peas the size of marbles were as green as they could be and exploded in your mouth with freshness. Finally there were new potatoes in their thin skin, as soft as mashed and dripping butter, veritable caviar to a family of mostly Irish ancestry.

The Silver Perch is gone—a victim of urban renewal. Urban renewal is when the government throws you out of your house at gunpoint, gives you half what it is worth, wrecks it, and builds something else. Now a statue of Fitz Hugh Lane sits where the Perch was. He paints one of his many Gloucester Harbor scenes.

The other bars and Houses of Joy that lined Duncan Street are all history. A bank sits in place of one whorehouse—they took a whorehouse and turned it into a bank. It just isn't fair. Some poor working stiff walks into a bank to borrow money for a house. Over twenty-five years he'll pay back twice what he borrowed and if he misses a payment the bank merely throws him out of the house, loans the money to somebody else, and they get it paid back twice. If nothing else, it remains a constant. Both the guy who walked into the pleasure palace back then and the guy who now walks into the bank to borrow money now get fucked, don't they?

Chapter 3 - Ted Williams: The Football Player

They called it the Warm Pot. It was scoured out at the intersection of two creeks—one coming from the northwest and the other from the northeast where they merged into one and dug out this swimming hole. Then one creek turned almost ninety degrees and continued on by Good Harbor Beach and into the ocean, hence the name. The Warm Pot was twenty yards in diameter and a full thirty feet deep at its center. From the deepest part of it, the sides sloped up in the same fashion as an old iron pot. At low tide the surface of the remaining water was heated by the sun making the Pot much warmer on the surface than the water on the beach. For this reason it attracted a lot of swimmers.

On this sunny Sunday afternoon the swimming hole is host to some thirty adults and more children. The kids, under the watchful eyes of moms and dads, swim and play noisily in the warm, dark water. Many collect shells, periwinkles, and sand dollars or try to catch small shrimp and minnows in the shallow periphery of the Warm Pot, as young children have since the beginning of time. Moms and dads sit on gaily colored beach towels in a circle on the warm, white sand that surrounds the Pot. They talk with many hand gestures vividly exchanging views. Couples engage in horseplay. Young men launch surprise attacks from under the water on their girlfriends who scream in mock terror. Two of the boys grab one of the girls by the hands and feet and swing her back and forth three times before catapulting her far out into the water. She screams all the way out and splashes down obviously enjoying the attention. These many eclectic sounds, along with the voices of thousands of bathers a few hundred yards away on Good Harbor Beach, create a loud buzz. The title to this Rockwellian scene could be "Swimming Hole, Anywhere, USA".

Somewhere in this perfect picture a nine-year-old boy begins to drown. He was either inadvertently kicked in the head or he made too many shallow water dives building up an excess of carbon dioxide in a phenomenon called "shallow water blackout". Either way he has become unconscious under water. So, in the middle of this sunny Sunday afternoon, with a gentle breeze blowing off the water in the shadow of thousands, little Tony Santos begins the slow descent toward the cold and forbidding bottom of the Warm Pot thirty feet below.

In the early Sixties it was believed that a person deprived of oxygen for just three minutes was brain dead. At just a few feet below the surface the air is compressed from Tony's lungs and he becomes negatively buoyant. Tony descends slowly at first but with the air exiting his mouth and nose, leaving trails of bubbles, he picks up speed. As he passes through the first three feet of water he leaves the warmth of the surface and enters a thermocline, a layer of much colder water. At just ten feet the water pressure is enough to rupture both of his ear drums. Perforated eardrums, however, are the least of Tony's problems as he moves faster and faster toward the inhospitable bottom of the Warm Pot. At twenty feet, with his hair gently moving back and forth like ripples on a pond, Tony's small body spins face up. His unseeing eyes face the surface, the sun, oxygen and life. With his arms and legs gently moving back and forth he picks up more speed. He enters the final thermocline and impacts the bottom of the Pot with enough force that a mushroom cloud of mud and silt erupts three feet off the bottom around him. Tony is thirty feet down in freezing water and his body has automatically gone into a state of hibernation. His life signs are all but nonexistent as his body diverts blood to his brain at the expense of his extremities. Tony's body fights to try to stay alive as long as possible. In the early Sixties this process had no name. It is now called "dive reflex". Children have been submerged in icy water for more than thirty minutes and been revived with no brain damage.

Tony has left the world of light, warmth, and laughter—the world of beings who walk on two legs and breathe air. Tony has entered a black, airless, cold liquid environment, a world foreign and unforgiving to those who inhabit the light world. In this world, this cold liquid world, the inhabitants of the light world above are viewed only as things to be pulled apart little by little and eaten.

Tony has entered the world of the crab.

Crabs are primitive creatures. They are not nearly high enough on the evolutionary scale to understand why they do what they do. They simply eat, excrete, and have primitive sex with other crabs. Crabs do not know much about the air and light world that exists above them other than the fact that most of what they eat floats down from above and ends up in their domain. Crabs are attracted to these objects quickly but through eons of time have learned to wait until they soften and become easy to pick apart and eat. Crabs cannot comprehend that this object that drifted down from the light world is a nine-year-old boy, a living, breathing being—a much more advanced life form than they, with the potential to grow, learn, think, and love. Tony is nothing more to them than food to eat. Absorbing its energy they will deposit what is left on the bottom of the Warm Pot.

The first crab to find Tony is a green one. Although not indigenous to this area, they came here mixed in seaweed from Japan sixty years ago. He carefully climbs up Tony's side and onto his tummy. He is joined shortly by a much larger red crab. They both test the flesh of Tony's stomach and determine it is still much too firm to tear apart. As the small boy's scent permeates further from him more and more crabs sense it. They close in on the boy. Creatures in greater number appear out of the dark and surround the motionless boy opening and closing their claws in anticipation. They have not eaten in a long time and are very hungry.

The boy has been legally dead for all intents and purposes for several minutes. It is just as well he is unconscious for what is about to happen to him has been one of mankind's worst nightmares since the beginning of time. He is to be slowly—oh, so slowly—ripped apart and eaten alive by hundreds of crabs, piece by little piece. It would be difficult at the moment because the body is still fresh and the flesh firm but in a matter of minutes the water will soften little Tony, tenderizing the little boy for them to pick apart. They will start by pulling pieces of skin off and thrusting it into their primitive mouths. In a matter of hours they will manage to punch through the skin of his stomach to get to the most succulent parts of him, his guts—the intestines and other internal organs.

In the interim the green crabs, armed with their razor sharp sickle-like pincer claws, will feast on a part of Tony that is soft enough for their immediate consumption. Several of them make their way up the side of his face toward the softest and tastiest part of the boy's anatomy. The green crabs are going to eat the little boy's eyes.

About this time Tony's mother notices he is missing. She begins yelling and gestures toward the center of the Warm Pot. When she doesn't receive the response she is hoping for she begins to scream hysterically. As she continues to scream everyone swimming in the water exits it as if they might be in danger of being implicated in some type of wrong-doing. It is as if the water has suddenly become an entity, a very evil thing, a thing no one wants to be in, let alone under. It's where a small boy lies drowning or maybe even dead. The swimming hole known as the Warm Pot has become a graveyard.

Mrs. Santos continues to scream, "My boy, my boy, for God's sake someone help me! My boy is down there. Please!"

Finally a couple of young men, perhaps urged by a mother's plea for help, or by chance to win favor with their girlfriends, enter the water and swim out to the center of the pool. After a couple of quick breaths, their legs rise vertically out of the water and they knife down into the darkness. Silence falls on the crowd of onlookers as they wait for the pair to surface. In less than thirty seconds both heads bob up, each gasping for air. White-faced and shivering they make their way despondently to shore. Shaking their heads and shivering in front of Mrs. Santos they mutter something about it being too dark to see on the bottom and too cold to stay there. She begins screaming as she runs down the creek bed toward Good Harbor Beach.

On the porch of the Williams Guest House, which overlooks the beach and the creek, a political discussion is taking place.

"I don't care, Father, he's a goddamned liberal." Shaking his finger for effect, he stands face to face with his friend Father Cunney, the parish priest.

"But, Ted, he's the Cardinal!"

"I don't care. He's a goddamned lefty. I tell you, Father, he's no damned good." Ted Williams's politics tend to be a touch right of center.

Sunday is a special day for the foreman of the Empire Fish Company. Monday through Friday the boss's work begins at 5: 30am and ends twelve hours later. Saturday is maintenance day. Sunday morning is spent doing yard work or whatever maintenance the Guest House needs. Sunday afternoons are spent either at the beach or barbecuing at the house.

On this early Sunday afternoon Ted and Father Cunney are on the porch of the house having a Budweiser or two and solving many world problems. Above the buzz from the thousands on Good Harbor Beach comes a sound out of the norm. It is the unmistakable sound of a mother whose child is in danger. It is low tide as Tony's Mom races away from the Warm Pot toward the Guest House screaming. As he crushes out his Kent cigarette and pulls on his beer, Ted Williams hears words that move him to act.

"Please help me, my boy is drowning."

As a high school All-State in football, Ted had a "full boat" (a full scholarship) to about every college in the country. He starred at Boston College before he went on to the NFL. Now, in his forties, working as a hands-on foreman, Ted is still a physical specimen. Running backs and safeties look like someone took a ten foot high, three hundred pile of bones and muscles and compacted them down to six feet and about two hundred pounds. They have a wound up look with the same bounce as a coiled up spring ready to explode. Rodney Harrison reminds me of my father—a little darker and better looking but with that same wound up look and bounce to his step.

He crushes his beer can and hurls it across the porch into a trash bucket.

"Well, Father, and we were having such a relaxing afternoon."

He explodes into action.

He jumps ten feet down to the side yard and again over the metal railing on top of the sea wall into the marsh. Displaying the distinctive characteristic of a pro football halfback, in three steps he is at full speed. Freed of his pads and helmet and in bare feet he flies. He covers twenty yards before the good priest is off the porch. Ted dodges the wood pilings in the marsh as he did tackles some twenty years before. Without losing speed he covers the remaining distance across the eel grass before turning ninety degrees left onto a sandy creek bed toward the distraught women. He sprints through a shallow pool of water about six inches deep, the splash from his feet kicking up behind him fully six feet into the air like machine gun hits from some World War II movie. Approaching the hysterical women he skids to a dead stop digging into the wet sand.

She screams and gestures that her son is missing in The Warm Pot. Ted nods and takes off toward the swimming hole a hundred yards away screeching to a halt at the edge of the hole.

When asked later about the short time it took him to get from the house to the hole he says, "I was running without a football, no pads, and eleven other guys trying to make a paraplegic of me, how the hell difficult is that?"

Below the red crab moves toward little Tony's eyes in search of some part of this large meal that is already soft enough to dig into and eat. The smaller green crab goes for his mouth for the same reason. They are both very hungry. The red crab kneads the little boy's eye testing for softness. Surrounding Tony in the murky darkness are many crabs moving ever closer as his motionless body seems less threatening and more enticing all the time. Several crabs climb onto his feet and prod, testing them for tenderness. It will not be long before they begin to consume the boy.

Breathing deeply Ted takes in the situation. As he regains his breath his first inclination is to dive in and search randomly but experience stops him. He knows his time on the bottom will be limited and the visibility almost zero. Searching almost totally by touch he cannot waste time going over the same areas. He disregards the many people pointing to different parts of The Pot—they are trying to help but no one really knows where the boy went down. Many of the bystanders, frustrated by their inability to help, walk away toward the beach as though to say, 'if I'm not here I cannot be held responsible if anything goes wrong.'

Growing up in Gloucester, Ted spent many days on Good

Harbor Beach and in the Warm Pot. He is quite familiar with the conditions at its bottom. As his breathing returns to normal he formulates a plan of action. He envisions the Pot as a clock with himself standing at six o'clock. He picks a spot on the far bank at about nine and aims a bit to the right of it reasoning that his stronger right arm would force him a little left. The enormity of the situation strikes Father Cunney as he arrives at the water's edge. Winded, he glances at Ted, and the other much-younger rescuers still on their knees gasping for air and vomiting. He knows that he and his friend are the little boy's only chance and that two men half their age have failed. Father Cunney calls on the one he has a bit more access to than most men. He calls in his ace. He asks God for help.

Ted takes several deep breaths and dives in. The Warm Pot is about thirty feet deep at its center. On the surface thirty feet doesn't seem very far—ten yards, a first down, two car lengths. The pitcher's mound is twice that distance from home plate. Field goals have been kicked from six times this distance in the NFL. Thirty feet under water is another matter—the pressure at thirty feet under water is almost twice the surface pressure. If you don't equalize the pressure in both your ears and sinus on the way down they will rupture and you will bleed profusely from both ears and your nose. If the surface water is a pleasant sixty degrees, after passing through a couple thermoclines it can be forty-five degrees or less on the bottom. You can pass out in forty-five degree water in fifteen minutes and be dead in thirty. Passing into water this cold can cause you to involuntarily inhale, not a good thing to do underwater.

In a full quarter-inch wetsuit, face mask, flippers and a weight belt, a thirty foot free dive is a test. Several free dives to this depth with little or no time on the surface will allow the carbon dioxide level in ones blood to go up which can result in shallow water black-out and drowning.

He dives and begins his descent into the cold darkness. His ears equalize naturally and he reminds himself that he will have a limited bottom time and must not search the same area twice. He pictures the clock in his head. Passing through the last thermocline and into almost total darkness his bones crackle with the numbing cold like Rice Krispies when you add milk. He fights the urge to inhale water and uses the breast stroke to glide along to the bottom, extending his arms all the way forward and then sweeping them back to his sides. Using this stroke also serves as a measurement. When arms are fully extended it is almost a perfect six feet between the two—fishermen have used this method to measure line for thousands of years, the distance is called a fathom. When he surfaces at nine o'clock in his imaginary clock, he has explored an area six feet wide from six to nine. For his second dive Ted moves two yards clockwise to approximately ten o'clock and eyes the location of five o'clock on the far bank. Breathing deeply he dives in and swims back toward the bank he started from. Many in the crowd of onlookers stand expressionless knowing all they can do is watch helplessly. Some begin to cry as they realize with each second the scene is closer to a tragic end.

On this second dive Ted passes almost directly through the center of the pool—the deepest and longest dive of the day. The icy water gives him a headache like the kind you get from eating ice cream on a hot day. His left calf muscle cramps severely and his entire left leg becomes useless. He continues on along the bottom in total darkness dragging his left leg continuing to do the breast stroke as he feels for the little boy. As he strokes back toward the surface the water turns from dark gray to dark blue to lighter blue until he breaks the surface at five o'clock. He pulls himself out of the pool and falls to his knees badly winded and vomiting.

"The boy is gone," someone in the crowd yells. "He's been down too long."

"For God's sake, don't kill yourself," another yells.

Father Cunney begins to pray out loud in Latin. Many in the crowd join in—some in Italian, some in Portuguese. Ted told me later that he came just that close to quitting but he looked at Mrs. Santos and wondered what he would say to her if he left her son to die. Some of the onlookers thought the older man should be physically restrained for his own good. Fortunately for them, they didn't try.

In his mid-forties he is a highly conditioned athlete much like the professional football player he had been twenty years before. He was one of those few people who could put a football under his arm and survive on an NFL football field. For twenty years he has worked hard at Empire. The strenuous labor has made him what, today, people would call "ripped".

But now he is in a bad way. His left leg is about paralyzed below the knee from a badly cramped calf muscle. He shivers uncontrollably and his teeth chatter. He will recall later that he is having trouble concentrating—it is a clear symptom of hypothermia. The next stage of hypothermia is unconsciousness. If he passes out under water he will die and he knows this. Without his glasses, the crowd around him is a blur but the constant buzz and the prayers of Father Cunney tell Ted he is not alone. He stands and walks slowly around the Pot. People back away, some with heads bowed praying, others offering encouragement. Some offer condolences. No one in the crowd expects him to enter the water a third time. He is a wreck and it is obvious that he has done enough. His breathing has returned almost to normal as he goes down on one knee at four on his imaginary clock. The early afternoon breeze, warm off the land, warms him. Tony's mother drapes a towel over his shoulders.

"Tony is gone," she sobs. "Thank you for trying to save him."

Ted has five children of his own. The house he owns at the corner of Bass Avenue and Nautilus Road is a blur in the distance. He thinks about his own responsibilities. Who would pay the mortgage and raise his children if he's not around? So far he has been running on adrenaline and the will to save a life. For the first time he realizes that he could die if he continues to search underwater and it would be a lonely death in the dark and freezing cold. He stands and tentatively takes a step toward the water dragging his left leg. The third part of the search, from four o'clock to eleven o'clock, although not the longest, is done in a very much weakened condition. He has a child Tony's age—me. Standing at the water's edge, Father Cunney continues to pray. The crowd for the most part is quiet. Some pray with bowed heads. Many of the girls cry. He stops staring into the water—he is all done. Mrs. Santos has released him from any responsibility he might have felt. Ted Williams is physically spent and he knows it.

"You can't make another dive, old man," one of the would-be rescuers yells. "Let it be."

The best way to get an Irishman to do something is to tell

him he can't. There were two things you never said to my father when he was in his forties—that he couldn't do it, or that he was an old man. Still shivering and dragging his left leg, he half walks and half stumbles into the water for the third time. He breaks the surface on the far side of the swimming hole a short time later. He collapses with his head between his knees vomiting. The priest and Mrs. Santos attend him.

One large red crab continues to knead Tony's eye as many more green crabs surround him. They crawl across his legs and all over his feet and stomach to test his flesh for softness. It's still just a little hard but salt water is a good tenderizer and they know it will just be a matter of time. Another large red crab appears out of the darkness. Many of the smaller crabs scatter, afraid of becoming food themselves. Crabs are cannibalistic. But the red crab, a full five inches in length, armed with a two inch serrated claws, has a much more important food source in mind. It scans for soft flesh on Tony's knees and feet. The crab rips flesh from the soft arch of the boy's foot. Blood mushrooms up and incites a feeding frenzy as every crab within thirty feet surges forward. Crabs begin to nibble on Tony's toes.

Above Ted regains his feet and his breath. He eyes the water in front of him. Only one part of the Pot has not been covered—the area from twelve o'clock to three. The boy has to be down there. Mrs. Santos puts a hand on Ted's shoulder.

"You have done enough," she tells him. "My boy is dead. Please don't go in the water again."

Year later Ted would say, "She just lost her child and she was worrying about me..."

"One more dive," he says enraged. "All I need is one more dive."

"No!" the priest stands in front of him. "If it is God's Will that the boy die today then let it be. You are not destined to die, too." He positions himself between Ted and the water.

"Father," Ted says, "I call few men my friend and you are one of them. I don't believe that it is God's Will that the boy drowns today. Now get out of my way."

He is shaking with rage. Rage warms him up. My father

knew how to use his rage, not only on the football field, but in numerous street fights on Gloucester's Portuguese Hill. His rage makes him go way beyond his capacity—and on this day it works for him and makes him return to that forbidden world where a small boy lies under thirty feet of water. With the priest chanting prayers in the background, people crying and the wail of fire engines growing ever louder, Ted makes one last dive. He thinks that it is a good thing to hear his friend's prayers as he dives as they may be the last thing he ever hears. He descends at an almost ninety degree angle. With a snap and a crackle in his shoulders he once again enters the thermocline and begins to shiver immediately. He can't remember which leg of the clock he is on and it doesn't matter because this is the last chance—he either finds the boy or it is all over. As before he sweeps his arms hoping to encounter the little body.

God, he prays, he has to be here—give me the strength to find him. He thinks about how much he wishes he had a cigarette and briefly promises God he will quit smoking and drinking beer if he can just find the child. He quickly revises this idea. "No need to panic," he tells me later. "Cigarettes, maybe—beer, never."

The big red crab is now sitting on little Tony's face. It neither knows nor cares what its claws will do to Tony's eye. For the crab an eye is just food. As its pincers close on the eye a striped bass senses its movement, flicks its tail, and blasts toward the movement. The bass smashes into the crab ripping it off Tony's cheek and crunches into the crab with surgical precision snapping it in two. The bass swallows then turns with another flick of his tail and snaps up the remainder of the crab as it darts by.

Ted sees spots before his eyes as he glides along the bottom. He fights the urge to swim back to the world of light and warmth as the signs of oxygen deprivation increase in this foreign and horrifying world. Commercial divers in thousands of dollars of high-tech gear have been known to cry for their mothers when they lose air at depth. I know I sure did. My father is alone. He is a man like most men with good and bad qualities but on this day my father is a very brave man.

The bass attack on the red crab causes a shock wave of water which resonates back, knocking aside the crabs nibbling on Tony's feet. The wave hits Ted right in the face and he instinctively swims right into the wave of water. His vision is almost zero but something silvery with stripes flashes by as he plows headlong into the unconscious boy. No time is left. He grabs the boy's wrist, braces himself on the bottom, arches his back and kicks off, pushing toward the surface. Slowed down by the weight of the boy the forces he has resisted until now take control and his oxygen starved body causes him to inhale water. My father is drowning. He's dying. "It's easy," he told me later, "you choke at first when you inhale and then the water just flows in and all the pain goes away."

The momentum of his push off the bottom keeps him moving toward the surface. Before he loses consciousness his life flashes before him. This is a thing I have experienced three times when working as a commercial diver and fisherman. For Ted it begins with the rocky shores of Baybull, Newfoundland where he was born with the monstrous, magnificent, blinding white icebergs just outside the harbor. Visions of his uncles in dories on the Grand Banks, his Uncle Patty, like many others, still there. He thinks about his wife. He effortlessly blazes past tackles on an NFL playing field. He wonders who will care for his children. He rises by inertia through the ever-lightening water, unconscious and still grasping the little boy. Ted Williams didn't know how to quit.

A crowd surrounds the water but only the priest wades out into it. To many the water has become an evil thing and they can't go near it. The priest, exhausted by his own diving efforts, wades in waist-deep water circling the periphery of the Pot keeping watch for his friend and the child. No one speaks above a whisper. Tony's mother sobs as women try to console her struggling to restrain their own tears. Men mumble to each other that there is nothing they could have done. The friendly swimming hole has the ambiance of a funeral—the funeral of a child, dead before his time.

Father Cunney grows agitated. This is the longest his friend has been down and the frightened priest raises his eyes to Heaven and begins to pray louder. As though on cue an arm breaks the surface right in front of him. The priest seizes the arm as many more rush into the water to help pull the unconscious, blue-lipped chalk-white man ashore. To everyone's astonishment the man has a death grip on the limp boy. A husky, bearded man slides his arms under Ted's shoulders and hauls him to safety. A little girl places a red beach ball under Tony's head. Tony lies limp and white with purple lips and nails, and widely dilated pupils. He does not breathe. He has no pulse. His feet ooze blood. All was for nothing, it seems—the little boy is dead.

Tony's mother kneels and cradles her child's cold body against her gently rocking him back and forth. "My Tony," she cries, "my poor baby, my Tony."

The crowd surrounds them praying in Italian and Portuguese, buzzing like insects with siren wails in the background.

Ted has begun to breathe. Throwing up water, he takes huge breaths of air as his color returns to normal. He struggles to sit up and makes his way to the sobbing woman.

"Thank you for trying," she cries. "My boy is dead but thank you for trying."

Emotionally spent, Ted begins to cry but his old ally, rage, fills him and he takes the child and turns him over slapping his back. "No," he screams, "no, I'm not finished yet." My father was never a good loser.

He turns the boy onto his back and begins to pump his arms up and down, the standard method of artificial respiration at the time. But the lifeless little body does not respond.

Ted read the Reader's Digest every month. "You can learn anything from a book," he used to tell his children. In the Sixties, mouth-to-mouth resuscitation was virtually unknown but Ted had read an article about it in the Reader's Digest and it came back to him. He places his hand under Tony's neck and lifts it making an airway. He pinches Tony's nose sealing it. He covers the cold blue mouth with his and breathes into it, trying to cheat death. The crowd watches anxiously. They have never seen anything like this.

"What the hell is he doing," someone calls. They don't realize they are watching the forerunner of CPR. Even the priest stops praying and watches Ted's every move.

With the first hard breath into the boy's lungs, the air comes back mixed with vomit. Ted, already terribly weakened, turns and empties his own stomach onto the sand. Later he tells me, "The kid had blueberry pancakes for breakfast."

The priest kneels beside his friend and copies the breathing method but he, too, becomes sick when the boy continues to vomit.

Both men cry in frustration but through the tears they notice a flush of red returning to the boy's face.

"Father," Ted gasps, "I think we've started something."

He tries again but the air keeps coming back in his face and he makes the quick, and very logical decision, that something is blocking the child's air passage. He opens the boy's mouth and hooks a finger far back into the throat. A small green crab scuttles up his arm and dives onto the sand where it quickly burrows down. With the air passage unblocked Ted continues to force his breath into the child's body until he feels the boy react and draw a breath on his own. He turns him to the side and white foam gushes from the little mouth. Tony has come back to life.

As the child lies on his side, each breath bringing more color into his face the crowd gasps and then begins to cheer, slapping each other on the back and clapping. Tony opens his eyes but they are unfocused. He does not see them and struggles to sit but appears to be unable to do anything. A hush falls and a murmur begins to circulate. What if the boy is brain damaged? What if all this work has only brought the boy back without the ability to think or function? Ted and Father Cunney kneel in the sand weeping with exhaustion. By now the firefighters have arrived and Joe Paynotta, a long-time friend of Ted's, drops to his knees beside the boy, talking to him, trying to encourage him to focus. Joe's partner Harold MacArthur joins them. The two firefighters have seen this before and they know if the boy can't focus soon he never will. Firefighters spend their lives saving others and they don't like losing—especially losing a child.

Tony's mother, who has been surrounded by women trying to support her, suddenly screams and pushes them aside. She hurls herself at her son. Elbowing the firefighters away she grabs the boy by his arms crying and screaming at the same time.

"Tony," she bellows, "Tony, you talk to me right now." She gives the boy a shake as the firefighters stare at her amazed.

"Please, God, please," Mrs. Santos prays and then shakes the boy again. "Tony, if you don't talk to me right now you are in some big trouble, do you hear me?" Everyone is stunned but the woman continues shaking her child. "Tony, you answer me or you are not going to sit down for a week."

Slowly, the boy's lips move. People strain forward as he whispers, "Mommy?"

"What, baby?" His mother holds him close.

"I'm thirsty, Mommy." The boy struggles against her and tries to stand. An electric shock ignites the crowd and applause, cheers and prayers rise through the summer afternoon. Ted and Father Cunney, still on their knees in exhaustion, stare in astonishment.

As the child recovers his senses amid shouts and cheers he asks his mother, "Who pulled me out of the cold."

"Those two men," she tells him pointing.

"Thank you, misters," Tony waves to them.

Ted and the priest wave back laughing and amazed as they try to help each other up.

"Well, Father," Ted says, still shaky on his feet, "this could drive me to a beer—not that it's ever a long trip on any occasion."

The two rescuers make their way through the crowd amid hand shakes and repeated congratulations. One of the young men who had made a first attempt with a single dive and then kept yelling doom and gloom says, "We were with you all the time."

"Well, son," Ted says, "that's what sustained us. Right, Father?"

"Absolutely," the priest retorts sarcastically.

Firefighters Paynotta and MacArthur come up to add congratulations.

"Would you gentlemen care to come to the house for a beer on this rather hot and eventful afternoon," Ted asks.

Joe's dark face splits in a grin. "We're on duty and we'd love to," both men chorused.

Before the four men can go far they are intercepted by Mrs. Santos. "Who are you guys?" she asks.

"This is my good friend Father Cunney. I'm Ted Williams."

"Ted Williams the baseball player?" she asks.

"No, ma'am, I was a football player."

"I know who you are," she says. "I saw you play for Boston College against Notre Dame."

"Really?" Ted grins. "Did I have a good game?"

"Not really," she laughs. "You kind of stunk. If you swam like you ran that day, Tony would still be underwater."

The four men burst into laughter as the grateful woman thanks him repeatedly.

Weary and still laughing they make their way toward the cold beers that await them.

Back on the porch of 136 Bass Avenue a church key is produced (long ago in the Paleolithic era, a church key was a popular name for a can opener) and four frosty cans of Budweiser are opened. Ted downs his in one long, grateful swallow, crumples it, lobs it into the trash barrel across the porch. He opens a fresh pack of Kents and lights one.

"You know, Father," he says, "these things are going to kill me."

"So quit, for heaven's sake," the priest replies.

"Well," Ted says, "I went without them for three days once and my wife Betty just walked in and bounced a whole carton off me. She said, 'Go back to them or I'm leaving' and she stormed out the door." He takes a long drag. "I guess my usually sparkling personality was a bit stretched."

"So it would seem," Father Cunney replied nodding.

All present chuckled and more beers were churched.

Back at the edge of The Warm Pot a small green crab digs his way to the surface of the wet sand and scampers back into the water. It slips down the side of the Pot away from the world of light, the world of warmth and sunshine. The world of monstrous two-legged creatures that stand erect and rarely venture down into the cold dark world where they do not rule. To the world where they only serve as food, to the world of the crab.

CHAPTER 4 - RATS
and the Art of the Off-Hand Rifle Shot

Trapped at the stern of the Black Sheep I watch with horror as the bloody salt water pools around me. I am no stranger to seeing men in pools of blood. The fact that it is mine is somewhat to the left of disconcerting. There is something about excruciating pain that heightens the senses and brings astonishing clarity—even clarity of hallucinations. He's standing there in his blue work suit with "Ted" on his left breast pocket, as real as the blood covering the deck. I can smell the cigarette he tosses to the floor and crushes out with his foot.

He is holding a rifle.

"This is a single shot, bolt action, .22 rimfire caliber rifle." He opens the bolt up and slides it back. Slowly, deliberately, he places a bullet in the chamber and pushes the bolt forward and down. "It is now loaded and ready to shoot. You understand everything I just did?"

I nodded.

He pointed the rifle out of the window. It cracked, there was some smoke, and the mud near the high water mark splashed up impressively.

"That's no BB gun," I said.

"No. It's not—and you remember that. This .22 rimfire is far from the most powerful rifle in the world but it is quite powerful enough to kill a person. Do you understand that?"

"Yes," I said.

"When I pulled the trigger, the firing pin snapped forward and impacted the rim of the shell causing a small amount of explosive material to go off and explode the powder. This forced the brass shell to expand to the size of the chamber propelling the bullet out of the chamber and into the barrel where it engaged the rifling, spinning it, as it traveled down the barrel and out. This spinning of the bullet is what makes it go so much straighter than the BB that comes out of your Daisy. It's the same with throwing a football in a spiral. This is a lot. Do you understand?"

I nodded.

"The reason I explain this is so that you'll understand that a gun is just a machine. It's not magic, it will do whatever you tell it to do." He ejected the empty shell and held the rifle up. "Now listen up," he said raising his voice. "This is a gun, a rifle. It doesn't have a brain, YOU do. You forget that for one second and someone could die."

He showed me how to use the safety and handed the gun to me. "There are certain rules that go with a gun. Rule Number One supersedes all other rules. Do you understand 'supersedes'?"

"Yes."

"What does it mean?"

"Goes beyond. It's the most important."

"Outstanding. Getting you the hell out of the Gloucester public nitwit school system with its New Math crap was the smartest thing I did this decade. The Sisters squared you right away." He looked at me and resumed. "Rule One. Never point the muzzle at any person or anything that you are not going to shoot at. What you do in these first and formative days of gun handling is to assume there is a continuous stream of bullets coming out of the barrel and point the rifle accordingly, usually up or down. Don't swing the barrel by anything."

"Okay. Up or down."

"Look, Ma-ah-k, I don't care if the gun is loaded or unloaded, if the safety is on or off, if the bolt is open or out of the gun altogether—don't you never point that gun at anything you shouldn't." He leaned down to make his point. "You have one chance. You make one mistake with Rule One and you are back to your BB gun, you roger how important what I'm saying is?"

I did then, I always have and I always will. I nodded. Thirty years later, while lowering an oily hammer, one-handed, on a .45 automatic, I blew a hole in the floor. I just sat there remembering the man who so long ago taught me the rule that saved me from putting a large hole through my ankle. Instinctively, thanks to him, I had kept the pistol pointed away from it.

"Don't shoot at the water unless you are shooting almost straight down," he continued. "The bullet can bounce off and go quite a distance. We don't want to hit someone across the harbor, now do we?"

I shook my head.

"Whenever you shoot, have a safe area behind to stop the bullet. I'll keep this simple. For the most part, if you follow Rule One you can't go wrong. That bullet can carry a mile so no shooting up in the air."

"Okay," I nodded. We were standing on the second floor of Empire Fish Company in the men's room which overlooked Gloucester Harbor. Directly across from us, in the part of town called The Fort, stood Cape Pond Ice. Years later, Sully and the boys took on ice there before they got weather nuked in the "perfect" storm. The Empire Fish building extends out into the harbor. The Building Center juts into the harbor on my right. Twenty yards of tidal mud flat separates them. This alley is roughly fifty yards from the window at low tide and twenty at tide. Norwegian brown rats, some as long as a foot, thrive in the alley. They dart back and forth from the rocks supporting the two buildings and move at varying speeds jogging in and out of the debris at the water's edge. The angle down to them was forty-five to sixty degrees, depending on the tide. With an iron-sighted .22 it was a challenging rifle shot. A rat scurried into the alley.

"Here's how it's done," the old man said, taking the rifle from me. He chambered a round, closed the bolt, tracked the rat, and splashed the mud directly behind it.

"I thought the idea was to hit them," I cracked.

"Okay, wise guy," he said, handing me the open-bolted rifle, "here. Load up."

As he watched me he smiled. "That's good, you keep your trigger finger outside the trigger guard until you're ready to shoot. That's smart. Where did you learn that?"

"I shot myself in the foot with my BB gun."

"Well, that's one way to learn." He grinned.

A big, old rat came out from under The Building Center wall. Two BB guns and thousands of BBs had taught me about sight picture, lead, and trigger pull. Resting my left elbow on the windowsill, I lead his center mass, the idea being to hit where he is going to be when the bullet gets there, not where he is when the trigger is pulled. I held the front sight down just a little in the rear notch to allow for the downward angle and touched the trigger back gently. The rat's head exploded. He shot up in the air about four feet and splashed back down in the mud very dead.

Pop took off his glasses and shook his head. "Were you trying to hit it in the head?"

"Left eye actually."

He laughed, then looked me in the eye. "You know, Ma-AH-k..." with that wicked long 'a' he had "...it's probably a good idea that you learn to shoot and shoot well."

Boy, was he right.

"Listen up. You are hereby sanctioned, within the confines of Empire Fish and in the alley between it and the Building Center, to shoot any and all rats and rats only. Leave the birds alone. Do you understand?"

"Yes, sir."

"Any breach of the rules will lead to an immediate confiscation of the rifle, do you understand?"

"Yes."

He leaned down again. "You screw up a little and you won't see that piece for a month. You fuck up big time and you'll never see it again in my lifetime."

Oh shit. When he used the f-word at that stage in my life, it was serious shit.

"Well. Then what's the cardinal rule of gun handling?"

"Watch the muzzle," I shot back.

"Outstanding." He handed me a box of bullets. "Here's forty-seven bullets. What's your goal?"

"To kill forty-seven rats."

"Excellent," he said and walked off.

I had a brand new Remington .22 and gold-colored bullets to shoot. I had been given the power of a gun and the responsibility that went with it. I was given the power of life and death. I was twelve years old. It was awesome.

On Saturdays there was no one at Empire save for my father and Bill Walima doing maintenance. Sometimes Mario LaMotta, the owner, came in, too. When I wasn't perched at the window in the men's room ambushing rats across the alley, I would roam other buildings seeking targets of opportunity. Moving from a smooth bored BB gun to a .22 rifle was like stepping out of a

WWI biplane and getting into a F14 Tomcat. In a matter of weeks I went from a fair shot with rest, maybe hitting one out of three targets, to a deadly killer. I prowled Empire taking out rats with nefarious efficiency, sometimes forty to forty-five out of fifty. I loved it. I was a rat killing machine. I shot them running between the buildings, knocked them down from overhead. I hit them in the head, in the front half—heart and lungs. I made frontal hits when there wasn't much area to hit and stern hits when they ran away from me weaving as they went. I nailed them eating and sleeping. With a downward shot I killed two with one shot while they were screwing. I knocked them off conveyor belts, wooden palettes, and dead seagulls. I was merciless. It was total war and the enemy couldn't shoot back. It was beautiful. I learned to shoot a rifle very fast and very well. No one had to teach me, I learned all by myself. I learned how much of the front sight to hold down into the rear sight at different distances on a downward shot, and on the occasional upward shot. I learned how much to lead a moving target at different distances. I learned to make one of the most difficult shots routinely—off-hand shot, no rest, downward angle, target moving at varying speeds, moving either right or left, zigzagging toward you and away with absolute lack of repetition of movement. Many times with three seconds to see the target and hit it. Target is sighted, rifle is raised, and safety snapped off. Correct sight picture is acquired, trigger is touched off—one, two, three. That stuff about squeezing the trigger is pure Hollywood bullshit. As soon as the sight picture is attained, the trigger is touched off. You try to do it without screwing up the sight picture but you never have enough time to squeeze it. You pull it directly back, quick and smooth. If you're lucky, you evolve to a higher plane of rifle shooting where you do squeeze the trigger but you start before you have the right sight picture and the race is on to get the correct sight picture just as the gun goes off.

Early in my decimation of the rodent population, Mario asked my father what I was shooting at. Pop handed him a trade journal article that explained that each and every rat in a factory the size of Empire did five dollars worth of damage every six months. Mario became my biggest fan. He bought me Remington .22 rimfire bullets in 500 lot bricks. The window from his office looked right out on the alley so he had a ringside seat for most of my kills. He could be in the middle of a high level meeting but at the crack of my .22 he would scoot his chair over to the window to witness the death-throws of a Norwegian Brown Rat. He would bang on his window in applause. Sometimes he would lower it and shout, "Good boy, good, that a boy, you shoot them all. You need more bullets, you just tell old Mario."

No wonder I became a good shot so young, I had an unlimited supply of ammo to practice with and targets to practice on. On one occasion I was returning to the men's room from a mission. Mario was behind me when, from the window, we saw a rat start into the alley.

"Oooh, ooh, shoot him," Mario said pointing.

"Wait." I tracked it to the center of the alley. CRACK! Dead rat.

"Good boy. Good boy." He shoved five bucks into my hand. "Why you wait so long to shoot?"

"If I let them get to the middle I can get another shot if I miss," I explained.

"You a smart boy," he said, patting my back.

While I kept my vigil in the window, he went into one of the stalls. I heard a considerable amount of muttering in Italian followed by the sound of a very large boulder hitting the water with a plop, the hissing of a high pressure hose, followed by a satisfied, "Ahhhhhhh."

The room was immediately filled with one of the most foul, obnoxious, toxic odors I was ever to smell. Even years later in my career as a commercial diver when I spent hours in the midst of liquids that would make a cesspool seem like a bottle of crystal, clear Poland Springs, I never encountered anything that smelled as vile as the grumpy Mario blew out that day. I started to hurl. I ran for the door and ended up with one hand on the wall projectile puking my strawberry pancakes like a fire hose. But I still managed to control the muzzle of my loaded .22 and not get any puke on it.

My father appeared. "Are you okay?"

"Yes."

"What happened? Don't tell me you were in there when Mario..."

I nodded.

"Run!" he yelled.

With the rifle at port arms and my father's hand on my left shoulder we ran down the stairs passing a very wide-eyed Bill Walima and out into the fresh air outside.

Out in the plant yard there was considerable laughing.

"He can really belt them out, can't he?" Pop said. "I always note when he goes upstairs and won't go in there for an hour—two if it's after he goes to lunch. I'll shit in a bucket before I go in there after him."

Bill Walima, who was curious as to why his boss and his rifle-carrying son had just come flying down the stairs, came out in the yard.

"Mark got caught in the head when Mario let one fly," Pop explained.

"You didn't warn him about that? I'm sorry, Ted, but I'd have to call that a triple P," Bill said, shaking his head.

"What?"

"Piss Poor Parenting," said the usually reserved mainte-nance man.

My father shrugged and Bill Walima walked away shaking his head.

"I'm going to hunt out on the wharf," I said.

"Good idea," Pop nodded. "It's after lunch—you'd best give it two hours."

When I made a confirmed kill, I'd save the brass. If Mario was around at the end of a hunting day, he'd find me, stick out his hand and I'd dump them into it. He would count every shell smiling with a look of sheer ecstasy on his face as he did it. If he wasn't around, I was instructed to put them in a glass bottle on his desk. As the glass bottle grew full, Mario took to watching me as I hunted—which led to a very fortuitous event. I was perched in the men's room window, Mario stood behind me smoking one of the world's most obnoxious cigars. Three rats emerged from The Build-ing Center and began their jig-jagging run across the alley. I took the first one out as they reached the middle.

"Get'em! Shoot, shoot," he yelled.

I had two more cartridges between the fingers of my left hand for easy access, a trick I learned watching a movie about big game hunting in Africa. I killed the second one but as fast as I reloaded rat number three scurried into the wall on the Empire side of the alley.

"That gun take too long to reload," Mario said.

"Well, at least I scared him."

"You not kill a lot of rats because you can't reload fast enough?"

"Yes," I nodded dejectedly.

He looked at me and left.

My father was with him when he returned carrying a box which he handed to me.

"You try this. It shoots a lot without reloading."

It was a Ruger 10/22 ten shot semi-automatic with a gold bead for a front sight and an adjustable notch for a rear. I can tell you now it was better looking than my last girlfriend. And she was a model. In hindsight the Ruger was definitely smarter, too, considering it didn't have a brain.

"You kill more rats with this," he said and walked out of the room.

My father looked at me seriously. "You can keep that rifle but the same rules that apply to the single shot, apply to it. Read the instruction manual. Run a patch with solvent on it through the bore then run one with oil through it. Get familiar with the safety and bear in mind that it will fire every time you pull the trigger." Pop's voice was extremely serious. "Listen to me—when you take the clip out there will still be a round in the chamber so it will still fire. A lot of people get shot by guns with the clip out." He leaned closer. "That would not happen if...."

"...they followed the first rule of gun handling."

He nodded. "Correct."

I nodded to show I understood how important this was. He turned and walked away.

I had a rifle that could shoot ten times as quick as I could pull the trigger. It was as if Daniel Boone had traded his flintlock for an M16.

I was devious. I baited them. I'd throw a dead seagull or fish into the middle of the alley and wait. Sometimes ten to twenty rats would wind up in my kill zone. I killed record numbers of rats but at the same time I noticed a strange phenomenon—my average went down. I was killing fewer rats per bullet than with the single shot. At first I dismissed it as being the result of having a new rifle with different sights but it continued, thirty-five out of fifty, give or take. Finally, I figured it out. With nine shots after the first, I wasn't being as careful in aiming. It was that attitude that led to a lot more misses. Years later I knew to call this "mind set". So then I went back to the mind set of one-shot/one-kill. When General George Armstrong Custer found himself and his two hundred and sixty troops surrounded by five thousand really pissed off Indians, they had single shot rifles. The Cheyenne and Sioux had lever action repeaters. Military intelligence, an oxymoron if ever there was one, had been slow to adapt a repeating rifle, believing that the boys would miss too many shots if they had a repeater. They were right.

A year or so later I was at the city dump one night, where the fires always burned, standing shoulder to shoulder with my friend Skip Arvilla. Skip was a lot older and given to informing me about certain great truths in life. We shot rats one after another until Skip turned to me.

"This is more fun than a date," he said, laughing. "Unless she fucks."

As my expertise with the Ruger increased, so did my confidence. I'd been ordered to confine my gun use to rat-killing but one day I heard screaming from the area of the wharf where my father had been working on a conveyor belt. Rifle in arm, I ran down the stairs to find my father pinned to the wall by two men. A third man lay unconscious on the floor as a fourth, brandishing a shovel approached my father. He cocked it back.

"Mark," Pop said, "the First Rule of gun handling is forthwith recanted."

"What does 'recanted' mean," I yelled, pointing my rifle at Shovel Boy's head, which showed I didn't know its meaning.

I was shaking so hard the rifle was bouncing in my hands

but I managed to train it on the man with the shovel.

"Drop the shovel," I shouted trying not to drop the rifle.

"You gonna shoot me, little boy?" the man hissed. He turned and stepped toward me. "You think that little rat gun will stop me? You shoot me and I'll bash your head in with this shovel." He took another step.

My father stared at me intently but said nothing.

"If you take another step, I will shoot," I said.

"You don't have the balls," he sneered.

I shot the shovel right in the head with a resounding clang and leveled the rifle at the head of the man who had been holding it. Evidently, not being stupid, he dropped it.

"Very timely," Pop yelled to me. "Gentlemen, this is my son, Mark, who is going to shoot you full of holes unless you vacate the area, right, Mark?"

"Yes, sir, much easier to hit than rats."

The two men on his arms released him. As he passed by shovel man he kicked him so hard in the groin it lifted him off the floor. The two men still capable of their own locomotion dragged the other two out of the door and across the street to The Silver Perch. Pop fired up a smoke.

"Splendid behavior," he said, patting me on the back.

"What was their beef?"

"Disgruntled, drunken ex-employees," he said smiling.

"Why didn't you tell me what to do?"

He knelt down, took off his glasses and looked me in the eye. "There are sometimes, Mark, when no one, not even I, can tell you what to do. This was one of those times."

"I don't know if I could have killed him."

"Well, fortunately, at the age of twelve, you didn't have to find out. Shooting the shovel was an excellent compromise. Real quick thinking. I'm proud of you." He squeezed my shoulder. "And, by the way, thanks."

"If I killed him, would I be a murderer?" Suddenly the impact of what I had just done, struck me.

"It wasn't necessary to take his life, but if you had to kill to protect your life or mine, you would be a killer, not a murderer. You may one day have to take a life to preserve your own or someone else's. Sometimes there is no other way. I hope you never have to find out but it is as it is."

Sometimes it's better to face a jury of your peers and let them decide whether you were right or wrong, than to face the alternative—death.

I became a regular figure prowling the piers of Empire, rifle in hand. One day as I made my rounds a long, black Cadillac pulled up.

"Hey! Boy. Come here." The passenger side window was rolled down and a very large Sicilian (even at a young age I could tell an Italian from a Sicilian) man with a broad-brimmed black hat motioned me over.

"What you shoot?" he asked.

"Rats." I made sure the rifle was pointed away from him.

"Two legged or four?"

A chorus of laughter rocked the car. There were five of them inside all dressed to the max with loud colored ties and bulges under their arms. There was also a girl next to the rear window and she powered it down.

"What a fine-looking little boy," she cooed. Her boobs bounced as she leaned out of the window toward me. I was mesmerized. They strained against the fabric of her dress for all they were worth. It held. Goddamit.

"Hey, boy, we shoot rats, too. The two legged kind."

Again laughter shook the car.

The girl leaned forward and both of those lovely boobs tried in vain to free themselves from bondage but, alas, they failed.

"Eh, guy, you looking at my woman?" said the man on her left.

"Ah, no," I stammered.

"Why not? She no pretty enough for you to look at?"

More laughter.

"You watch it, guy, I have a gun, too."

As usual, when scared shitless, I'm at my best. "Yes, sir, I'm sure you do. But mine is in my hand and I don't see yours."

Total silence.

The one riding shotgun, who had first addressed me, started laughing. "He don't seem too afraid of you, Joe."

Everyone laughed and Joe laughed the loudest.

"No, Anthony, he ain't. Hey, kid," Joe said, "I'll let it go this time. Forget about it."

"You got a name, tough guy?" Anthony asked.

"Mark Williams."

"Wait, wait. You not Teddy's boy?"

"Yes, sir."

"Hey, guys," he turned to the others. "This is Teddy's boy."

The nattily attired men were what I called wise guys, even back then, because that's the way they acted. I was young then but I knew what a wise guy was, and what they did for a living.

"Mark," said Anthony. "Would you do me a favor and go tell Mario the boys are here."

I nodded and took off up the stairs barging into Mario's office interrupting his phone call.

"Mario," I panted, "Mario, the mob is here. They're looking for you."

"What you say?"

"Five of them in a big black car. Outside in the yard. They've got a girl with them."

He hung up and went to the window. "That's my brother Anthony. Go tell them to come on up."

"Okay."

I ran back to the car. "He says to go on up."

"That's the good boy," Mario's brother said. "Here, buy you some bullets."

He handed me a hundred dollar bill.

"Mario buys all my bullets," I said like a dummy.

"Then go buy some candy."

I just stood staring, wide-eyed, at the bill.

"What's the matter, kid? You never had a hundred bucks before?" the one called Jay asked.

"Nope," I stammered.

"I tell you what—here's another." He handed me another brand new hundred dollar bill. "Now you can buy a whole shit load of candy. You can buy enough candy to get fat like me, ech?"

They all laughed.

"Kid, we got to go talk business with Mario. You look after

Kris while we went, okay?"

"You betcha," I blurted.

"Anyone mess with her, you shoot him."

"For two hundred bucks I'll run the clip on him," I said trying to sound as much like an adult as possible. They all busted up laughing.

"Hey, that Teddy's boy—he okay," they said as they started up the stairs laughing.

"Thanks for the money," I yelled after them.

"Hey, forget about it," they yelled back.

The pretty girl called Kris got out of the car. "Mark, will you show me around the wharf?"

"Sure!"

She was extremely pretty—with long blond hair worn down, a perfect body, big breasts, and long legs. My head came about to her belly button. In my later years looking up at that particular view became my favorite way to look at a girl—and usually assured me of a second date. You figure it out.

She took my right hand and I carried the rifle in my left as we walked out to the front of Empire to look at the boats. I think that somehow I got imprinted or something that day because ever since then I've always enjoyed having a pretty girl and a rifle around, go figure.

"Where do you shoot the rats?" she asked.

"Mostly from the men's room window."

"Really?"

"Yes, ma'am."

"Call me Kris," she cooed. "Will you show me?"

This was just too cool—getting to take a girl into the men's room! Just as we looked out of the window in the men's room a rat started across the alley. As distracting as pretty females can be, even to a boy of twelve, I aimed my rifle and killed it.

"That was very cool." She gave me a big kiss and pulled me close in a hug. "I hate rats." I put my arm around to hug back and, since I was rather height-challenged at the time, my hand came to rest on her nice tight butt.

"Young lady! Just what exactly are you doing with my son." My father appeared out of nowhere.

Drat, I thought. I hated when he did that—the bastard.

"He just shot a rat," she said.

"He did, did he?"

"This is Kris," I said to my father.

She floated over with her hand out and he shook it.

"Very pleased to make your acquaintance, young lady."

"Are you Ted Williams, the football player?"

"I was," he answered. "Now I'm Ted Williams, the boss of Empire Fish."

"I've heard about you," she gushed.

He looked at me and, before he finished lowering his glasses, I blurted, "I'm protecting her!"

"Ah-huh," he said. He smiled at her. "Such a fine looking young lady most certainly needs protection. A lot of unsavory characters drain over here from The Silver Perch." He turned to me, "Do continue. I'm all ears."

"They gave me two hundred dollars," I told him.

"How much?"

I pulled the two C-notes out of my pocket and showed them to him.

"Well, that's the easiest money you'll ever make," he said smiling at Kris. "You can keep the money, it's yours fair and square and you do have a loaded weapon. But I want you to understand that the individual who gave it to you acquired it by rather dubious means which I will explain to you when you're a little older. Now I have to run uptown for about fifteen minutes. I trust you can keep yourself amused in my absence?"

I nodded. "Can I keep Kris?"

She moved over and slid her hand around my shoulder.

He nodded holding back a smile. "You can keep Kris as long as Kris wants to be kept."

"We'll be here or hereabouts," she said smiling.

"I can't really shoot anyone, can I?"

"No, you can't." He smiled back at Kris, started toward the door and then stopped. "On the other hand it's Saturday and some of those stiffs standing outside the Perch used to work for me. We are, shall we say, on less than friendly terms. They have been drinking all day and even in their inebriated state they are bound to see me leave and do something stupid like come over here." He studied her. "Kris is an exceptionally pretty female and as such she will attract drunken males like seagulls to dead fish. No offense," he said to her.

"None taken."

"If, in fact, one of those idiots is stupid enough to come over here and bother her, uhhhh, shoot him in the foot."

"Which one?" I asked eagerly.

"Your choice." He winked at both of us, walked toward the door, then turned back to Kris. "Young lady, don't get him too wound up, if you please. He might shoot himself or something."

While we waited at the window for another target, she rubbed my back. Mark liked.

I asked her if she was going to marry Jay. She said he didn't want to marry her.

"He's stupid," I blurted, stunned by such an incomprehensible idea.

BAM! Big old kiss right on the lips! I was still dizzy from the kiss, and another look at those lovely boobs, when I spotted something out in the alley.

"Holy shit!"

"Is it another rat?"

"Look..." I pointed, wondering if the kiss had messed up my vision.

"That's the biggest rat I've ever seen!" we both said at the same time.

We're talking a Chernobyl nuclear rat here! The thing was fully three feet long with a head the size of a softball. It started across the alley and I thought that it was a really strange rat. Every few feet it would stand up on its hind legs presenting a really nice target.

CRACK. Head shot. He goes down. One very large, very dead rat.

Just as I was feeling tremendous satisfaction a window in The Building Center flew up and a man's head popped out. He was screaming all kinds of foul stuff. Kris and I looked at each other. We had no idea what he was screaming about. The head disappeared and the window slammed down.

Kris excused herself and went across the hall to the little girl's room so I took the opportunity to do the same. I was just zipping back up, my rifle leaning against the wall, when I was wrenched backward, seized by the throat, and slammed up against the wall. The crazy man gripped me by the throat, his black eyes blazing and his stinking breath assaulted me as he screamed maniacally into my face.

"YOU LITTLE PRICK! Do you know how long it took me to train that weasel to kill rats, you little fuck???"

My legs turned to rubber and I would have slid down the wall if he didn't have me with both hands by the throat. I was beginning to see spots when the man's head was yanked back and, suddenly, a full, right-hand punch crunched right into his face. Kris stepped back as he flew back into the corner. Rubbing her fist, she grabbed me and shoved me behind her.

He shook his head and staggered to his feet screaming, "I'm gonna pound both of you."

"RUN!" Kris screamed but the crazed man was between me and the door.

They seemed to appear out of nowhere. The hammers of four shining, silver-plated forty-five automatics clicked in unison as they pointed at his head. The boys had arrived.

"We seldom miss at this distance, asshole," one of them said.

My, I thought, didn't Weasel Man just calm right down!

"You all right, kid?"

I nodded, my shirt was ripped but that was all.

"Kris?"

She nodded.

"What is going on here?" Mario demanded.

"I came back from the little girl's room and this idiot had Mark pinned up against the wall, so I hit him," Kris explained.

The guy's nose was smashed and bleeding profusely. The guys all started howling with laughter.

"I guess to hell you did," Mario said. He turned to the bleeding man. "You get beaten up by girls often, cupcake?"

The boys laughed again.

Mario moved closer to him. "Now, what the fuck you put

your hands on that boy for? And it better be good."

"He killed my weasel."

Mario looked at the other men frowning. "Is this guy all right in the head?"

They all shrugged their shoulders.

"What the fuck is a weasel, anyway?" one asked.

"Ain't it some kind of animal or somthin?" another said.

"Yeah, it's an animal about this long," said Weasel Man holding his hands three feet apart. "I taught it to kill rats. The Building Center hires me to get rid of rats."

"I never heard such bullshit," Mario said.

"He shot my weasel in the head." He pointed an accusatory finger at me.

"Mark," Mario turned to me. "Did you shoot a fucking trained weasel in the alley?"

"Nope. Just a big rat. Right, Kris?"

"Biggest rat I've ever heard of, let alone seen," she agreed.

Mario and the boys approached the window. I pointed out the big rat.

"Looks like a big rat to me," said Mario.

The wise guys were all chuckling.

"It's the biggest fucking rat I ever seen, you kill it, kid?"

I nodded.

"He shot it once in the head," Kris said.

"It's a good thing you shoot it in the head," said the guy called Jay. "Otherwise it mighta got mad and come up here and eat you."

Everyone laughed.

"Jesus," another said, "I've shot some two-legged rats that weren't as big as that."

"It's not a rat!" screamed Weasel Man. "It's a goddamned trained weasel, you assholes."

Boy, did it get quiet. It's not a good idea to raise your voice to wise guys. Stupidly, Weasel Man kept yelling, "That little prick killed my prize weasel and that bitch broke my nose."

Before any of the men could do anything, Kris took two steps forward and smashed him in the face again. He shook his head trying to clear it as his knees wobbled and fresh blood flowed. Boy, could that girl throw a punch. The wise guys applauded.

"That's my girl," said Jay.

I think this was the second imprinting of the day. To this day, I love a really pretty female capable of extreme violence. Fortunately, Gloucester is full of them.

Weasel man wasn't getting any smarter. He lunged at her again and again three .45s clicked in unison as they were aimed at his head. He came to his senses.

"He was the best rat-killing weasel I ever had," he moaned almost in tears.

Mario pointed to me. "I have him to kill rats. Why the fuck don't you get a gun and kill rats like a man instead of some crazy bullshit, trained, big, fucking rat?"

"It's a weasel, not a rat," he pleaded.

Mario pulled his hat forward and looked at the man intently. "Now let me get this straight, you have what looks like a big rat that you call a weasel. You take this weasel what looks just like a big rat, you turn him loose around a bunch of rats and the boy here, who is killing these rats for me, shoots it in the head. What the fuck you think is gonna happen? And you have the balls to come into my fish plant and swear at him and put your hands on him and scare him and a girl who beat you up???"

"It took me two years to train him!"

"I don't give a rat's ass!"

That brought more laughter.

"Why you not get some white paint and paint 'WEASEL' on the side of it so Mark will know what it is and not shoot it? Maybe you could make a circus act out of it. Get out of my plant."

As Weasel Man started to walk away he turned and pointed his finger at me. "I'll catch you sometime when you're alone."

I blew him a kiss. How someone with a mouth like mine ever lived long enough for its body to get big enough to protect it, is a constant source of amazement to me.

"You didn't just threaten Mark, did you?" Mario asked.

As men have done from the beginning of time, Weasel Man had tried to salvage some manhood in front of the girl. It went south fast.

"Okay, okay," Mario said, "did you guys hear him threaten the kid?"

All nodded.

"You come into my plant and threaten this kid because he shoots your trained fucking circus animal that looks like a rat because that's what I hire him to do, you dumb, stupid asshole."

BAM! Mario smashed him in the face driving him back five feet into the wall with a thud as blood gushed everywhere.

Mario walked slowly toward him, speaking low, becoming more enraged with every step. "You threaten a child. I show you."

He grabbed him by the shirt collar with his left hand and began hammering him with his right hand. Bam, bam, bam. Blood was spraying all over the walls.

Over the years that I knew Mario LaMotta I was to see him on a few occasions when he became this enraged. There was beating someone up and there was killing someone. With Mario, I discovered, that line could get crossed very fast.

I hollered for him to stop—so did Kris. Two of the wise guys finally intervened and, grabbing him by each arm, managed to drag him off. In the midst of the beating, my father appeared and Mario stopped struggling.

Weasel man slumped down to the floor, semiconscious, bleeding everywhere.

"Well," said the old man. "I bet there's a story here."

All the men fired up tobacco of one type or another.

"Are you all right?" he asked me.

I nodded. "Kris smacked that guy when he grabbed me. She broke his nose."

"She did?" His eyes opened wide. "An extremely pretty woman, capable of violence. How alluring." He winked. That's it! I got it from him!

"She's Jay's girl," I blurted, "but he won't marry her."

A bemused silence ensued.

"I should think that's Jay's big mistake," he said nodding at Jay.

"Then these guys pointed guns at him."

"Gentlemen," Pop nodded at the men. They nodded back. "And thank you, Kris. Are you all right?"

"Just super, thank you, Mr. Williams," she said rubbing the knuckles of her right hand.

"Would someone care to enlighten me as to why this individual, who lies in a rather bad way, would come in here and assault my son?"

They all started talking at once recounting the story of the rat-killing weasel mistaken for a rat. I stood by the window, a portrait of innocence.

When they finished, Pop turned to me. "Didn't I tell you exactly what you could shoot and what you could not?"

"I thought it was a big rat," I said pointing out the window.

He motioned me out of the way taking the .22 out of my hands and leaning it against the wall. Lowering his glasses he peered out into the alley then turned back to the room.

"I'd have to call that an honest mistake. That thing looks like the biggest goddamned rat I ever did see."

Everyone chuckled.

He handed the .22 back to me. "Carry on."

Weasel man had come to and was struggling to his feet.

My father walked over to him. "Are you all right, sir?"

The man moved his jaw back and forth and moved his head from side to side. "Yeah."

"How much was your trained rat... er... weasel worth?"

Oh no, I thought. I could see it coming. Shit.

Pop walked over to me and snapped his fingers holding out his hand not saying a word. I gave him one of the hundred dollar bills I had so briefly possessed. He put it in his pocket and snapped his fingers again. I gave him the other one.

"Easy come, easy go," he said.

A new bike and Reese's Peanut Butter Cups, cigarettes, and Playboys for a year flashed in front of my eyes. Gone. The bastard. I was ripped.

He handed the money to the man. Mario and the other guys each chipped in a hundred dollar bill. With a beaming smile on his bloody face, he left.

A flask appeared and was passed around. I stood at the window next to Kris. I was pissed. Shouldering the rifle I shot out the window three times. All heads snapped toward me.

"Rats?" Mario asked.

"No," I said. "I shot the damn weasel again. It just cost me a fortune."

"That won't bring the two hundred bucks back," my father said with a stern look. "And it's a waste of ammunition."

"I know," I grumbled. "But it sure felt good."

"Yeah, kid," said one of the wise guys, "I know the feeling." Laughter echoed through the men's room of Empire Fish Company and two of the men's hats fell off as they belly laughed.

"Your son sure is a kick," one said to my father.

"Oh, he's a star." He scowled at me but I knew he was trying not to laugh. He finally gave in to a smile. "Young man. Make sure the next thing you shoot is alive and try not to kill any more weasels today."

"Yes, sir." I faced back to the alley.

Kris bent down, her fantastic breasts dancing in front of me. "It's okay, Mark, you'll get more money some day."

I melted.

"Young lady," my father cut in, "please be careful you don't poke him in the eye with one of those beauties. And, Mark, try not to shoot yourself in the foot. Okay?"

As I turned red the room filled with laughter and another flask appeared and was passed around.

I was distracted from my embarrassment by an eruption of squealing from the alley. A bunch of rats was feasting on the weasel. I raised my rifle.

"Wait!" Mario said. "Come here, guys, and watch this kid shoot."

They all crowded around me. Six rats fought over the carcass, squealing and screaming as they ripped it apart. Crack, crack, crack. I moved my sights from rat to rat killing them.

Mario was beside himself. "Oh. Oh, good. Good. Kill them all. Get them."

I killed three and the other three ran for The Building Center. I killed one then tracked the other one shooting right in front of him. He turned and ran for the Empire side. I let him run for a few yards then shot right in front of him. He again reversed direction. The boys caught on and thought it was hilarious. Hell, I was having fun and would have done it a few more times when I caught my father's less than approving look. I got the message and killed the rat with the next shot.

The laughter continued.

"That wasn't very nice," Pop said, fighting back a laugh.

"Can this kid shoot or can this kid shoot?" said Mario patting me on the shoulder.

"Hey, kid, you want a job," said one smiling. "Guys, there's another rat on that thing. Let's see how you shoot."

One moved me out of the way and all four stepped to the window. Four silver .45 automatics were drawn from shoulder holsters and cocked. Two were thrust out of the front of the window and one was on each side. Pop motioned for me to back up and pointed at his ears. I got the message, leaned the rifle against the wall, and plugged my ears. In the confines of the room, the blasts were incredible. Shockwaves rolled back onto us. I felt my hair blow back and squinted at blinding muzzle blasts as smoke filled the room. Golden brass shell casings flew everywhere, ka-chinking down on the cement floor as the slides on the four pistols slammed back and forth, hurling a shell every time as each pistol bounced up and down. Two windows on the Empire side blew up and one in The Building Center. Glass scattered all over the alley. The hits around the weasel splashed mud fully ten feet in the air—it was just so cool.

Some of the dead rats flew up in the air and plopped back down—killed twice, no doubt. The biggest target, Gloucester Harbor, took a few hits, its water splashing up and cascading down. Two passing gulls fell out of the air leaving a trail of feathers and floated on the water. Shells continued to clink down into the sinks and urinal and off my head. At almost the same time four slides locked back on the automatics. The acrid smoke rendered the air almost unbreathable.

The rat disappeared into The Building Center wall unscathed. My father and Mario tried not to laugh. Kris and I kept straight faces. It was a Hollywood shooting—lots of noise and no hits. You couldn't take a step without stepping on spent brass.

"I guess people are easier to hit," I said. Mario and my father smiled.

"Hey," Mario said, "if I had you guys to shoot rats, I'd be out of business."

"Hey, forget about it," one said.

All of them stood shaking their heads as they dropped empty magazines onto the floor with a clang. New magazines were inserted into the pistols, slides slapped forward, hammers thumbed down, and the automatics were slid back into their respective holders.

One of them turned to me. "Hey, wise guy, you think you could hit anything with this?" He patted his holster.

I looked at the old man.

He lowered his glasses. "Remember the first rule."

"Hey, kid, come here." He bent down and took his beautiful silver gun out. He held it in his right hand, dropped the clip into his left, and pocketed it. He pulled the slide back hard, ejecting the bullet and caught it in one practiced move. He went down on one knee and we were face to face. He handed it to me butt first. It was wicked heavy.

He pointed at the slide. "That is going to come smashing back. You don't want to have your fingers in the way. Capice?"

I pointed it at the wall with my right hand on the grip, finger extended down the trigger guard. The heel of the grip rested on the palm of my left. Using two hands, I cocked the hammer and dry fired it a few times.

"Hey, kid, I bet you no can hit that weasel."

"I bet you five hundred small that my boy here can hit that damn big, ah, rat, ah, weasel, whatever the shit it is," Mario replied.

Mario is rumored to have bet $250,000 on the Red Sox to win the Series in the early Fifties. Funny. Mario never impressed me as stupid but, Jesus, to bet that much money on the Sox???

All eyes were on Mario. My father lowered his glasses.

"He's never fired a pistol before. Hitting something with a pistol is a lot harder than with a rifle. He'll do well just to hit the harbor."

"Yeah, Teddy, you right. Boys, let's have some odds, if you please."

"How about two to one?"

"Four to one!"

"Three," Mario shot back.

The boys all nodded, except Anthony. "I'll bet with my brother. I think the kid might maybe hit that fucking thing."

A gazillion one hundred dollar bills came out.

"Three to one he gets it in one shot."

Kris held out five hundreds. "I bet this on Mark."

"Taken."

"Hit that thing," she said to me.

One of the wise guys shoved a clip into his pistol. It locked with a click. "Okay, kid, all you have to do is pull the slide all the way to the rear. Let it go and you're ready to dance."

I nodded.

"Keep your finger off the trigger until you're ready to shoot," said the old man.

I held the grip tight with my right hand and grabbed the grooves at the rear of the slide with the left. I couldn't move it. The boys chuckled. Mario and my father rolled their eyes back. Anthony bent over and whispered,

"Cock it first. It will make it easier to pull the slide back."

I did, then pulled the slide all the way to the rear and let it go. It snapped forward chambering a round and leaving the weapon cocked. I held a loaded, cocked .45 automatic. I was twelve years old.

I stood at the window and tried to get a sight picture holding the gun with two hands. I might as well have been at full gallop on a horse, the sights danced all over the place. I tried to get front blade aligned in the rear notch and get the weasel on top of the front blade to no avail. Then I did what smart shooters have done since peasants with matchlocks tried to hit knights on horseback, I took a rest. I rested both of my elbows on the sill of the window. With the pistol still pointed out, I glanced back at my father, Mario, and my pretty new friend, Kris.

"Take your best shot," she replied.

The other two nodded their approval. I felt no pressure. Yeah, right.

"Hey, kid, what's the matter? That great big gun too much for you?" one of the boys said. The others chuckled.

My friends, few that they are, can laugh and make fun of me at will. But to this day, if I don't know you, it's not a good idea to laugh at me. I get royally pissed, then I calm down and watch out.

"Why don't you guys shut the fuck up and let the kid take his shot?" said Anthony. "I've known you dipshits all my life and when you were his age none of you could hit the toilet with a stream of piss holding your little pecker with both hands. Go ahead, kid, take your best shot."

I rested the pistol on my left hand which lay on the sill and pulled it in while pushing my right hand out. The pistol steadied down. I got the weasel perched on top of the front blade and centered in the rear. I lowered the front a little to allow for the downward angle and started to take up the slack of the trigger. Easy, easy. Musn't screw up the sight picture by moving the pistol. Take in the trigger slack. Keep the weasel on top of the front blade, more slack, weasel steady on, more slack, easy, more.

KA-BOOM!

The blast was louder than a sonic boom. I had both eyes open when the gun exploded, I was blinded by the muzzle blast. The gun rocked up and twisted to my left. My father, Mario and Kris applauded as the weasel jumped a full foot into the air. A hit!

I stepped back from the window and suddenly slipped on the brass shells all over the floor. My trigger finger did a bad thing—it went inside the trigger guard and BOOM! I blew the window out!

The recoil knocked me down and slapped my finger back again.

BOOM! The mirror over the sink exploded spraying shards of glass all over the place. The wise guys, my father, Mario and Kris were all seeking cover in a big way! Hats flew everywhere.

What happened is called "machine gunning". Each discharge knocked my finger back into the trigger, firing the pistol. The ivory colored urinal exploded and turned to dust that drifted everywhere. The fluorescent light above blew up and drifted down over me like snow. The hats, asses, and elbows flew everywhere. Getting shot at is nothing new for wise guys. They litter the floor, staying as low as possible. The last round traveled the length of the room and shot out the street side window. The place was covered with prostrate men and one woman, dust and gun smoke. I ended up on my back with that big old .45 on my chest, slide locked back, empty.

The old man appeared over me. He took the gun.

"Are you alright?"

"Sparkling," I replied.

"Everyone alright?"

There was a chorus of affirmations.

"Mark," he said. "I think this is a bit too much gun for you at the present time."

"Do you think?" I said.

The boys started laughing.

"Hey! You gonna stay in that stall all day?" one called.

"I ain't coming out until Anthony tells me I can shoot back!"

"So, you gonna lie there with your leg in what's left of the pisser with white powder all over you?"

"Those goddamn buttons keep you too high off the floor," said another getting up and dusting off.

"Are you all right?" asked Kris giving me a hug. I could really get used to those hugs and the view that went with them.

"Maybe we shouldn't have put a full clip in, huh?" said the guy whose pistol it was as my father handed it back to him.

"Probably not the best of ideas," my father replied.

All the men lit up smokes—Mario lit a cigar—and tobacco smoke soon replaced the gun smoke.

"Pay up," Mario announced.

They all handed Mario and Anthony what looked to me like a million dollars. The one with the wicked husky voice slapped me on the back.

"Good shot, kid. Real sweet. Teddy, you sure you don't want him to come work for us in a few years?"

"Thanks but no," Pop replied.

Mario walked over to me. "I knew you could make that shot." Patting me on the shoulder he handed me a wad of hundred dollar bills. I counted five—I was rich!!!

"Mario," Pop said, "that's way too much money for him."

"Aw, let the kid keep it," Anthony said.

I vigorously nodded my head in agreement with him.

The old man stuck his hand out and I reluctantly handed him the wad. He took three bills and stuck them in his pocket.

"Tuition at St. Mel's," he said returning the rest to me.

Wow. Two bills! That was more than I had ever had.

The wise guys filed by me on their way out saying goodbye. Kris gave me another big kiss right on the lips.

"Bye, Mark," she cooed. "Thanks for looking after me." If my father hadn't held onto my shirt collar I would have followed her right out of the building and wherever she wanted to go.

One of the wise guys had a wicked husky voice. Years later I thought I recognized it in the trial of a well-known mobster. The story was that there was a million dollar open hit on him. That means if anybody killed him the boys would find you and pay you off. For awhile he was held out on Thacher Island, protected by the Coast Guard. My brother Ted and I figured it was probably too long a shot from shore. I'm not sure but I think he was put in the witness protection program where his safety was guaranteed by the government. He was killed some time later. Anthony did thirty years in jail for a murder he didn't do but was then released.

That evening on the way home in the car, I got the usual disclaimer.

"Now, Ma-AH-k, we don't have to tell your mother about the day's festivities, do we?"

"Absolutely not," I answered immediately.

CHAPTER 5 - SISTER MARY ROSE

I was in the fourth grade and nothing made sense. I couldn't even add numbers. At East Gloucester Elementary I spent my time daydreaming about P51s and B17s and air battles because I figured a kid who couldn't even add numbers like twenty-five plus thirty-five was just stupid.

I can close my eyes and see her face in front of me. Oh no, it must be a vision of hell! Her face, beet red with bulging, blood-shot eyes, and snorting through both nostrils as, white-knuckled, she brandished a three foot wooden pointer as thick as a broomstick. The white fabric of her habit heaving furiously up and down on her chest as she inhaled and exhaled vigorously screaming.

"You people must have woolies in your heads!!!"

Sister Mary Rose. Big globs of sweat rolled from her forehead, down her nose and splashed on the classroom floor.

I raised my hand.

"Yes, Mr. Williams."

"What are woolies, Sister?"

"Woolies, Mr. Williams, are the dust balls one finds under one's bed."

"Thank you, Sister."

"You are quite welcome, Mr. Williams," she hissed with a look that could melt glass.

Sister Mary Rose was my teacher at St. Mel's Day School. In my first four years in the public school all my grades were D's and F's. The classes were too big for the teachers and they were trying to implement newer, more liberal teaching methods and some foolishness called New Math. Report card time at the Williams house was not a happy time for me.

"Too much TV!" my father announced. "Well, I can remedy that."

Click. No television for two weeks.

"Don't you have home work?" he would say to me.

"Nope."

"Well, then I'll give you some. Where's that math test that you flunked and I had to sign."

I got it.

He pointed to one of the equations. "Add that."

I got it wrong.

"Add it again," he said. "Only this time THINK! You god-damn well pay attention to what you are doing and think." He pounded the table with his fist. My father swore at work all the time but when he swore at home, I had learned to seek cover.

I added the equation.

"Right!"

He pointed to another one and I added it.

"Right!"

I then proceeded to get every wrong one right.

"Now," he said, "why did you get all of these wrong yester-day and get them right today?"

I shrugged. "I don't know."

"I do," he said. "You're not dumb or special. You're just lazy. You need the proper motivation and the public school system is a catastrophe. You're going to a Catholic school. The nuns will take care of your failings just like they did mine."

Unfortunately, Catholic schools cost more money than public schools. My father began coming home late one day a week. He would give mother a handful of bills. He had found someone on the waterfront who would pay him piece meal to fillet fish not by the hour. He could fillet fish as fast or faster than the best cutters on the waterfront.

This went on for a month or so. Then one day he showed up at one of my Little League practices in the middle of the after-noon still in his blue work coveralls.

"You get fired again?" I asked.

"Yep," he replied nonchalantly.

Every once in awhile he would get into it with his boss, Mario LaMotta. They would yell and scream at each other and call each other names in front of the entire fish plant. Mario would then fire him. And the old man would walk out. Long before there were such expressions as "employment security" Pop had it figured so that God himself couldn't run that plant without him.

The place would be in chaos in an hour and Mario would start to see profits draining away big time. He would hire him back—always within a day. And always with an appropriate raise.

Pop was hitting flies to the outfielders when Mario pulled up in a big old black Cadillac. Pop handed off the bat and glanced at his watch as he walked by me.

"Well, let me see. Three o'clock. That's two hours. That will cost him an extra fifty bucks a week," he said winking at me.

"Oh, and Mark," he turned back to me. "Tell mother I'll be an hour or so late for dinner. I can personally guarantee that the fish plant is A.F.U."

"What's A.F.U.?"

"That means that the fish plant is running in somewhat of a chaotic manner."

"Okay."

Mario didn't even get out of the car. They both waved to me as they drove off. Pop didn't need to cut fish once a week any longer.

I was in one of the more hazardous seats in Sister Mary Rose's class at St. Mel's. It was located at the very front of the room. When she would snort through her nose I had all I could do not to burst out laughing. I knew instinctively that being a poor student put me on the list no one in their right mind would want to be on—her shit list. Combine that with the fact that I was male, I shuddered to think what would happen if I laughed at her. Still I resisted her attempts to teach me. I was quite the little rebel.

"Mr. Williams, did you study your homework?"

"Yes, Sister."

"Well then, if I were to ask you to multiply twelve times twelve, what would I have?"

I had no idea.

"Well?" she said mashing the pointer into her left hand with her right. "I'm waiting..."

It seemed like I went out of myself. Like someone else was

in control of my mouth. It just came out of me like an involuntary burp.

"Are you going somewhere, Sister?"

Her rosy face went beet red. In an instant her chest and her monstrous bosoms began to heave. Her dark eyes grew black and they locked on me. Her breath came in gasps. All the normal classroom noises ceased. Not a foot was shuffled. She took a great, deep breath through her nose and blew out spraying gobs of green snot all over the front of her spotless, white habit.

I couldn't help it. I burst out laughing. The rest of the class, obviously more intelligent than I, remained silent. She took a step toward me and raised the pointer as high and as far back as she could. In a booming voice that reverberated off the walls and shook the classroom windows she bellowed, "Young Mr. Williams, while you are at St. Mel's you may not learn to fear the Lord thy God but you will most certainly learn to fear me!"

The rest of the class hunkered down, they were safe. I was the one that was the target.

Ka-BOOM! She brought that pointer down and smashed me right across the face. Damn, she was fast. I didn't even get a hand up in front of me. The smack blew me out of the chair and onto the floor where I lay on my back, motionless, dazed, tasting my own salty blood.

A face appeared through the fog. My new friend, Elizabeth Curtis, later Dr. Elizabeth Curtis. She helped me to my chair with words of wisdom.

"You better start paying attention and learn to read or that old woman will kill you."

Dinner at the Williams house that night was a somber one.

"Ma-AH-k," Pop said, "I got a call from your principal today. She said that maybe that teacher of yours ... uh ... Sister Mary Rose, she maybe could have hit you a little hard today."

Half my face was covered by a huge bandage and I was fighting to hold back more of the big crocodile tears I had shed earlier in the day.

"Sister really hurt me today," I said.

"Really?" He looked at me.

Mother intervened. "Are you going to sit by and let them hit him like that?"

He looked at me and then at mother. He shook his head and looked at all of us around the table. Mother stared at him intently. He took a bite and swallowed hard, then a sip of water. A blank look came over his face. He picked up the bowl of lima beans and held it out.

"More limas anyone?"

"Did you say anything to the principal at all?" Mother asked.

"Yes, I sure did. I told her to tell Sister Mary Rose not to break anything if possible. More haddock anyone?" He lifted the plate of fish.

Mother gave him a disgusted look.

By the end of the school year I went from being a D and F student to being an A and B student. I got the Most Improved Student Award. To this day I can learn anything from a book—I didn't really need to go to high school, or college, for that matter. Everything I have learned through all these years I have learned because I can read. I don't think I ever did thank that cranky, old, man-hating nun, so I believe I will now. Wherever you are, Sister Mary Rose, thank you, ma'am.

My father decided to do something about the public school system. He ran for and won a seat on the school committee. Blazingly honest, brutally truthful, with staunch beliefs that something was either right or wrong, and with no tolerance for bullshit, he was doomed as an American politician from the start.

While on the committee he was asked at a meeting by a fellow member, a local medical doctor, what he thought of the present system of teaching kids the basics of reading and writing.

"The old method worked fine. Your new math isn't worth a tinker's damn and you liberal, left-wing dimwits, are going to be responsible for the American public school system going nowhere but down. We have all here tonight agreed, that since it was instituted it has, indeed, gone nowhere but down," he stated.

"Mr. Williams," the doctor replied, "how is it that a man of your limited education and whose only claim to fame is that he played professional football but now works in a fish plant, feels justified in giving any type of valuable opinion on the education of children?"

My father had graduated from Boston College but, because he was there on a football scholarship, he had, as has always been the case with athletes, spent more time on sports than on his education. Before he could respond he was halfway to his feet. Before he could inflict any physical damage his life-long friend and retired Captain, Harry H. Curtis, put his hand on his shoulder to stop him. Other than my mother, the Captain was the only man who could save someone from my father when his trigger was tripped.

Once he was seated in his chair, Captain Curtis turned to the doctor.

"Let me ask you something, doctor. I'm just an old sea captain and I go to you with an ailment. You treat me and tell me that I am going to get better. A short time later I come back to you, still in pain and, in fact, the pain has gotten worse. Again, you treat me and tell me I am going to get better. A few weeks go by and I am a hurting son of a bitch, do you really think I need four years of pre-med, four years of medical school an internship and a medical residency to come to the very logical conclusion that as a doctor, you are woefully lacking at best and, at worst, a total cluster fuck?" He looked at the infuriated doctor as the rest of the school committee sniggered. "Forgive my colorful language but having listened to the liberal drivel the doctor has spewed here tonight, I'm afraid I've just run out of ways to express myself."

It was generally agreed that he had made his point.

CHAPTER 6 - CURRENT

A s it has for hundreds of thousands of years, the sun warmed water recedes exposing the green eel grass in the marsh behind Good Harbor Beach. It funnels from the wide area of the marsh to the narrower creek which parallels Nautilus Road. It passes the Williams Guest House picking up speed as the marsh empties into the creek and flows on underneath the first of two wooden footbridges that span the creek connecting the road with the beach. It is a cloudless, sunny Saturday afternoon in August. Thousands of people frolic on the beach and in the water, which is uncharacteristically warm for New England, it's at least sixty degrees.

The creek carries on, turning left at an almost perfect right angle. As it narrows again it picks up even more speed and rushes dead away from land at over four knots directly out to sea. Passing the majestic Hess house sitting high on the rocks overlooking the churning waves, the creek empties into the ocean. Young boys have always been attracted to the sun-warmed waters of the creek, much warmer than the ocean waters. The water here is sensuous and inviting on a warm summer afternoon.

Because I grew up on Good Harbor Beach, I had been beach tested at an early age. At the age of nine or ten I decided I could handle the beach alone and asked permission from my father.

"Can you swim?" He looked at me over the top of his glasses.

"Yes."

"Come with me."

At low tide we would go to the Warm Pot, at high tide it would be to the creek in front of the house. On this day we were at the Warm Pot.

"You did say you could swim?"

"Yes." I squeaked.

Suddenly I was ten feet from shore and three feet under-water. I surfaced and swam to the shore. I earned the right to free range of Good Harbor Beach—alone.

On warm summer days the Williams family took full advantage of proximity to the beach. A hole would be dug and rocks were heated as our ancestors had done here centuries before us. When the rocks were radiantly red with heat they were covered with wet seaweed on which lobsters and clams were placed. More seaweed was added and then fresh corn still in its husks, potatoes and small, whole chickens, hot dogs and Italian sausages, more seaweed and the whole thing was covered and left to steam. It was time for boys to have a swim.

It was an unusual day. The moon was full and the tide was stronger than I had ever known it to be. Though I had spent many hours in the creek in my young life this was a particularly powerful current and, before I knew what happened, I found myself caught in it. I swam as hard as I could but this was a ripping tide and my small body was no match for it. I knew immediately that I was no match for it. I was swimming hard, my breath coming in gasps as I held my head above the water, eyes wide open as someone in trouble in the water will try to do. The harder I swam, the more desperate my situation seemed. I knew I was in a bad way and the rocks below the Hess house were looming up before me very fast.

There were shouts coming from the shore. Someone had seen that I was in trouble and began hollering. All I could see was the rocks, if I could just grab on to one of them maybe... My body seemed to be getting heavier and heavier. I knew I couldn't stay afloat much longer. Then, through my fear and panic, I heard that familiar voice.

"Ma-AH-k!!!"

His voice was the only sound in my ears.

"Here" he called. "Swim here."

He stood in the water ten yards from me. I turned and did as I was told.

"Swim," he called encouragement. "You can do it. Swim here." He pointed.

I swam as hard as I could and before I knew it he was right in front of me.

He bent down and helped me out of the water. "There you go," he said putting an arm around me. "Don't try to swim into the current. Just turn left or right and get out of it. Think. Don't panic—think. When you panic you're dead."

"Yes," I said tremulously as I walked beside his reassuring presence. We returned to the part of the beach where the family was beginning their picnic.

In a big galvanized washtub, a block of ice was cooling steel cans of Budwiser and PBR Beer and bottles of Coca-Cola.

"What was all the commotion over there?" Mother asked looking up at us.

"Nothing," Pop said handing me a Coke and opening a Bud for himself. He knew how tenuous my beach rights were with her. "Someone got caught in the current but they got out okay." He smiled at me. "No problem, right, Mark?"

"Yes," I said taking a long drink.

My close call that day made a dinner that was already excellent even better. The steaming corn, lobsters and chicken all with their juices sealed inside had that faint taste of the ocean. Our ancestors had it right. Most chefs overcook things but, long before the invention of the New England Clambake, the earliest Americans were serving food just like this on Good Harbor Beach.

It was a memorable afternoon. Throughout the day I would look up to see my father tapping his temple with a forefinger and the words he spoke to me that day and on so many others still come back to me.

"Think, Mark. Reason your way out. As long as you don't panic you always have an option."

Chapter 7 - Good Harbor Beach Dog Squall

I remember back to the first time I was scared—really scared. I was seven or eight and somehow I had gotten caught in a summer white squall on Good Harbor Beach. I was the only one on the beach except for this monstrous, ugly-assed dog that had been stalking me all day. I'd had problems with this dog before. On more than one occasion the dog surprised me by putting both its feet on my back, knocking the breath out of me as I hit the ground, and then it proceeded to scratch my back. Its moron of an owner would talk to it like it was a person, like moron owners of dogs will do, and act so surprised that it didn't answer back. Its breath stank and the only way I could ever escape it was by taking to the water.

It was a weekday and few people were on the beach when I had enough of the monster and its sharp paws. The few that saw us probably thought that the little boy was playing with the nice dog. How cute. I, however, was petrified with fear of the thing and the pain in my back forced me to act. When it approached me for the third time, I threw a handful of sand in its face then grabbed a rock and bounced it off the fucking thing's ugly head with a resounding thump. While the dog tried to figure out what just happened, I took off. I made commendable speed all the way home.

When my mother saw the condition of my back, she called the owners of the dog. Naturally, they took no responsibility and said I must have teased it. Since I was used to spending the better part of every day roaming the beach this was a bad situation. I became increasingly afraid of the heinous thing and began avoiding the beach out of fear of what it might do to me next. Finally my father was apprised of the situation.

I returned to the beach on Sunday. There it was again—big, ugly, and in everyone's way. It spotted me from a hundred yards away and started right for me. I escaped into the water. I knew that dog wanted to kill me. It was only through many long swims under the water that I managed to avoid the dog and by noon he had disappeared. I assumed he went off to eat small boys somewhere else. Probably where they were easier to catch.

This day was the first one in which I was to be effected by the weather phenomenon known as a white squall. After a prolonged stay in the creek, I lay on my stomach in the warm white sand and pulled it around me like the reverse of a snow angel, the way small boys have on Good Harbor Beach since the look-outs scanned the woods for Saber-toothed Tigers. Belly down in the warm white sand I immediately fell fast asleep as only little boys and old men can do. My last conscious thought was that I was really tired from trying to avoid that fucking dog.

BA-BOOM!

I awoke suddenly with sand smashing into me feeling like a million bee stings all at once. The thunder was so loud that my ears hurt and wind-whipped sand stung my eyes when I tried to open them. The flash of lightening was blinding even with my eyes closed and was instantly followed by a roaring crash that pounded my eardrums. I put my hands over my eyes to protect them from the stinging sand and squinted.

Shit. There it was in front of me again. The fucking dog, snarling and all teeth. I knew this time he was going to eat me alive. And then it really got bad—it started raining.

The squall exploded all around me. My world went from the dark of night to blazing light when the lightening split the air. The wind whipped the sand against my bare skin and rain fell in a continuous sheet horizontally. I couldn't move. I screamed at the evil beast in front of me. Drool oozed from it's ugly mouth and mixed with the rain as it fell to the ground. It's eyes were black. Time stopped and I stood completely paralyzed. Amid the booms of thunder and howling wind there was another sound, the smash of the glass front storm door of the Williams house. My father, when he was told that I was missing, had slammed the door open and pieces of glass were later found across the street. I did the only thing I could do, I took off like a deer as fast as my legs would carry me with the dog at my heels. I could hear my father yelling for me. I couldn't stop trying to run toward his calls, the dog snapping at my heels. The swirling sand and pelting rain made visibility negligible, but I ran as hard as I could.

The dog jumped up and scratched the shit out of my shoulder spinning me back towards my house. Just as lightening flashed, I saw my father running like the pro football halfback he once was through the water kicking up spouts of water as though leaving a picket fence in his wake. I jumped up and headed for him, the dog in hot pursuit. The dog reared up and I heard my father yell "Duck!" as he sailed over me, smashing into the dog and knocking it back several yards.

My father was the first to regain his feet, the dog right after him. An ungodly hellish sound emanated from the dog as he bared his teeth. Then a scream came from my father that rivaled the dogs. They stood eye to eye for what seemed like a month. The dog lunged at him. They rolled on the sand, arms, legs, and paws intertwined. The dogs teeth flashed as they clamped on his shoulder. He screamed as he grabbed the dog by the throat and held it at arms length. Its legs pumped on empty air helplessly. With two hands he literally ripped its throat apart. A flash of light illuminated Salt Island and the twin lights of Thacher Island as blood gushed over his arms. Horizontal sheets of rain washed the blood away as he tossed the dog aside like a piece of wood. He raised his head and screamed at the storm. Suddenly the pain in my shoulder was gone and I suddenly found myself perched atop his shoulders. Lightening flashed, cutting the blackness of the afternoon and thunder roared. Atop my father's shoulders I screamed at the thunder boomers with him. Like him I dared the sons of bitches to hit me. None had the balls.

CHAPTER 8 - LITTLE LEAGUE

Boys all over the field—throwing, catching, fielding grounders. Baseballs everywhere. The whack of the baseball on wood reverberates throughout the ballfield. Many taking batting practice, others pitching. Older men walking among the Little League hopefuls writing down the numbers of any kid displaying any talent. It was Little League tryouts. The air was filled with the smell of sweat, leather, and fresh cut grass.

What a disgrace if I wasn't picked up. The tryouts were almost over. I was a terrible hitter and a poor fielder. The hand-eye coordination that would later be one of my greatest assets had yet to manifest and I was smart enough to know it. I was sure no one had noticed me. I was positive no team would pick me. When no one was looking, I tossed a ball over the fence in centerfield.

The whistle went off and all the hopefuls were called in around home plate. The coaches huddled halfway between home plate and the pitcher's mound. I stopped in centerfield to tie my shoes. I was the last one in and the coaches were waiting for me to get there.

"A ball went over the fence," I hollered as I stood up.

"What?"

"A ball went over the fence," I screamed. "A new one."

One of the coaches waved at me to get it. I jumped the fence and picked up the new white ball. By this time everyone was looking at me. I knew this was my only hope.

A year before, several of my cronies and I declared war on a summer house near the bridge at Good Harbor Beach. That in itself was painful enough but grew categorically worse when one of my fellow conspirators, in an attempt to gain favorable treatment, ratted me out. Since I was the only one of the group who could hit the third floor windows with a rock, Mark's Dad, who most assuredly did practice corporal punishment, had to pay for all the windows on said floor. The only good memory I had of that experience was later when my Dad said, "Well, at least you've got a good right arm."

I had whacked enough airborne gulls with stones to know he was right about that.

With the eyes of all kids and adults on me, I took a step and let the ball fly. I was about ten feet beyond the centerfield fence and the ball was caught on the fly just beyond home plate. Notebooks were raised and pencils flew. I was drafted in the first round by the Dodgers, the worst team in the league—of course.

I don't remember much of my first year other than that my coach had me riding the bench a lot. I played outfield. Mostly I spent my time learning the basics—like the position of left field was determined facing out from home plate, not facing in. I got a few tries at pitching, usually late in the game when the Dodgers were hopelessly behind, not an uncommon occurrence. I could throw a lot harder than most any of the other kids my age or even those a few years older. In the vernacular of the day, I had a gun for a right arm. There was, however, a small problem with control.

In my first formative days as a pitcher I seldom gave up a hit. Problem was I seldom got close enough to the strike zone for the batter to reach the ball with the bat. I couldn't get a base hit myself to save my life. Pitching a baseball is like playing golf, it's all about rhythm and timing. I might not have had any hand-eye coordination but I sure could hum a baseball. I was just never sure where it would end up. Mostly what I hit were opposing batters and the players on deck. I knocked over bats stacked together and smashed the piles of batting helmets. I made the opposing coach duck. I made my coach duck. I hit people in the stands. I sent the opposing team's mascot to the vet—unconscious. The most embarrassing thing was to bang the ball off the backstop right back to me in one bounce. Catcherless pitching, I called that.

"Please try not to kill any of your team-mates," our new coach, Tom Latoff, would say to me before I was to pitch at batting practice.

The opposing players seldom razzed me. If they knew how safe they were from an intentional beaning, they would have let loose on me with a verbal barrage without fear.

Once after a resounding defeat at the hands of Officer Duke

Ryan's Braves, he gave me a ride home and explained that just a few years earlier the Dodgers had won the Little League World Series and that they might one day win another. At the time, I thought that was about as plausible as the Patriots winning the Super Bowl or the Red Sox beating the Yankees and the winning the World Series in the bottom of the ninth in the seventh game.

My second year was better and so were the Dodgers. I strengthened my arm more over the winter by throwing big, heavy, wet snowballs for hours on end. In the Spring I threw rocks, at bottles, at cans, at low-flying seagulls, and at my friend Bobby Noonan. I threw at whatever target presented itself. I had gained enough accuracy that the opposing team sometimes let their mascot out of the dugout when I was pitching. I never once hit the opposing coach and only made mine duck a few times. I mainly just hit opposing players—on the hands and feet mostly. I did manage to hit one hapless individual right smack on the helmet and, yes, it was the chicken who ratted on me about the third story window and, no, it was not an accident. Plus the ball made second base on the rebound. He got the message and refused to get into the batter's box against me. Even for a rat he was not stupid. I was most vindictive as a young man.

For some unfathomable reason known only to himself, one player actually turned away from one of my speedier endeavors and took it right in the middle of his back. A resounding KA-thump and he lay crumpled in the dust, screaming something awful as he twisted around trying unsuccessfully to reach his hand around to where he had been hit. No one was seriously hurt, well, physically anyway. I suspect some of those hit had problems sleeping at night as small white spheroids would come hurtling out of the dark at them. As far as the razzing went, when I was on the mound the opposing team was as quiet as little bitty church mice.

What I really remember from my years of playing Little League was the wire fence at the field called the Oval. It appears in front of me at night in my dreams and always I react the same, to hell with the fence just catch the ball.

The Oval was one of two fields we played on. The field at Stage Fort Park had an old wood boarded flat fence. The Oval had brand new chain link wire all around the outfield. I was in the right field that day having, by this time, figured out that when you stand at home plate and face out, right field was the field of play to the literal right of the pitcher's mound. Who knew?

The Dodgers were ahead but the score was close. The batter connected and up, up, and away it carried toward right center, higher and higher. I kept it in front of me as long as I could. Suddenly it was right over me and I was acutely aware that the fence was coming up ahead of me fast.

Slow down, I thought, it's a home run. Let it go.

As the fence grew larger and larger and the ball was a little beyond me I made a conscious decision, Fence be damned. CATCH THE FREAKING BALL!

At the last moment I simultaneously extended my glove over the fence, the ball slammed into my glove, and I smashed into the fence at top speed. I turned toward home plate stunned and toppled back against the fence. Blood flowed down my face and into my mouth. It was all I could feel. I slid down the fence to my knees. I couldn't think. There was something I needed to do. I toppled over onto my side and curled up in the fetal position. But... what was I doing? Oh, yeah, the ball. My mouth was full of the salty taste of blood but I managed to pluck the ball from my glove and hold it up. A roar cut through the fog closing in on me. There were too many people on the field. I couldn't think. I just held the ball up and lay there watching the people running toward me. What were they all doing on the field? They had no business being there. Tom Latoff was running at full speed right at me and beside him was... no, I thought, that's all wrong. What's my father doing running on the field? That made no sense. Behind them I made out the opposing coach and two umpires running as well. Get off the field, Pop, I thought. You'll get in trouble.

Suddenly Tom and my father were there bending down as the others arrived. They were all talking but I couldn't hear them. A handkerchief appeared and was held against my nose. I tried to get up but many hands held me down. All I wanted was to stand up. Little puppy dog tears ran down my cheeks. I struggled to stand. I heard my father's voice and the hands were removed. I got shakily to my feet.

"Outstanding," my father's voice cut through the cheers

and screams. "Outstanding," he repeated.

"Best catch I've seen on a Little League field in twenty years," the opposing coach said.

The applause came from everywhere but all I could think of was the pain in my face. I felt my father's hand on my shoulder guiding me back across the field and into the car. At Addison Gilbert Hospital he stayed beside me as they stitched me up.

When the doctor and nurses left us alone my father turned to me.

"Excellent." He lowered his glasses, always a sign to either duck, seek cover, or listen closely. "As you go through life, Mark, situations will occur where, if you do the right thing, you might get hurt or even killed."

I sniffed but said nothing.

"Trust me, doing the right thing is often the most difficult choice to make. But I want you to always be a man and do the right thing, do you understand?"

"I think so," I replied.

"You think so? By the way you plowed into that fence with reckless abandon pulling down that ball, I'd say you are well on your way to becoming quite the man." He put his hand on my still-trembling shoulder. "I'm proud of you."

We all become shaped into who we are by a few incidents in the course of our lives, whether we are a person of worth or have the worth of a dead dog. That catch was one of mine. Those few times in my life when I had to take a chance on getting hurt or killed to do the right thing, I prayed something like this, "Dear God in heaven, please give me the courage to conduct myself in the correct manner. The way I was taught by my father."

Good teacher, wasn't he?

Thirty years later I was in Josie D's Restaurant when one of my teammates, Jimmy Muniz, approached me shaking his head.

"That was one hell of a catch," he said.

Though thirty years had passed I knew exactly what he was talking about.

My father taught me a lot about courage and honor. However it was my Uncle Howie who taught me about eating lobster—unfortunately not in time. There's an old belief that if you eat a lobster that was dead when you cooked it, you will get sick to your stomach. Watch any cooking show on television and you'll hear world-renowned seafood chefs promoting this belief but they are wrong. Lobsters are often caught by draggers. Considering that they are scraped up off the bottom and dragged for a few hours smashing around with all the other debris that the net picks up it's not surprising that they are dead when they are pulled up. For a million years the fishermen on draggers would cook dead lobsters at sea and sell the meat shore side. This led to the moderately illegal practice of cooking the smaller, immature lobsters and the extremely illegal, immoral and ungodly practice of cooking the female egg-bearing ones. Once the shells are dumped over the side and the meat is diced there was no way to tell the size or sex of the lobster that the meat came from. Your federal and state governments were all over this in their usual state of awareness of what's going on in the fishing industry. It only took them forty or so years to make it against the law to cook lobsters on a fishing boat. Your taxes at work. Johnny on the spot, as usual.

When I was eleven I went to work at my Uncle Howie's Lobster Pool on Pirate's Lane in East Gloucester. Every night five or ten lobsters out of a thousand would die and every morning I would cook them. Uncle Howie only had to show me a bad one from a good one once. It's diver-proof. The meat of a good one is pink and firm, a bad one is white and flaky. I never had breakfast before going to work at the lobster pool because I knew I'd have lobsters to cook and a pound or two of lobster meat for someone who loves lobster meat is a grand way to start the day. On some days Uncle Howie would help with the de-meating and on those days there was considerably more meat than on the days when he didn't help. I don't believe he ever caught on.

Before I had this knowledge of telling good from bad lobsters, however, I ate a bad one. Bobby Noonan and I had been skin diving the day before the Little League championship game. We were off the back shore when we found one of those wooden crates that a lobsterman was nice enough to leave in about fifteen feet of water for us. It had seven keepers in it. We sold three to a widow woman who lived near Bobby's summer house on the back shore.

She gave us fifty cents for them. This was merely the continuation of a practice that began when fishermen on the Sea of Galilee docked their boats at the end of the day and were paid far less than their fish was worth. Fishermen have, historically and traditionally, been given the short end of the stick. Fish dealers call it boat price—if there is a way to screw with the fishermen the dealers will use it—I call it stealing.

Perhaps it was justice but it turned out that one of the ones we ate had died and gone bad. The worst part was I was pitching for the Dodgers in the championship and I woke up on the day of the big game with stomach cramps and diarrhea like I have never had before or since. I could barely walk. It was too soon for the other pitcher to throw and we flat didn't have anyone else who could pitch. This game was the one that would determine if we went to the Little League World Series. Over the objections of both my parents I showed up at the ballpark looking like a fish that had been dead in the water for about a week.

One look at me and my coach thought I should go to the hospital. My team-mates were crestfallen. I could barely walk out to the mound but I did and for six innings I spit up bile, soiled my pants, almost passed out once an inning, but managed to throw baseballs past a sufficient number of Pirates so that at the end of the day the Dodgers had the most runs on the scoreboard. I was a genuine, bonafide hero to my team-mates. My father, who allowed me to play despite my mother's and the coach's objections, lowered his glasses and nodded his approval.

I don't remember much of the first World Series game except that we won it and the opposing pitcher was a lefty with a wicked sidearm delivery that nobody could hit very well. Myself, I had the same problem with lefties that I had with righties, I just plain could not hit at all. My arm had developed, and I had managed to develop enough control that opposing batters were no longer handed a blindfold on their way to the plate. Every now and again, I'd intentionally bounce a pitch off the backboard or send the on-deck batter sprawling, just as I did in my first and formative days as a pitcher. The occasional wild one kept the batters from crowding the plate, leaving the outside corner the place to throw to. A little fear in a batter is a beautiful thing. Not bad for a twelve year old, eh?

I didn't pitch the second game. We lost. The third game in a three game series was the same as the seventh game of the World Series, winner takes all.

It was the last half of the last inning and the Dodgers were at bat. Their last at-bat. I had pitched a good game, allowing only one run. Unfortunately, the opposing pitcher had likewise allowed only one run. We had a man on third base, one man out and Pitcher Williams was on deck.

I remember exuding self-confidence at the prospect of going to bat with the fate of the game in my hands: Oh, God, no! Don't make me have to bat. Don't make me have to go out there!

I don't remember what my batting average was that summer but I bet it would make a good golf score. Tom Latoff gave me a look of confidence. He was a good coach and, in this case, a good actor. He knew better, so did the rest of the team. If they had to depend on Williams to get this guy home, they knew we were all done. One of the best pitchers in the league was one of the worst hitters. I was pumping so much adrenaline that I could hardly walk or take a practice swing. My breath came in gasps.

Ted was leaning on the fence smoking one of his Kents. He nodded at me confidently.

Yeah, right, faker, I thought. He knew that I couldn't hit a basketball thrown by that wicked, hard-throwing, left-handed, side-armed terror. The noise level around the field was at a fever pitch. The sounds, no matter how eclectic, melted into one deafening buzz. The parking lot was filled with cars and cars were pulled over on either side of the road passing the field.

I concentrated on the kid at bat ahead of me. Please get a hit, I begged in my mind. Please get a hit so I won't have to. I was that batter's biggest fan. He was down two strikes. The pitcher wound and unleashed with that wicked devious sidearm delivery.

POP! The ball smacked into the catcher's mitt which erupted in a puff of dust.

"STRIKE THREE!" A called strike. He didn't even swing. Oh shit. The buzz intensified.

As if in slow motion I put on a batting helmet. It weighed a ton. I glanced at the old man through eyes stinging from the nervous sweat running into them. His mouth was moving but I couldn't hear anything but the buzz. My team was all out of the dug-out, jumping up and down and cheering wildly. I could hardly put one foot in front of the other and the bat felt like it was full of lead. Coach Latoff appeared at my side trying to look supportive.

"Just take a good cut at it," he tried to reassure me.

I felt like I was being sent over the top into interlocking fields of machine gun fire. My chest heaved. Adrenaline pumped through every vein and capillary. I wished I was anywhere but there. My mouth and throat were devoid of any and all moisture whatsoever. I tried to swallow but all I got was the taste of old copper pennies. The two kids tending the scoreboard sat with their legs dangling. I wished I was out there. A plane sailed by overhead. I wished I was on it. I wished I was anywhere else—on Good Harbor Beach, fishing off the back shore, shooting rats at Empire Fish, anywhere but here.

"Batter up!" the executioner yelled.

I stumbled to the left hand batters box and proceeded to wave the bat over the plate in a couple of half-hearted swings. I cocked the bat over my left shoulder. The pitcher coiled snake-like and a wickedly vicious fastball appeared from his left side. A little white spot, no bigger than a golf ball, it appeared out of nowhere and expanded at an extraordinarily fast rate. It grew in size and seemed to sizzle—s-s-s-s-s-s-s-s-s—as it blew by me and smashed into the catcher's mitt. It sounded like a gunshot.

"Ball!" the umpire yelled raising his left hand for effect. I could not have hit that pitch in a million years.

Maybe, I thought, I can just stand here and get walked out of this mess.

As the catcher threw the ball to the pitcher I looked around the crowd. Their mouths were all moving but I couldn't hear them. In back of the fence surrounding the outfield, there was a steep, grassy hill that rose sharply. Small boys chased each other in and out among the blankets where families had settled to picnic while watching the game.

The pitcher took a full windup and launched another hideously vicious fastball that screamed by me, low and away. I didn't bother swinging. I couldn't have hit that ball with a tennis racket.

"STRIKE ONE!"

Great. One and one.

Again he unwound and uncorked like a spring. He launched another bullet inside and low.

"Ball!"

Wonderful. Two and one. I was pumping so much adrenaline I felt like I was melting. Again he rocketed one at me. That pitch I picked up when it was about halfway to the plate. I swung as it flashed by smack over the middle of the plate exactly where I put the bat. Unfortunately I put it there long after the ball had passed.

"STRIKE TWO!"

My swing was more like a half-hearted farewell wave to the ball as it smacked into the catcher's mitt. The count was two and two.

He set up to throw again. It appeared out of nowhere—s-s-s-s-s—and sailed by high.

"Ball!"

Three and two. One pitch from disaster.

As far as coaches go, I never had one who was only fair. They were either very good or useless. Tommy Latoff was a very good one who took time off from his busy oil business to coach Little League.

"Time!" he called and yelled encouragement to me.

My father called me over to the fence. As I approached him it was as though the sound on a television set had been turned back on full. Grown men were screaming at me.

"The batter is no good."

"What a loser!"

"Is that the best you've got?"

Things no adult should be allowed to say to a twelve year old.

My father just stared at them with that no-nonsense stare of his. He motioned me closer.

"Mark, don't be listening to those morons. Frustrated athletes are like bad weather, they'll always be with us." It got real quiet real quick.

I stared at the ground wishing I could just disappear.

"Ma-AH-k, you listen to me."

I looked up.

"You step back into that batter's box all the way and you dig in with your left foot. Coil up like a spring." He tapped his forehead for emphasis. "You concentrate, you hear me?"

"Yes," I mumbled.

He took a knee and looked directly at me over his glasses. "You think," he repeated. "You don't see anything but the ball. You don't hear anything. Listen to me. You focus one hundred percent on the baseball and if it comes so much as near the plate you swing at it as hard as you can. You swing right at it and take your best cut and what happens happens. Whatever does, I'll be here for you."

I nodded.

I was a scared little boy when I walked away from the plate but, as I walked back, I had one reason to exist—to hit that ball. I was a razor. I cocked the bat over my shoulder as I walked back to the plate. Everything was silent. Mouths moved but I didn't hear a thing except my father's words. Hands gestured and everyone was on their feet. Those people who stood immediately behind the wire fence had their fingers hooked through the wire and leaned toward the field like they were hanging on in a strong wind. It was a sunny day and the wind blew northwest scudding billowing clouds across the sky. I could smell resin and the leathery, sweaty smell of the catcher's mitt as I stepped into the left-handed batter's box. I noticed that the lines defining it were much less worn than those in the right-handed box. There were many more right handed hitters than lefties. I focused my attention on the pitcher. I moved to the very rear of box and moved my left foot back and forth. The rubber cleats on my shoe planted my foot nicely. I took one practice swing and coiled the bat back over my left shoulder. I was coiled, ready to strike. I focused. I heard nothing and saw only the ball in the pitcher's hand. He held it across the seam as he rocked back to start his wind up.

Just try to blow that ball by me, asshole. Come on, shithead, show me the heat.

The ball disappeared into his glove and I concentrated on the glove it disappeared into. Up over his head. His right leg is raised. He starts forward and the leg comes down. His arm whipped forward. Even the pitcher disappeared. All I thought about was that ball.

It came whipping forward about waist high. I see you. I see you. The seams spun vertically. It grew in size. It came right down the middle of the plate.

Wait. Wait.

The bat exploded off of my shoulder. I watched the bat meet the ball.

CRACK!

The ball blasts off the bat and smacks into and then out of the first baseman's glove. It rolled into right field and he took off after it. I blasted off for first base. I flew and focused on the bag.

He had the ball and headed for the bag. It was a foot race now with the game as the prize. It was close. My foot hit the bag a second before his as I hurled by and into right field. The umpire waved his hand in front of him.

"SAFE! The runner was safe!" he reaffirmed at the same time the runner from third base made it home. The rule was a base hit. The ball was too hot to handle.

The Dodgers won the World Series.

Sometimes my right shoulder pains me. I wiped my shoulder out pitching on two days' rest in high school. I became all-state my senior year but it cost me my arm. I've had the bends and it really smarts but I wouldn't trade one moment of the memories of that last afternoon as a Little Leaguer to escape all he pain in the world—not one second.

CHAPTER 9 - MACKEREL

Growing up on Good Harbor Beach, most of my childhood was spent on the beach, in the tidal marshes, and in the tidal pools and creeks formed by the ebb and flow of the ocean. It was a landscape of constant change and unending discoveries. When I was about twelve the creek that flowed into the Warm Pot behind our house traversed a distance of roughly thirty yards and was about ten yards wide sloping up from a depth of four feet to a sand beach on one side. On this day, as I walked past the Warm Pot, the pool was loaded with fish swimming back and forth. At first I thought they were pollock, a bland, white meat fish but then I saw the black stripes on their backs. Those ain't no pollocks!

The tide was a moon tide, which rushes in higher and faster than a normal tide, often carrying unsuspecting fish with it. When you hear about sharks and other ocean wildlife showing up in tidal pools and streams it is often an abnormally high or strong full moon tide that is responsible. On this occasion a large school of mackerel had been trapped here and would stay until the returning tide picked them up and carried them back out to the ocean. They were probably chasing smaller fish—or being chased by a larger fish. Either way I was ecstatic, as macks were great food fish.

Mackerel at that time were an underutilized species not processed at Empire Fish. I grew up on haddock and other white meat that my father brought home. Macks were a rare treat. Their dark meat is even darker toward the skin and is far more succulent than white fish. They are a pretty fish, shiny with silver bellies and dark green backs with black stripes for camouflage from above. In the old days they were split, salted and packed into barrels then shipped all over the world where they titillated pallets and raised blood pressures. But in the Williams house they were most often barbecued in aluminum foil topped with onions. Butter was overkill—they were food fit for a king.

The problem was to get them out of the water and onto the bank with nothing but bare hands. I plunged in among them and moved to the deepest part of the creek, about waist deep, where most of the fish were. I tried to catch them with one hand and then with two but to no avail. The water unfortunately was too deep for me to move fast enough. I tried to stay in the densest grouping of fish but they immediately sped off in every direction like bullets. Frustrated I walked back to the dry creek bed to mull the situation over.

As I sat I drifted into a trance-like state as images of this marsh a thousand years earlier flashed through my mind. I watched as an Indian boy, the same age as me, hid behind a rock just below my house. It was the perfect blind from which he could watch large black ducks pass a few feet in front of him, totally unaware of his presence. Armed with a bow and arrow, he watched and waited until he had an easy shot. From behind this rock he supplied his family with food. I still find his arrowheads to this day.

I used the rock in the same way. No one ever showed me how to do this, but armed with a CO2 pellet gun I had shot many a duck from this same perfect ambush spot. Was there some ancient connection between us, I wondered. How did I know how to use this spot if no one ever showed me? When spearing monkfish off the Eastern Point breakwater, how did I know to aim under the fish, allowing for refraction? As a baby dropped in the water, how did I know not to breathe? I knew when a man bent down and I looked into his black, lifeless eyes that he was a bad man and meant me harm. Years later when a girl took her clothes off in front of me, I knew exactly what to do. Those primitive instincts still live in me. I can sit for hours and look into a fire.

As I sat with the images cascading before me a group of people arrived from the beach. They must have been local folks because they knew, as I did, that a lot of free dinners were swimming around in the deep end of the creek. They pushed me aside.

"Get out of the way, boy, we'll show you how it's done."

They plunged into the water and pandemonium ensued. As they tripped over one another one fish was flipped out of the water and caused much pushing and shouted claims to ownership. In the meantime the fish flipped back into the water. After about fifteen minutes of this craziness, six people had landed no fish and were contemplating a stop at the fish market on their way home. They returned to the beach. Obviously sunbathing was more suited to them than catching mackerel by hand.

The only thing they had accomplished was getting the water so stirred up that it was now impossible to see the fish. As I stood staring into the water it was as though someone else took over my mind and body. I waded back into the lagoon. All that mattered was catching some fish to feed my family.

"It's impossible, little boy," one of the failed fishermen yelled.

"Don't," one of the girls said, "he's so cute, let him try."

"Give it up, kid," another guy hollered laughing.

The fish were bumping against my legs and suddenly it just came to me. I put my hands under the water, palms out, waving them back and forth as I walked from the deep part of the creek up the bank. As the water became shallower, I moved faster. Some of the fish moved back and forth to my left and right. I grabbed at them but the water resistance made me woefully slow. I went nuts, screaming. When the water was at my ankles several fish appeared in front of me, twisting and turning back and forth. The frustrated fishermen were silently watching me. Finally one fish was left in front of me. I grabbed for it but it slipped out of my hand and returned to the safety of the deep end of the creek.

I was beyond bullshit. The bystanders began to hoot and holler. Adrenaline surged through my whole existence, my senses seemed magnified. My whole body tensed with anticipation and I returned to the deep part of the creek. I was on the edge—feeling everything and seeing everything. The unseen fish bumped into me. With my hands in the water I walked parallel to the bank. I moved until the fish were bumping into me in the greatest number then turned toward the bank once again. This time I ended up with ten fish in front of me in very shallow water. More people were watching and some of those who had made fun of me before were now shouting encouragement. I crouched and launched myself up and forward screaming with reckless abandon. With knees and elbows I smashed down on the fish.

"Kid's crazy," someone observed. Everyone else was silent.

I came up from wherever it was that I went to and was aware that I had fish pinned under both knees and one under my left elbow. With my right hand I removed three large fish and tossed them far up onto the bank.

The crowd broke into applause as I jumped up and down in glee while the three fish tried to wriggle back to the water. To my audience it was amusing. To me it was a celebration of life genetically imprinted on me in that, like my ancestors who fished and hunted in this marsh thousands of years earlier, I could catch food and live.

An older couple—they had to be in their thirties—with heavy New York accents, a large man wearing a cowboy hat and his wife, and a pretty blond girl with little or no bathing suit on and her macho boyfriend, all approached me.

"Son," the cowboy said, "are those fish good eating?"

"The best," I retorted.

"Would you show me and the missus how you got those three on the bank," he drawled.

"Sure!"

"I'd like some free fish, too," the man from New York said. "Show me, too."

"Honey," the blonde said to her boyfriend. "I like mackerel. Maybe the little boy would show you too." She smiled at me.

The guy snorted. "I don't need no little pup to show me how to fish. I'm a Gloucester fisherman."

He strode confidently into the water where he entertained us all for a few minutes before falling face first into the water without catching a fish. Those on shore hooted at his antics. He was pissed at embarrassing himself in front of his girlfriend. Turns out he was a guinea draggerman. Naturally.

"The idea is to get them on the bank," I said.

He sneered and gave me a push.

"Son, don't you be pushing that boy around," the Texan said. He towered over the draggerman.

"Honey, you listen to this little boy," the blonde said bending down, affording me a great view of her two lovely boobs, nipples and all. I was a horny little shit long before I even had pubic hair. Some things you never outgrow.

"Come on, son," said Tex. "Let's all pay attention to this kid and catch us some fish."

"Bullshit," the draggerman sneered glaring at me.

"Did you say you fish for a living?" Tex asked.

"Yeah. What of it?"

"Well," I said, "you must be poor as a church mouse is all I can say."

Everyone chuckled.

"Aw, why don't you go..."

"Son," the Texan interjected, "you best not be finishin that sentence if you know what's good for you."

"Now, Sugar," the Texan's wife interjected, "we're not at home. Don't you go breakin up anyone."

"Yes, dear."

The New Yorker, whose name was Irving, spoke up. "Would you please show us how you did it?"

"Sure," I said, "come with me."

The three couples entered the water.

"How do you know where those fish have been?" Irving's wife asked. "The water is all dirty. I don't know if I want to eat fish that have been swimming in such dirty water."

She followed him into the water hesitantly then jumped back.

"Goodness! One just bumped my leg."

"Come on, dear," Irving coaxed. "These fish are five cents a pound in the market back on Long Island."

That did it, in she came. I got them all in a semicircle in the deep part holding their hands in the water.

"Now just walk towards shore as fast as you can," I said.

With several people moving toward shore the shock wave was so much greater than with one that few of the fish could escape back to the deep.

"These here fish don't have spines like a catfish, do they, son?" asked the Texan.

"Nope."

One swam up Irving's wife's bathing suit near her ample butt and she freaked out.

"That fish is attacking me," she screamed. Irving stopped to lend aid to his endangered wife. Everyone else continued on to the beach. The scene was crazy, fish were flying everywhere. Some flew way up onto the bank.

As the wall of people approached the shore a phenomenon occurred that I was later to see many times. When we were in about a half foot of water, as if turned off like a faucet, the fish began to well up out of the water moving very slowly as if by being packed so close together they lost all sense of direction. Some freaked and jumped right out of the water onto the beach but most just lay paralyzed in a pile. Tex and the others started yelling as they plowed into the fish, hurling them far up onto the bank. A shovel or pitchfork would have been perfect but hands were all that was needed.

With fifty or so fish on the bank we stopped. That was all that was needed. Coolers and bags were pulled out and we each took about five fish then flung the live ones back into the water. Even the draggerman uncharacteristically helped put the live ones back.

Tex slapped me on the back. "Hell of a time, son. I haven't had so much fun since me and the boys got smoked and went diller grabbing." (Whatever the hell that meant.) "Thanks for showing the missus and I how y'all fish up here in the land of the Bunker Hill Retreat."

They headed back to the beach with their fish.

"Are you sure we can eat them?" asked Irving's wife. "They weren't bought in a store and they have sand all over them and I hope you don't think I'm going to eat them with their heads still on. You better believe that you're the one who is going to take the guts out of them."

Irving sighed and looked at me with the look of a man who has enough patience to fill an ocean. He waved me over and, with his wife safely out of earshot said, "You did me a favor. I'll do you one." He lowered his voice. "When you are older and thinking about getting married, don't." He patted my shoulder. "Bye."

"Are you going to keep me waiting here all day," Mrs. Irving called. "I'm getting cold and the water is coming in and my arms are about to fall off from all that work catching these fish."

He flashed me a see-what-I-mean look and headed back to the beach, his wife talking to him all the way.

The blonde bent down giving me a final perfect glance at her lovely boobs.

"Thank you," she said. Her boyfriend just snarled something indistinct as they headed back to the beach.

I had no way to carry all those fish back home so the Williams family could enjoy a dinner of grilled mackerel that evening. I finally improvised using several long pieces of eel grass and twisted them together to run through the gills and out the mouth of the fish. With them safely strung up, as they had been for thousands of years, I slung them over my back and headed home.

No one had to teach me how to do it, I just knew.

Chapter 10 - The Warm Pot Shark

As kids, my cronies and I spent a good part of the summer at the Warm Pot. It was probably thirty feet wide and a good thirty feet deep with barely a foot of visibility and a sheer drop off that was a constant source of amusement to us. As a likely looking couple would walk up the creek from the beach we would all exit the water and let our victims approach. Teenage couples were best as they walked hand and hand cooing sweet nothings to each other and, from the ankle deep creek they'd take one step and —WHOOSH!—right under! It was cool to watch.

Of course the guy always got blamed. In those first and formative years I learned that in any issue between males and females, the guy is always to blame.

On one occasion I took pity on an approaching couple but they disregarded my warning and both splashed down, hats floated, cigarettes were soaked, sunglasses floated down toward the bottom. We were all in stitches. His girlfriend had red lipstick smeared all over her face and she looked like an Indian so we, of course, began dancing around her yelping like Braves. She ran back to the beach crying. The guy took severe umbrage and lit out after me. He was fortuitously slow.

As we got a little older and the female factor came into play we modified our behavior. As a couple approached we would exit the water so as not to give away its depth. With any luck the unsuspecting girl wouldn't be able to swim and my friends and I would valiantly swim to her aid. The approved rescue method was the cross-chest carry and, of course, we'd manage to slide our hands into her suit so a serious feel was copped. If the female being rescued had large boobs, the trip to shore could take quite some time to the point where some of the older and better developed girls were near hypothermic by the time they were rescued and returned, thanking us profusely, to the shallows.

One day I was the first to arrive at the Warm Pot after an unusually high moon tide. I had a dive mask with me and planned to explore the bottom of the pot while the water was still clear. I put the mask on and was ready to jump in when I was overcome by an unknown feeling the likes of which I had never experienced before, but have had experience with since. Everything became intense. The sun shone brilliantly. The marsh grass, still dripping from its tidal immersion was golden and glistening. The gulls drifted by silent save for the rustle of feathers. It was unbelievable as the houses and cars and all other evidence of modern time seemed to disappear. I felt like a boy from a time long gone. A boy who hunted and fished in this marsh thousands of years before and as if his visions were passed on to me and triggered by this strange feeling. Through the eyes of this ancient time my peripheral vision seemed to vanish. My total focus was on the water in the pool. The water in the Warm Pot seemed to move slowly in a counterclockwise circle as though being stirred by an unseen finger. I stared at the spiraling water as a distant voice whispered its message, "Don't go in the water."

I listened closer but the houses and cars were coming back into my awareness. I had dropped my mask and as I bent to retrieve it something came hurtling out of the water right at me, fast as a bullet. Mouth wide open he flew right over my head and landed five feet up on the bank. A large striped bass. What a catch! I knew he was either chasing or being chased. The water continued to move in a strange, circular pattern. I wondered if a seal was in there, that happened sometimes, but, no, seals have to come up for air. Blue fish hadn't made it as far north as Gloucester in those days. I stepped back from the water's edge. I thought I saw a shadow but it wasn't clear.

I could put my mask on and jump in. Even though I wasn't always very smart at that age I wasn't entirely stupid. I scooped up the bass and took my prize home to be baked. I told a few people that there was something in the water that day that made a three foot bass jump five feet out of the water and on to the shore. But, in time, I came to believe it was my imagination—there was nothing in the water.

Many years later I was standing in back of my house after

the second "storm of the century" occurred after the one thirteen years earlier. I watched the creek rushing back to the ocean. There was little more than a foot or two of water left in it and it was moving fast. A fin and tail, about three feet apart, rushed past me and flowed out to sea before I managed to get out so much as a "holy shit".

Chapter 11 - Pop and the Porgies

It was a weird day on Good Harbor Beach. The waters of the creek that flows between the ocean and the marshes behind our house becomes sun-warmed after hours of flowing shallow and wide-spread. I was ten and watched, fascinated, as thousands of porgies filled the shallow creek and literally were pushed out of the water onto the beach by striped bass which chased them, smashing into them with reckless abandon. The porgies, pushed together in a foot or two of water, seemed to lose all sense of direction and swam very slowly counterclockwise. The bottom fish forced the ones above them up and out of the water. They welled up and out like bubbles from an aerator. Suddenly one of the pursuing fish overshot his target and blasted out of the water in a four foot arc and landed on the sand. His tail pounded the beach like a jackhammer.

It was a fish I had never seen. Living on the edge of the ocean as we did, I had grown up on this beach and knew most fish by sight but this one was new to me. It looked like a blue barracuda, sleek as a jet fighter, with a head that was all teeth. Another blasted out of the water, then another, flapping around violently and regurgitating bloody bits of porgies. I was astonished.

They were bluefish and they had arrived in Gloucester after having migrated a little further north each year. Bluefish, I was to learn, were a treat. Screw stripped bass. They fight like a shoe and taste as bland as most white fish. Bluefish fight like Saxons, all day and through the night, and taste like a tender steak with enough Omega oil to make a lot of heart doctors change specialties.

As I approached the foot bridge that connects the beach with Nautilus Road I heard a woman scream, "Look out, you fool!"

There was Pop wading out into three feet of water appearing oblivious to the swell of harmless porgies welling up around him. A choir of warnings were shouted from the bridge.

"Mommy, will the fish bite the man?" a little girl asked.

"Oh, yes," I said. "They are vicious fish."

Everyone watched the fish churning around my father as he waded back and forth. People shouted warnings and urged him to seek safety.

"For God's sake, look out," someone screamed. Cars stopped and some beeped their horns trying to warn the hapless man being surrounded by fish. As the water churned with fish around him it looked as though they are eating him alive.

"Oh, no," Pop screamed, his arms flailing, "what's happening to me?"

"Don't just stand there," a lady screamed at me. "Go help him!"

I couldn't help myself. I busted up laughing.

"Help me, help me," Pop carried on thrashing about. "Oh, God! They're eating me alive!"

Mothers turned their children's faces away from the terrible spectacle unfolding before them. I was laughing so hard I could barely stand up, everyone stared at me as though I was insane.

The mass of fish, with my father at the center, moved slowly down the creek toward the ocean. People began moving away from the crazy man on the bridge who was laughing at the horrible scene before him. I decided to join the ruse.

"Hey," I yelled, "Isn't someone going to help him?"

People averted their eyes and turned away. Pop, in the meantime, had begun screaming horribly and sinking down among the swarm of fish as though they had devoured his legs and all that was left was his head and wildly flailing arms above the quivering mass of fish. With a blood-curdling shriek his head sank below the water. One arm was all that was left waving madly and then it too disappeared. Everyone was silent as they stared blankly at the spot where he disappeared. I couldn't help myself, I started laughing again. They stared at me with complete disgust.

Just then Pop rose out of the water, all six feet of him. He was laughing uproariously as he walked back toward where I stood on the bridge. I don't know which of us was laughing harder.

"Tourists," he laughed. "It's the little things that make it all worthwhile."

Part Two

A Gloucester Fisherman

CHAPTER 12 - TOURIST TOUR
The Afternoon of the Shark & Contagious Panic

The first trap of the trawl broke the surface and I hauled it aboard. I had an audience. A bunch of tourists were with me on a lobster tour. There were two very attractive young women in their twenties, Katie and Beth; a sixty-something couple, the husband's baseball cap read "USMC"; a thirty-ish farm couple from the heartland—Kansas, I think; and, finally, a couple in their forties—the husband informed me he was a psychiatrist. Great.

As I opened the trap door they all crowded around with looks of fascination. I removed an empty Budweiser can and held it up.

"This is why there are fewer lobsters than there used to be."

"Pollution," someone said.

"No," I replied, "beer drinking during the day, the lobsters have all become alcoholics."

Chuckles.

"I read that there are fewer lobsters because there are too many lobster traps." The farmer's wife had dark hair and was very handsome. She was also smart.

I stopped the hauler and addressed the group. "In the last four or five years the total catch has stayed about the same while the number of traps in the water has increased ten times and the number of lobstermen have doubled. What does that tell you?"

"It tells me that more lobstermen and traps caught fewer lobsters per man and per trap, so you made less money as the lobstermen and traps increased."

"Correct, pretty dark-haired lady from Kansas." I smiled at her and she stepped closer to her husband. "We're all in competition with each other so if the guy fishing next to me goes up a hundred traps, so do I. Before you know it you've gone from four hundred traps to a thousand."

"Why don't they just make a trap limit?" asked the shrink.

"Your federal government, as usual, a day late and a dollar short, is working on it."

"Has pollution hurt the lobster industry?" asked the girl called Beth. She stood next to her equally blond friend. Both were easy to look at.

"A lot less than draggers."

"What's a dragger?"

"A dragger is a boat that drags a net along the bottom and kills far too many little fish for every legal size fish it brings to the surface."

"Well," her friend shrugged, "why don't they just throw the little fish back?"

"Most die of air embolism on the way up. The federal government says fish stocks are down because of over fishing but even little babies in Gloucester know it is method of fishing and not over-fishing that's the problem."

The old Marine squinted at me. "Do those draggers, as you call them, catch lobsters?"

"Yes, and they destroy the bottom where lobsters live. They smash and kill a lot more. In Maine, draggers are not allowed to take lobsters. Up there the cry is 'by trap alone'."

"So you think the draggers are mostly responsible for the depletion of the fish stocks?"

"It started in the Thirties when they took the sails down, put in a diesel engine, and began dragging a net along the bottom. Like I said, too many little fish die for every fish that is kept, it's just that simple. Do you people really want to hear this?"

They all nodded.

"In the Seventies and Eighties as the draggers wiped out one species of fish after another, what did the federal government do? Regulate? Hell no. They gave fishermen loans to get bigger boats and more sophisticated electronics which they used to catch what fish were left. And since it was the government doing this, where did the money come from?"

"My tax dollar," grumbled the old Marine.

"Exactly. Then when the fisheries were further depleted and the boats started to go belly up—those few that weren't sunk for the insurance—your government bureaucracies, in their infinite capacity to further fuck up an already fucked up situation, stepped in and bought back the boats and the licenses with what?"

"Our tax dollars," he repeated. "Where the hell was Sixty Minutes, for Christ's sake?"

"Oh, it's not over there. After selling their boats and licenses, some of the boys bought other boats and licenses and continued to fish."

The farmer's wife, whose name I had learned was Brenda, frowned, thinking. "So, it sounds like the federal bureaucracies that are making laws to safe guard the fisheries now were either stupid or..."

I looked at her and nodded.

"...or bought off," she concluded in a low voice.

All eyes turned to her and I saw heads nod in agreement.

"Son," the old Marine folded his arms over his chest. "You don't seem to think much of the federal government."

"Sir, I believe that I live in the best country on earth and I think it proves how great it is by surviving the cluster fuck of bureaucracies that have grown in it like a proverbial cancer." I had noticed the psychiatrist's wife tendency to roll her eyes at my language.

"Now that's enough history and politics for one day. In the words of those first Gloucester Men, three hundred years ago, 'let's go fishing!'" I pulled the next trap aboard. Several lobsters flipped around in the parlor head. The people crowded around.

"Are all those legal?" the farmer asked.

"Nope." I picked the largest lobster in the trap up. "This is a seeder."

The pretty blonde named Katie had managed to work her way closer to me.

"A female egg-bearing lobster. It will have eggs all over the bottom of its tail." I flipped it over and thousands of eggs were clumped all over the underside of the tail. I heard the "ahhs" from the crowd as I held the lobster out to Katie.

"Here," I said, "hold it."

Tentatively she held her hand out and as I leaned toward her, I pretended to trip, losing control of the lobster which soared overboard—just as I intended it to do.

Katie flushed. "Oh! I am like so sorry."

I gave her my best you-dumbass look then grinned. "I had to throw it back. It's illegal."

She flushed even deeper. "You are such a shit," she said.

Maybe this day wasn't a waste of time.

"You take the largest lobsters and the seeders out of the trap first so they don't kill the smaller ones," I explained removing the two that I was sure were of legal size.

"This is so cool," cooed Beth.

I removed four small lobsters I was sure were shorts and flipped them over the side after the seeder.

"How can you tell those two are legal size?" asked the farmer.

I wrapped my left hand around the claws of the largest lobster to control them and held up the measuring gage. "This gage is three and one quarter inches long from prong to prong. You hook one end of it in the eye socket like this... and hold it parallel to the center of the top of its body shell down toward the tail. If the second prong hits the body shell, it's legal. If it hits the tail it's a short." I fitted the gage into place and held it out. "As you can see this lobster is way legal." I repeated the measurement with the second one. "Two quarters," I told them. "Not bad."

"Why do you call it a 'quarter'?"

"Because it weighs in at one and a quarter pounds. It's a common weight for lobsters. Sometimes the gage will just slide to the end of the body. The body is exactly three and a quarter inches long."

"So, it's legal?" the farmer's wife asked.

"Nope. It's a tie. Just like Las Vegas and baseball—ties go to the house or to the runner." I slipped rubber bands over the claws of the two on the table in front of me.

"Why do you do that?" Beth asked looking at me with big, wide eyes. "Isn't that cruel?"

"Nope. It keeps them from smashing each other up in the pool. In the days of old they would stick wooden pegs into each claw so they wouldn't open. The rubber band is kinder and gentler."

All eight of them clustered around the table looking at the two quarters. Katie managed to squeeze past Beth and get next to me.

"The one on the left is a male," I said. "The other is female."

They looked skeptical.

"Okay," Katie said with a toss of that blond head of hers, "I give up. How do you tell the boy lobster from the girl?"

"Look at the one aft." I pointed and they all leaned closer. "That's the flat end of the boat as opposed to the bow—or pointy end." I said to Katie who was looking in the wrong direction.

Bang! Shoulder slap.

"Where that one's tail begins it is much fatter than the one forward whose tail begins much narrower. The one with the fat tail is the female."

"Just like humans," the Marine bravely offered. His wife smacked him on the shoulder.

"Yes, sir. The females have fatter asses than the males." I laughed.

Katie feigned shock and swatted at me again like the Marine's wife had done.

"You, young lady, would be an exception," I said.

She giggled. "You two are terrible."

When my crew settled down I grinned at them. "Do you want to know the real reason that lobsters are not more abundant? I have to warn you, the answer is a bit lewd."

There was a moment of uncertain silence then the Marine said, "I think you can go ahead and shock us."

I cleared my throat. "The lobster was doomed from day one because quite simply the male lobster has..." I held the narrow-tailed crustacean up before me. "... two penises."

Looks of quizzical amusement spread over the faces of the men and the farmer's wife. The two blondes laughed. The shrink's wife made a face of disgust.

"That's right, people," I said, "two dicks. There it is—lock, stock, and barrel. They have been doomed from the start. I'm amazed that they didn't become extinct a million years ago with a handicap like that."

I turned to the two giggling blondes and thrust the lobster toward them. They recoiled in mock fear. When I pointed to the two appendages on the underside of the tail they huddled together.

"Come on," I teased, "don't you want to touch them?"

They squealed and hugged each other. All the men noticed and enjoyed as all men everywhere do.

"Chicken."

"I am not..." the one named Katie said.

"Hey, girl, when you go home to..."

"California," she said hastily.

"When you go home to California you can tell everyone that while you were in Gloucester you touched a lobster's penis—two of them, in fact." I grinned at her. "I'll bet you'll be the only girl in town with that distinction."

She gave me a look that clearly signaled she was up for the challenge. Reaching out, she carefully touched both penises. The boat was raucous with laughter. She stepped back and took a bow. Everyone applauded.

I raised the lobster for all of them to see it. "Okay, people, what do we have here?"

"A very happy lobster," the Marine quipped. "Hell, look at him smiling." His wife swatted him again. Everyone laughed and Katie shot me a look that was hard to mistake.

"I know what you're thinking, girl," I turned to her.

"Who me?"

"Yes, you. What's your name again?"

"Katie."

"I know what Katie's thinking." I watched her.

"You do not!"

"Yes, I do."

"Okay, smarty pants, what am I thinking?"

"Katie's thinking I wish my boyfriend had two penises."

She gave a mock gasp. "Stop picking on me!"

I shrugged and turned away.

"Why would I want that?" she asked hastily.

"Think about it," I said looking her in the eye, "one's up, one's down, one's up." Her eyes widened and I turned to the group. "So what would that make Katie?"

"A happy camper," the Marine answered.

Katie covered her face feigning embarrassment.

"Wait," I said. "It gets better."

"How could it get any better?" Everyone turned in astonishment to the wife of the Marine who had just spoken. Her husband stared at her, his mouth open but nothing coming out in reaction to her bold statement.

"Well, ma'am," I smiled at her and she returned my smile without reservation. "It's like this—BANG—they're both up at the same time. Oh yeah. Just think, lucky Katie could have legal and illegal sex at the same time."

She laughed and my audience cracked up.

"Just think of the legal conundrum. 'Your honor, it is possible to have both legal and illegal sex at the same time. My client is innocent'. It could be very dangerous for our poor Katie, though. Just think, right in the middle of the best time she ever had in her life, if she were to sneeze... well... being pretty much air-tight... BOOM!"

Everybody howled and Katie whacked me in the shoulder.

"Oh no," I continued looking right at her, "poor little Katie, stuck to the ceiling, bits and pieces of her all over the bedroom." She whacked me again. "Her honey would feel terrible and probably develop some kind of sex problem." Whack! "My God, what a tragedy. Man, that would really suck."

"Leave me alone," she said smiling.

I winked at her and turned back to my audience. "Think about it seriously, people. Suppose millions of years ago we developed two of them instead of the lobster—think of the ramifications. Sure there'd be a lot of happy girls out there. Just look at Katie, she can't stop thinking about it..."

"Stop picking on me!"

"So, guys, think about how much trouble having just one dick has gotten you into." The men laughed loudly. "Think of all the fights you got into, think of all the money you spent. Divorces, alimony, child support, kids growing up with only one parent and all that caused by having just one dick. Do you think you could have survived with two of these beauties?"

The farmer and the Marine were cackling as were their wives.

"Young man," the psychiatrist spoke up, "perhaps I could trade you the cost of this tour for an hour on my couch. It might do you some good."

"No really, doc, if we developed two penises first, Darwin's

Theory of Evolution would have rendered us extinct. If we'd had two before the lobsters, the lobsters would be standing on this boat watching us flap our tails and bite each other inside the traps. They'd be the ones getting ready to drop us into boiling water, break us to pieces, and eat us."

Katie giggled and nudged her friend.

"Not that some of us don't look good enough to eat," I said to them.

"Promises, promises." Katie smiled.

"Anyway," I turned back to the group. "Shall we carry on with the time honored practice of fishing?"

I hauled the next trap and watched the looks of disgust as the crew stepped back. The girls pointed at it and covered their mouths.

"Son," the Marine was the first to recover, "That is the ugliest... I don't even know if it could be called a fish ... that's the ugliest thing I've ever seen. What the hell is it?"

I flipped the trap onto the table and turned it for them to get a better look.

"That, ladies and gentlemen, is an ocean catfish. Also known as a wolf fish."

"Its head is all teeth," Brenda said slightly horrified.

"Folks, if the guy who designed the monster in the movie 'Alien' didn't get the idea from this fish, I'll eat it raw."

"Hey," Katie piped up, "I thought I had first dibs on that, Mr. Fisherman."

Beth and the psychiatrist's wife looked at her in shock. The farmer and the Marine snickered.

"You are a delicate flower to be sure." No doubt in my mind now.

The cat was a seven or eight pounder, a big one. It slunk back and forth like a snake, its teeth were easily an inch long and protruded out of its mouth with the upper and lower jaw interlocking. When codfish come up in a trap they will push against the far side of the trap trying to get away from you. Not so with catfish. A cat will come right up to you snapping with those two rows of massive teeth which click when they snap together as though to say, Okay, asshole, you caught me. Now let's see if you can get me out of here and still have ten fingers.

Katie wiggled in beside me and approached the trap. As she extended a finger toward the fish it lunged at her. Its teeth crunched down on the wire mesh with a weird tooth-on-metal sound. She jumped backwards and clutched my arm.

"Oooo," she squealed, "he tried to eat me..."

"Well, we can't blame him for that, can we?"

She giggled and slapped at me still hanging onto my arm. I looked down at her and let myself think briefly about an appetizer for that evening's grilled catfish dinner.

I disentangled myself and took hold of the trap. "In my first and formative days of lobstering, I'd use two hands to try and get them out of the trap. That just got me a world of hurt so I tried other methods—I tried stabbing them in the head but it takes them fifteen minutes to die. Same thing when I shot them with a .22...."

"You shot it with a gun?" Beth stared at me in shock.

"Yep. When the .22 didn't work I tried a .45 automatic but those things take forever to die and I can't stand around waiting for a damn fish to die. Besides shooting them is woefully hard on the trap and boat plus it gets expensive. So..." I turned the trap and the ugly beast inside lunged at my hand. The girls squealed. "...I learned to be bold and fast. I just shoot in with one hand, grab them behind the head like a snake and yank them out fast before it can turn and crush my hand. The other thing you have to look out for is if the damn thing hooks its tail in the mesh of the trap, it makes it a real bitch to pull out."

"Really? You're that fast?" Katie chirped.

I held up my hand and wiggled my fingers. "Still got ten."

She took a deep breath. That was fun to watch.

"Okay, people," I said. "Step back." With the ease acquired by years of practice, I shot my hand into the trap, grabbed the fish and ripped it out, jamming it straight up and smashing its mouth into the wood of the roof overhead. Predictably, its teeth clapped down crunching into the wood. I let go and it swung back and forth unable to open its jaw. I stepped back with a flourish amid gasps and expressions of delighted horror.

"Son, just what are you going to do with it?" asked the Marine.

"Sir, he will be barbecued with peppers, onions, and potatoes and eaten by me."

"Is he good eating?" asked the farmer.

"Well, sir, the reason that ugly son of a bitch has those weapons for teeth is that he eats mostly shell fish. Lobsters, scallops, crabs, sea clams. For Christ's sake, his regular feed is what makes up the menus of the finest restaurants in the world. Just look at the bottom of that trap." I pointed indicating the crushed lobster shells on its floor. "If you ate like that, you'd taste good, too."

"Hey, Mr. Fisherman, don't fill yourself up. Remember..."

"Are you going to let that fish just hang there?" the shrink and his wife had edged toward the far end of my boat.

"Nope. Stand back, folks." In one well-practiced motion I jerked an eighteen inch steaking knife out and upward slashing the fish from its butthole to its head, splitting it vertically and spilling its guts onto the deck in a bloody mess. Swinging the knife horizontally and spinning in my best Russell Crowe impersonation, I severed the body from the head which remained dangling from the wood. The eviscerated body landed with a thump on the deck. I scooped it up and tossed it into the lobster tank to wash it then smacked the head with the side of the knife. It plopped into the water a few yards over the side. My audience was dead silent.

As I cleaned the blade of my knife I heard the Marine chuckle and heard the whack as his wife swatted him again. The girls were staring open-mouthed and the shrink and his wife wore faces of astonishment.

"That was really good," the farmer said in a low voice.

"It certainly was," his wife added.

"Just fixing the food for dinner," I said to him. "There's not a whole lot of difference between those of us who catch your food and those who grow it. If you want to eat, it's a really good idea not to fuck too much with either, is it? You really want to trust me on this point."

The farmer nodded agreement. The psychiatrist cleared his throat. "I'll tell you what. I'll give you a free hour on my couch any time you want it."

I laughed. "Only if Katie will lay on it with me." I looked right at her and she took an unconscious step forward.

The next trap on deck had a lot of lobster shells in it and three shorts.

"Come on over, people. This is what I call Mark's Rule of Lobstering." They gathered around. "This trap had one three-pound male and three little shit-assed shorts like those. The larger, slower lobster will always lose to the smaller, much quicker shorts out of water. That costs me about ten bills. Just like in humans, the smaller, quicker guys will always take out the big, slow guys." They all watched the three shorts running all around the trap through the broken shells. "The other part of Mark's Law goes like this: 'When I swing a trap onboard with many lobsters in it, the crunching sound I hear is always little illegal sized lobsters crunching up the legal sized ones and costing me money'."

The next trap on board has no lobsters in it.

"How come there are no lobsters in this one?" the farmer asked.

I motioned him to come closer.

"See this? One of the nylon squares in the mesh between has been cut in the mesh between the kitchen head and the parlor head and a two inch square hole is the result."

"You mean the lobsters can find their way out through that one little hole?"

"Yes, sir, every last one of them."

"Not exactly stupid, are they?"

"Nope, not at all, I'm bound to say."

The next trap onboard elicits another chorus of "ooohs" and "ahhs". What appears to be another alien space creature swishes back and forth in the parlor head of the trap. Like the catfish, its head is all teeth but its body tapers out from head to tail, more like a snake than a fish. Sliding quickly through the trap it is one nasty creature. Because of its tendency to enter lobster traps and kill everything in there it is called a lot of things by fishermen.

"That, folks, is a Conger Eel." I said as they inched closer to get a better look. As it swished back and forth its head moved rapidly from side to side constantly looking for a way out. It reminds you of one of those creatures from miles under the sea. Its face is little more than long, ugly teeth. "The problem with the eel is a lot like that with the catfish. As you can see..." I pointed to the crushed up lobster shells in the trap "...it's had a lunch of what I'd bet were two quarters and a two pound female. The Conger Eel is smart enough to know that catching lobsters in a trap is a whole lot easier than chasing them when they're running free. Plus they're a real pain in the ass to get out."

The shrink's wife made a disgusted sound and turned away. I guessed she was anticipating a repeat of the cat evisceration.

"Being an eel it has a slime coating. Trust me, it's just as nasty as it looks. It can really slip around in the trap and it can wrap its tail around the trap holes so tight you can pick the trap right up in the air trying to jerk them out." I heard sounds of disgust from the two girls. "Just like with the catfish, as soon as the trap breaks the surface, if there are lobsters and an eel, the race is on to get the good lobsters out before that sickening crunch—like nails on a chalkboard. Good lobsters being smashed. Usually there are no lobsters left so you can take your time getting it out."

"You can't grab it like you did the catfish, can you?" Brenda asked fascinated.

"Not exactly," I said. "Too slimy. For a time I simply turned the trap over and let the damn thing fall out but after hauling a couple of hundred traps you really don't feel like doing extra work because of a stupid eel. I would simply stick the thing between the eyes and leave it in the trap." The girls squealed loudly. "Brilliant bastard that I am, after hauling a few hundred traps with the dead eel, and not so much as a short lobster in them, I figured out that the traps with a dead eel didn't fish. Think about it. If you were a lobster in my kitchen head, would you enter a parlor with your natural enemy in it? Nope, no way."

They were listening apparently enthralled. Dealing with wolf fish and Conger Eels was an everyday nuisance to me but my audience was captivated.

"So," I continued, "I tried leaving the door open in the hopes that the seagulls would take care of it but, nope. Seagulls are among God's stupidest feathered creatures but are not dumb enough to go near a Conger Eel. Finally, I settled on this course of action..."

I saw them shift closer both fascinated and afraid of what they were about to witness. I took a six inch serrated knife in my left hand and flashed in with my right hand grabbing the eel behind the neck and shoving the knife between its eyes up to the hilt. Ripping the creature out of the trap I held it up to the startled crew. The tail of the eel wrapped in circles around my arm down to the elbow and tried, for all it was worth, to twist its head and take a chunk out of me. Naturally, I got the most mileage out of it by pretending to throw it at the girls who squeaked and grabbed each other. I then smashed its head on the rail of the boat and unceremoniously tossed it overboard. Conger Eels are not good eating.

"That, people, is how an eel is removed from a lobster trap. Stimulating, isn't it?"

"Do you enjoy pulling the wings off of living flies?" asked the psychiatrist.

"Do you ever see seals out here?" asked Beth.

There was no good way to tell the truth.

"You're hauling traps in the summer. It's hot, muggy, no wind and you have the bottom half of a Grundy on. It, as you can see, is made of rubber—so are my boots. Not the coolest of materials to work in. Your clothes are soaked through after hauling the first trawl, you have twenty more to haul. Wearing a bandana is not a fashion statement, or part of gang colors, it's a necessity. It keeps the sweat from running into your eyes and blinding you, not a state you want your eyes to be in while at sea, now is it? Your boots fill with sweat and you squeak with each step. At the end of each day you have the beginning of a classic case of trenchfoot. The waves are two to fours with intermittent sixes and eights. The waves hit the boat from all directions in no set pattern. Your work platform moves horizontally, vertically, and laterally with no rhythm whatsoever. We even have a name for it—classic Mass Bay slop. It knocks you all over the place and it's where lobstermen spend most of their life. The corporate bullshit world would call lobstering 'labor intensive'." I saw the farmer and his wife nod in empathy. Farmers know about intensive labor.

"Imagine you have to shovel wet snow up a forty-five degree incline in a hurry for fifteen or twenty minutes with the floor jumping all over the place. Take five off and then you have to do it again, twenty times in a row. That might give you an idea of what it's like to lobster alone in the North Atlantic." I noticed that the psychiatrist was looking a bit green. Good. "If you take your mind off what you are doing you can run your fingers through the hauler or even fall overboard. If you go over, you die."

Beth and Katie gasped. I turned to them. "George Clooney might be able to swim in rubber overalls," I told them making reference to a scene in the movie "The Perfect Storm", "but in the real world, if you go over in rubber and boots you might as well be wearing an anchor. You're going one place—down."

Both of the girls had wide eyes. The shrink's wife appeared mildly concerned.

"So, you pull up to a trawl. In between pulling the traps onboard and turning them sideways which, with the wood runners, is a pain, you are dropping the boat in and out of gear trying not to tangle in a buoy line which will end your day in a hurry. You're removing the few good lobsters and throwing the shorts and the other shit back overboard. You're re-baiting, closing the door and running the traps all over the boat. Trust me, you can get into one foul mood. So you pull in a trawl and the first two traps have five lobsters each. The third is empty, the door is open and the bait-bag is gone and you know from experience that the rest are going to be in the same condition. It's a sickening feeling that punches you in the stomach and sends rage through every vein in your body. With every subsequent trap that comes out of the water in the same state your rage grows. You know you have been 'sealed'."

"'Sealed'?" asks Brenda.

"Yup. One of those cute little bastards that everybody loves has found your trawl line and had a feast. You pull trap after empty trap and the rage festers. You pull five, ten-pot trawls all sealed. What state of mind are you in?"

"Deadly," says the farmer.

"Thank you, Kansas. So think about this, you just put back the last sealed trap which you have not only had to re-bait but also replace the bait bag. Just as you are jotting down the loran bearings, five yards off your stern up pops the adorable little head of a seal looking like a puppy dog. The cute little thing has wiped out one fourth of your day's pay by ripping the bait out of them and, having found a good, easy food source, is right there waiting for you to re-bait so he can do it again. What would you do?"

The farmer folded his arms over his chest. "I believe I'd

shoot the damn thing."

"You'd kill a seal?" shrieked the girls hysterically.

"I believe I would," the farmer repeated. "Quick as I'd kill a fox in my henhouse or a mad dog."

Brenda nodded in agreement with her husband.

Katie turned to me. "You wouldn't kill a baby seal, would you?"

"Of course not," I replied with a straight face. Not if it would change her plans for me I wouldn't. I turned back to the farmer.

"You see, Kansas, killing a seal is moderately illegal. At one time there was a bounty on them but now your Federal government in its usual H.U.A. fashion, takes a dim view of popping the little sons of... the cuddly little seals."

"What does H.U.A. mean?" asked the Marine.

"Sir, it means 'head up ass'."

"What's the punishment for killing seals?"

"They smash into your house with a tank and burn you to death."

The shrink's wife gasped.

"Just kidding. But they might as well. They confiscate your boat, fine you and throw you in jail."

"Just for killing one seal?" the farmer was flabbergasted.

"Yes, sir. Your tax dollars at work protect them there seals. Worse than that, folks, is that in the past thirty years every food fish from the haddock to the monkfish has been systematically depleted by draggers while your federal government has been busy protecting the seals. And it gets worse, the biologists say that the intermediary host for a deadly codfish parasite is the seal. This parasite has contributed to the demise of the codfish as much as the draggers. The thing is, the cod is a food fish but does anyone eat seals? Which is more important?"

"So it sounds to me like the federal government has screwed up pretty bad here, Mark," the old veteran said.

"Well, I tell ya, sir, I'm not quite ready to join some inbred militia and screw cows but their record of managing the fishing industry in the northeast has been decrepit to the point of criminally negligent going back thirty years."

"So, Mark, do you gun them seals?" the farmer asked.

A lot of eyes went to full open.

"No, sir, I'm a law and order man. But I know one lobster-man who has been shooting at them for twenty years."

"He kills seals??" the two girls sobbed.

"I said he shoots at them. He doesn't hit them, not that he doesn't try."

The farmer chuckled. "That don't surprise me. You Yankees are not really known for your prowess with a rifle."

"Tell me, sir, what is this boat doing as we speak?"

The farmer thought for a moment. "I guess it's moving some."

"Yes it is. It's a calm day, southwest wind is maybe five knots, waves are less than a foot. It's a veritable mill pond out here. Trust me, this is not a normal day on the North Atlantic. Imagine if it was blowing fifteen to twenty and the waves were two to four feet the way it usually is. Imagine how much the boat would be bouncing around."

The farmer considered that. "It would be like hitting something off of the back of a horse at full gallop—almost impossible."

"You got it, Kansas." I turned to the two older men. "Marine, Kansas, do you figure you guys are fair shots?"

"Qualified expert in the service," the farmer said.

"Same here," said the Marine who had informed me he had been at the Chosen Reservoir. He was one of the frozen chosen.

"So you can both hit an elephant if you are sitting on it?" I said smiling at them. "I mean, you can shoot."

Both nodded.

"Gentlemen, what's the most difficult shot?"

"A moving target below you or above you," said the farmer.

"How about if the platform the shooter is standing on and the target both move horizontally, vertically and laterally with no rhythm whatsoever—like maybe a lobster boat in classic Mass Bay Slop?"

"That would be the second hardest target, sonny," the Marine said fixing me with a look that said he knew what he was talking about.

"What would the first be?"

"All those things you describe, only the target would be a North Korean with a rifle trying to kill you."

"I stand corrected," I agreed.

"So your friend hasn't hit a seal in ten years," Katie interjected.

"My friend can hit a quart of beer, off-hand, a football field away on land but off a moving deck... forget it. If he comes close enough to scare a seal he figures he's made a good shot. Shooting and missing is his vent."

"He tells me that sometimes after he misses one, when he is in the middle of the next trawl and an adorable little puppy-like seal head pops up right next to his boat, winks, and smiles before diving away. He says he doesn't know whether to go for his gun or bust up laughing."

"Son, why not get you a shotgun and 00 buck the damn thing?" asked the very practical farmer.

"Because I might hit one."

"Oh, big, tough lobster man," Katie said. Everyone laughed.

"Let me tell you a story," I said leaning back against the trap table and they gathered around. "I was in the restaurant of a health club watching a National Geographic Special. Somewhere on a beach in South America there was a seal rookery with a little river running through the middle of it located along a beach. Seals are running to and fro. There were three girls sitting at a table watching, too. They kept 'oh-ing' and 'ah-ing' over them. 'They're so cute,' said one. 'I want one for a pet.' Another one said, 'oh look at the cute little seals playing.' One baby seal is looking for its mommy and yelps mournfully. It falls into the stream and is pulled toward the ocean. A collective sigh comes from the girls. Two more babies end up in the stream headed for the ocean. 'Oh, look out, little seals,' the girls cry."

"What happened?" Katie and Beth ask simultaneously, their eyes huge.

"At the mouth of the stream the little seals are trying to get back to the shore when—WHA-BOOM! Orcas appear from nowhere and smash into the cute little seals, their jaws crushing down on them. They ripped them apart, shaking them as blood and guts fly everywhere. One of the seals is swallowed whole. Two of the orcas play catch with the eviscerated, limp body of one as though it was a beach ball."

Katie and Beth had their hands over their mouths in horror. The shrink was taking notes. The farmer and the Marine were doing their damndest not to laugh out loud.

"That's horrible," the shrink's wife blurted. The Marine's wife and Brenda rolled their eyes at her.

"I was on my feet cheering with a couple of other guys as if the Sox had scored a home run. 'What?' I yelled 'No A-1 Sauce?' The girls at the next table were crying—actually a lot like you girls," I said.

"How can you be so insensitive?" Mrs. Shrink gasped.

"Easy," I said. "I hate the goddamned things. Just then an Orca barreled out of the water onto the beach and snatched another baby seal, tossed it in the air, swallowed it whole, and rolled back into the water."

"You're disgusting," she snarled.

I nodded in agreement. "Yup. While the two Orcas played catch with Andre the girls stormed out of the club. Probably headed to a salad bar for dinner."

"What did you do?" asked Beth.

"Me? I had another glass of wine and went home and renewed my subscription to National Geographic."

It was too much for Kansas and the Marine. They busted up laughing. I went back to hauling trawls.

The first trap of the next trawl comes up devoid of any life whatsoever. "Okay, people," I said holding up the bait bag that looked like it had been sliced with a knife, "what happened?"

"Sealed," said the shrink—much to my surprise.

"Good guess but wrong," I said. "This one was birded."

There is a long silence.

"How the hell would a bird get into your trap under water," asked the Marine shaking his head in disbelief.

"You are like, such a bullshit artist," Katie said.

I grinned at her. "I find such an excellent girl swearing so alluring."

She made a face at me. "You'd find a girl sitting on a toilet alluring."

"I just knew she was kinky," I said to my crew. They laughed.

I held the bag aloft. "What's different?"

Brenda shrugged. "Looks the same as the one that you described as 'sealed'."

"Nope. Look closer. Some guys lobster for twenty years and never learn the difference. Seals rip the bag apart. This looks like it was cut with a knife."

"What kind of bird could do that?" the Marine's wife asked.

"Well, I'd like to tell you that I figured it out through some brilliant deductive reasoning..." I continued. "But the truth is I thought it was seals, too, right up until I found a sliced bait bag and a dead cormorant who had taken a wrong turn and ended up in the parlor head."

"I like suppose you have a 'friend' who shoots the birds, too," Katie said.

"God, you are feisty," I stared at her.

"Yeah? Play your cards right and you'll find out just how feisty I can be."

I turned back to my crew.

"Folks, the seal wrecks a whole trawl. The bird might get one or two traps but they don't cause enough trouble to worry about. There was one time however when a friend of mine had his whole trawl birded and he was seriously pissed. Lo and behold there was a big old cormorant sitting in the water licking his beak and looking so guilty. Well, damn if my friend didn't take off after it banging away with a big old .45 automatic. Well, as Providence would have it, that old bird was so full of fish he couldn't get off the water. He chased him banging away at an all but impossible target, right by two other boats hauling gear. The captain and the stern man on each of the boats stopped hauling and started clapping. Evidently that bird had pissed off a lot of people that day."

Kansas laughed and the Marine gave me a grin.

"My buddy finally ran out of bullets, returned to sanity, and went back to fishing. He told me that both of those boats called him and asked if they were on the right side of his boat or the left. In the world of a lobsterman, the right side means you're a good guy—like the Republican right wing—and the left side means you're a bad guy, a Democrat liberal left. Just like in the real world."

There were disgruntled mumbles from Mr. and Mrs. Shrink but everyone else laughed. I leaned over and hauled the next trap on board.

"Now that is rare! I haven't seen one of those trap up in years, they're usually far too smart to trap up."

"What is it?" the girls chorused.

I turned around with a wad of crumpled aluminum foil in my hand. "Look everyone, it's a lobster roll—heavy on the onions and mayo."

Both girls smacked me on the arm while the others laughed.

"Oh, you, you..." Beth stammered.

"...you jerk," Katie finished for her.

The next trap I pulled brought a collective gasp and a little whimper from Mrs. Freud.

"Oh God!" The girls hugged each other wide-eyed. They had a habit of doing that and I wasn't the only one who noticed it. Both the farmer and the Marine seemed to enjoy it too. I nodded to each of them and they nodded back in agreement—it was certainly appealing.

"Is that a shark?" asked the shrink in disbelief at the three foot long creature squirming inside my trap.

"No, doc, it's a dog fish."

"It's a what?" the Marine's wife asked.

"Come over to the table, folks, and I'll show you a diver-proof way of telling a shark from a dog fish."

They crowded around. "Believe it or not, this is the fish part of your classic British fish'n'chips," I said flipping the fish out for them to look at.

"You're not serious," Mrs. Shrink said.

"Serious I am and mighty fine tasting these puppies be, too." I turned the still wiggling creature around to face them. "Lots of people panic when they see that dorsal fin. To most people it looks like a shark. Ever since the movie "Jaws" these guys have been wrecking havoc among people who have never seen them before. But see how small its mouth is? That means it's a dog fish. On a shark the mouth would spread like a grin from ear to ear—sort of like the face of a man who had just had sex with Katie here."

WHAM! The size of the black and blue mark on my arm was increasing proportionately to the movement of my mouth.

"Did I hurt you?" Katie pouted.

"No," I grinned at her, "yes, I mean. But it was a good hurt."

She gave me another flash of those eyes. I shook my head to clear it. Suddenly, it was as if I had a vision.

"Hey," I said, "you people want to have some fun?"

There was a hesitant silence while each member of my crew let their minds wander to what my idea of fun might be.

"What devious and depraved scheme has your brain devised, young man," asked Sigmund.

"Come on," I said dropping the dog fish into the live well and setting back the trawl. "Let's head over to the beach."

I headed toward Good Harbor Beach two miles distant. On a hot mid-August, Sunday afternoon like this one it would be packed with thousands of people basking in the sand and splashing in the waves. When we were about a mile from the beach I called to my crew, "How can you tell the water is warm today without touching it?"

"At this distance, son, not a clue," the Marine said when no one spoke up.

"See all those people in the water?"

"Yes, does that mean that the water is warm?"

"Not by itself."

"What then?"

"The give away is that they're all in over their crotches."

Everyone chuckled.

"It's that simple? I'll be damned."

I took the boat out of gear and walked to the stern. "If it's hot outside and the beach is crowded but no one is in the water over their ankles you can bet it's bone, frickin cold. Brilliant bastard, aren't I?" I said.

"Very logical," the shrink nodded.

As I approached the beach, I slowed to a crawl and right at the point where the lifeguards raised their whistles to warn me off, I went hard over to the right and began to parallel the beach just to the right of the point where the creek empties into the ocean.

"Now, ladies and gentlemen, if this here dogfish that looks

like a shark will cooperate, I believe I can create a condition which could best be described as contagious panic along the full length of this here beach."

I picked up the weakened but very much alive dog fish and discreetly dropped him into the water on the beach side of the boat.

"Ya see, folks, when the doggy fish is weak, he tends to swim on the surface—normally these guys are bottom feeders so most people never see them—but if my guess is right he's just weak enough..."

I saw mischievous grins spread across the faces of the two older men as they caught on. The others looked puzzled. Katie moved beside me and whispered, "Just what are you trying to do?"

I leaned down so only she could hear me, "With you later or on the beach now."

She gave me a "yes" smile if ever there was one. Great. One "yes" smile out of twenty tries may be about my average but I'd take it.

Meanwhile the dog fish, as if by remote control, swam right at the beach. The first person to spot it was a large, burly man with more body hair than a gorilla who had waded into the water up to his waist. His eyes nearly popped out of his skull.

"SHARK!" he shrieked back-pedaling so hard he toppled backwards onto his bodacious ass creating such a wave that it sent two small children flying.

It is a fact known by those who live here, and especially those of us who make our leaving at sea, that these waters have killed over five thousand Gloucester fishermen. This is a point not lost on most visitors either and prudent mothers keep sharp eyes on their little ones when they venture into the water here. The mothers of these two kids smashed into the water with the force a couple of NFL corner-backs and scooped them out. Hair-boy flailed about trying to stand and accomplishing little more than another resounding splash.

"You are like so evil," Katie said whacking my black and blue shoulder again.

"You don't know the half of it," I said to her. She flushed.

Aboard the Black Sheep there was considerable laughter but not so in the water. It was awe-inspiring. A wave of total and complete panic spread through those in the water as the killer from the deep swam, weak and confused, into their midst. The poor fish, completely baffled by the commotion, headed toward the beach then turned hard to its right about ten feet from shore and ran parallel as people shrieked, "SHARK! SHARK! SHARK!"

From the Sheep it looked as though a strong wind blew every man, woman and child out of the water in mortal fear of the three-foot-long monster. Mothers pulled small children so fast their feet couldn't keep up and they wound up dragging the poor kids through the water and ten yards up onto the beach as though the fish could scuttle out of the water and nab them. Screaming, crying, pleading, and ubiquitous exclamations of "oh my God" filled the sunny afternoon. Little kids stood crying at the water's edge and bikini-clad girls leapt onto the backs of their boyfriends. From all compass points on the beach the cavalry arrived. Husbands, fathers and boyfriends stormed the surf yanking terrified women and children to safety from certain death at the jaws of the vicious man-eater.

God, I loved being a Gloucester fisherman. It was the little things that made it all like so worthwhile. My only concern was that I had no oxygen aboard as it was beginning to look like Mr. & Mrs. Semper Fi could be in need of some. Everyone, even the politically correct Freuds, roared with laughter.

Back on shore the lifeguards had been alerted. They capped off their whistles and pulled out their bullhorns as the disoriented dog fish swam aimlessly down the beach, its fin knifing ominously through the water.

"SHARKS!" The cry went up. "Everyone out of the water. For God's sake, OUT OF THE WATER! MANY SHARKS!"

People ran for their lives, some began packing up and heading for their cars while others, edged slowly back toward the surf in hopes of getting a glimpse of the nefarious killing machine in the water.

"Has anyone got a gun?"

"Call the Coast Guard."

"Where are the police, for God's sake?"

Their cries echoed across the water to a fishing boat filled with eight hysterically laughing tourists.

By the time the police arrived not one person among the

thousands on the beach was so much as touching the water. The lifeguards walked in ankle deep water as though they were in a minefield warning off the swimmers with their bull horns.

"The beach is closed due to shark attack. I repeat, attacking sharks, the beach is closed."

In the midst of the pandemonium, the poor dog fish managed to get his bearings and head out to sea. I wished him a long life and a full tummy. He was, without a doubt, the most entertaining fish I ever met.

On shore, as the threat appeared to subside, mothers kissed the children they almost lost. Girlfriends hugged and kissed their hero boyfriends—who would be thanked more intensely later, I hoped—for snatching the fair damsels from the jaws of death. Men shook hands and slapped shoulders. People bonded in the way they only can after sharing a near death experience. It was touching.

"You are such a stinky," Katie said, holding her sides as she laughed.

"Haven't had so much fun since the hogs et my baby brother," the farmer howled. Whatever the hell that meant, I thought.

"That was beautiful," the Marine laughed trying to catch his breath.

"So, doc," I said, "would you call that 'contagious panic' or what?"

"Well," he was doing a poor job of trying to keep a straight face, "In my professional opinion, it was a classic case." He couldn't stop laughing which earned him a ball-breaking glare from his wife. At least someone else on the Sheep had earned the wrath of a female.

"Listen up, folks," I hollered, "this concludes our lobster tour aboard the Gloucester Fishing Vessel Black Sheep for today. I hope it has been educational as well as entertaining."

Applause broke out and continued as I put the Sheep in gear and prepared to head back in. Just then Katie tapped me on the shoulder.

"Why does that man on the boat with an orange stripe on it have a gun?"

I turned to face a Coast Guard forty-one footer. I checked it out and turned to her.

"It's a pirate boat and that pirate is going to come aboard and ... you know what they say about pirates. Your rape is imminent."

She stared at me, "Are you going to let him carry me off?"

"No, ma'am," I said with absolute conviction.

An official U.S. Coast Guard vessel full of official U.S. Coast Guard personnel pulled up to the Sheep. A Petty Officer and two seamen stepped onto my boat. The Petty Officer spoke.

"Excuse me, sir, do you mind if we inspect your boat?"

"Oh, please do. It's a fine, flat, calm day and even a Coasty could pull that there forty-one footer up to a fishing boat," I replied.

"I don't know, sir. We have an officer at the helm today and he is rather shaky."

"Is it him?" yelled the officer from the 41.

The Petty Officer turned to him and shrugged with hands out, palms up.

The seaman carrying the notebook appeared to be the low man on the totem pole. He stared at the Petty Officer. "Sir," he sputtered, "we're looking for a thirty to forty foot Novi with a gray hull and a blue cabin with seven or eight people on board, for Christ's sake." He pointed at me. "This has got to be him."

The Petty Officer glared at him. "Boot, when I want your opinion I will tell you what it is. You roger that, sonny?" He turned to me. "F.N.G."

"What does F.N.G.. mean?" Katie piped up.

The Petty Officer turned to her and smiled. "Freakin New Guy, in polite society. The other F-word elsewhere, ma'am."

"Oh."

"Are you the master of this vessel?" He turned back to me.

"Masturbator and master of the Black Sheep, I be, sir." Katie giggled. The other women moved to the far side of the boat keeping wary eyes on the proceedings.

He extended his hand. "I'm Chief Petty Officer Chris Benton." He nodded to the older of the two seamen. "This is Seamanforever Mike Moriarity and this is Apprentice Seaman... what's your name again, boot?"

"Lane, Petty Officer," the kid stammered.

"Lane. Seaman Lane is right out of Basic and we are educating him."

"Lucky him," I replied.

"Okay, Cap. Do you have any firearms onboard?"

"Who are you? Sara Fucking Brady?"

The boots eyes grew enormous as the other two hid their smiles. My crew watched nervously.

"The Petty Officer asked if you had any weapons onboard," chipped the young seaman.

"I heard him, you little puppy ass mother fucker. Keep your shit little slit closed or I'll put you in the next fifty traps I fish, you read me?" I responded.

The kid stared at me in astonishment.

"Answer him, boot," Petty Officer Benton snapped.

"Yes, sir," he said to me.

Smart Coasties learned long ago that they may have the right to be pushy, but never do to Gloucester Fishermen on their own boats while at sea.

"Actually," I lowered my tone. "I do have a few weapons onboard."

"W-where would they be?" the boot stammered.

"There's a M1 Garand and a .45 automatic down below," I said looking him straight in the eye. "And another one right here." I slapped my hip pocket.

The boot backed up a step and reflexively unsnapped his pistol and reached for it.

"Hey, boot, keep your hand away from that pistol," shot the Petty Officer. He and Mike had stepped back so the kid couldn't see them laughing.

"You like to take it to the edge, there, don't you, Cap?" Chris said to me.

I stepped closer to the boot and gave him the once over. He looked to be about fourteen.

"Does your mother know you carry a handgun?" I said giving him my most intense look and trying desperately not to let the grins of the other two Coasties make me smile and blow my act.

"Aw, geez," the kid stammered.

My crew were unsuccessfully trying to stifle laughter. The poor kid turned beet red.

I turned my attention back to Chris. "There may be a few

other guns around, Petty Officer."

"And where would they be, Cap?"

"Well," I said, "All over the place. The Gatling gun isn't working so I had to put it down below with the other machine guns."

Chris raised his eyebrows. "Lobstering a little competitive this year, is it, Cap?"

I shrugged. "You know what they say, it's better to have them and not need them than to need them and not have them."

Chris nodded. "We'll check them out when we finish up here. Do you have life preservers for everyone onboard?"

"Of course. Somewhere."

"Check them off on the list, boot."

The boot stared back and forth between us. "Aren't you going to have him show you?"

"Check the friggin list, boot! Do you have flares onboard."

"Sure." I scratched my neck. "I saw a box of them around here a year or so ago... Somewhere."

"Excellent. Check 'em off, boot."

"But... but, sir..."

Chris glared at him.

"Checked, sir." He made a show of putting a large check-mark on his list.

"Good boy. You're learning. I speak and you do."

"But, sir..."

"Seaman Lane, your mother really doesn't know that you carry that big old handgun, now does she?" Chris repeated.

Katie and Beth giggled and the kid turned an even brighter shade of red.

Chris turned back to me. "Of course you have a bell onboard."

I gave him a look of surprise that was almost sincere. "Did I miss a few months or something? Is it friggin Christmas already?"

"Anything that sounds like a bell will do, Cap."

I thought a moment then walked over to the trap table, picked up a hammer and rapped the exhaust pipe a couple of times.

"One bell, Seaman Lane."

"Sir..."

"A check mark, if you please, Seaman Lane!" Chris turned to me. "There for a minute I thought we were making progress. How about a life-ring, Captain Williams?"

"Oh sure," I said rolling my eyes at my crew. "Guys like me that fish alone can't do without a life-ring. I mean, my God, if I fell overboard what would happen if I didn't have a life-ring to throw to myself, for Christ's sake?"

I heard the Marine and the farmer start to lose it again.

"Please, Captain Williams," Seaman Moriarity interjected. "We have to follow official Coast Guard policy for fishing boats under fifty feet. We are acutely aware that it was written by some legal bureaucrat dimwit officer who most assuredly grew up in a landlocked state and who has never been on a fishing boat, has no idea how to run one, and who will, in all probability, retire an admiral after a full career of writing stupid rules and regulations." He took a deep breath. "Nonetheless, the dumb rules are the dumb rules."

I held up an ancient life-ring that looked like it had the flotation potential of a sledgehammer.

"Checking the life-ring," sang the boot. "However, sir, I feel I would be negligent if I didn't point out that your life-ring is not attached to a line and as such is unacceptable."

"Holy shit, Seaman Moriarity," Chris chipped. "Not much gets by our boy, Lane, there does it?"

Moriarity nodded. "He's officer material if ever I seen it." He turned to Lane. "Seaman Lane, if you'll venture a good look at the Captain there, you may notice that he's wearing rubber Grundys and rubber boots like all lobstermen. If he falls overboard he's going straight down, we find empty lobster boats steaming in circles more often than we want to. Do you really think a ring is going to help him?"

The boot cleared his throat and bravely continued. "Ah, Captain Williams, are these paying passengers?"

I glared. "Are you accusing me of something dishonest?"

"No, no, of course not. Uh... do you have a survival suit onboard."

"That I have." I went below and returned with a state-of-the-art survival suit which I handed to Seaman Lane. His jaw dropped open as he took it from me.

"That looks like one of our Mustangs," he said turning it over. The words "Coast Guard Station Gloucester" were stenciled on the back in reflective tape.

"There goes our boy again," said Chris in wonder. "He's just all over this thing, ain't he?"

"Good God boy shit howdy, he don't miss much I'm bound to say," said Mike.

Lane stared at me. "This is an official Coast Guard Mustang. How the hell did a civilian get hold of this? You could get in a lot of trouble for possessing this," he said to me.

"Seaman Lane, I don't as a rule feel the need to explain myself to a lot of people ashore and fewer out here. But you're a boot and I'll make an exception." I looked at Chris and Mike and they nodded assent.

"Two friends of mine gave that to me still in factory wrap some years ago. You see, my first boat had gone down in February and I nearly died of hypothermia because I didn't have one on board. I couldn't afford one, you see, and even if I could, the ones available to civilians, as you call me, were no damn good anyway. Now, puppy, would you like to take a guess at which two guys on this boat took a chance at getting thrown out of the Coast Guard, or even going to jail, to give their friend a chance at staying alive in the North Atlantic in winter if his fucking boat should happen to sink? I'll give you a hint—they both have on uniforms."

He looked at Chris then at Mike and took a deep breath.

"Checking survival suit, Petty Officer..." he said with resignation. "And I didn't see a thing, did I, sir?"

"Mikey, did you hear our boy here?" Chris said delighted.

"I sure did and, my, didn't his stay at Station Gloucester just become so much more educational and easy?"

"Indeed. In two months the kid could run a boat like a Gloucester Fisherman and trust me, few Coasties ever reach that level."

"Sir," Lane said to me, "why don't you wear the survival suit all the time?"

"Very simple, Seaman Lane. In the winter I would be too hot and in the summer I would die of heat exhaustion. Unlike you Coasties..." I nodded toward Chris and Mike "... I don't just motor around on a million dollar boat saving Gloucester Fishermen from drowning. I have to work for a living and it is what the yuppie pukes would call 'labor intensive'."

"Cap," interrupted Chris, "do you have all the appropriate fishing licenses, federal permits, state permits, and assorted bullshit paperwork that your federal and state bullshit-know-nothing-about-the-real-world government bureaucracies require you to have under punishment of death?"

"Absolutely," I said. "I have stacks and stacks of useless paperwork, yes, I do."

Lane sighed. "I know, sir, check paperwork."

"Outstanding, Lane," Chris grinned, "you continue to surprise me."

With the inspection completed Chris fixed me with his best imitation of a stern look. I tried to act like I was taking it seriously.

"Now then, Captain Williams, are you aware that there was a shark scare at Good Harbor Beach this afternoon?"

"Sharks? Really?" I made my eyes as wide as I could. "Good God, that's terrible. Was anyone eaten?" I turned to my crew. "Did any of you see any sharks today?"

They all shook their heads and shrugged their shoulders as if they were choreographed. I was so proud of them.

"What happened, Petty Officer?" I asked.

"It seems one swam the entire length of the beach causing quite a stir."

"I'm shocked. Did it bite anyone?"

"No, sir," Chris replied. "There were no physical injuries."

"Well, thank God for that," I said. My crew were doing an admirable job of staying somber.

Chris cleared his throat. "There was a problem though, Captain Williams."

"Really? What was that?"

"It seems, Cap, that a number of individuals are claiming it was so traumatic that they may need psychiatric assistance."

"Well, I'll be," I said trying to look as concerned as possible.

"There were numerous reports of acts of extreme bravery on the part of individuals hauling children to safety from certain death when Jaws tried to rip them apart." He cracked and let a smile slip.

"You don't say." I stayed in control.

"Yes. The news pukes are all over it and starting to sniff around and there may be a problem."

"And that would be…"

"Well, it seems a swimmer perchanced to observe someone on a thirty to forty foot gray hulled Novi-styled boat with a blue cabin and several people onboard toss what he described as a shark-shaped object into the water near the beach. Said swimmer claimed the panic started a short time later."

"That's hard to believe. Who would do a thing like that?"

"Sir, you should be aware that this individual throwing a shark in the water could be brought up on charges."

"Charges?" I asked. "What charges? Inciting stupidity among tourists?"

"No, sir, inciting a riot, that's a felony."

"Really?" I considered that. "Well, Petty Officer, all I can say is I hope you catch the bastard."

"I do, too." Chris nodded agreement. "Now then, Cap, all we need to do is check down below for illegal substances."

"Trying to add to Michael's stash, are we?" I asked.

"Only if it's good shit," Michael chipped in.

"Follow me gentlemen." As I started below with Chris and Mike following I motioned to Kansas and the Marine to join us. The shrink ignored my offer.

"Lane," Chris ordered, "you keep a sharp eye out for that shark-throwing platform and, Lane, do keep an eye on our officer on the 41, okay?"

"Yes, Petty Officer."

"Good man," said Chris as he disappeared below.

The two California girls started to join us.

"I'm really sorry, ladies," I said, "but females are not allowed below deck on the Black Sheep. It's a bad luck thing."

Katie stared at me. "Oh, that's a story!"

"Sorry," I repeated.

"Honey," it was Mrs. Semper Fi speaking, "whenever men

pack up like that, there's a good reason and it's best to leave them alone."

Katie gave her a skeptical look. "Is it that male bonding thing."

The Marine's wife chuckled. "Probably they are just going to drink and swap lies but it's best to let them have their space."

She was a smart lady, I thought. Probably had to be.

As soon as we slid the door shut Chris and Mike exploded with laughter. "Did you throw a dogfish in the water near the beach?"

I nodded. "I did. And the beautiful little fuck swam the full length of the beach. Best one I've ever done."

"You should have been at the station," Chris laughed. "It went nuts! 'Killer sharks among the swimmers at Good Harbor Beach'—it was crazy."

"Pandelirium," I said.

"Pandelirium for sure," Mike agreed.

"Got something to show you," I said to the men. "You're not going to believe what I trapped up last week."

I retrieved an extremely old bottle of Jamieson's Irish Whiskey from the cabinet.

"Some toy boat apparently wanted some lobsters. He endtrapped me and was ethical enough to leave payment."

"I hope to shout he left payment," Mike said reaching for the bottle and examining the label with reverence. "That's a hundred dollar bottle of aged Irish whiskey."

"You of all people would know, Mike," I said.

"Yes, I certainly would..."

"Gentlemen," I announced, "let us see that this whiskey ages no more."

"Can't fault that logic," Seaman-forever Moriarity said.

I passed around plastic cups and the seal was broken.

"Killer sharks!" Chris said holding up his cup.

"Killer sharks," the rest of us chorused and we drank and refilled.

"Marine?" said Chris to the veteran.

"Korean War," he nodded.

"Were you at the Cosine River Retreat like my uncle was?"

"Son," the old Marine said, "Marines don't retreat. We just fight in another direction."

"I stand corrected," Chris replied. And we filled our cups again.

The vet pointed to Chris's handgun. "What the hell kind of a gun is that, son?"

"It's the new Beretta." He removed the gun from his holster, dropped the clip into his hand and offered it, butt first, to him.

"How many rounds does that clip hold?"

"Seventeen."

"But they only let Coasties have one bullet and they are only allowed to load after someone shoots at them." I try never to miss an opportunity to mess with my friends.

"What's that?" the Marine asked.

"That's the de-cocking lever, sir."

"Go on," he stared at it. "A de-cocking lever?"

"Yes, sir."

"What do you need that for? In the old days we would hold the hammer with two fingers, pull the trigger, and lower the hammer. Isn't a de-cocking lever just one more dumb thing to malfunction? The .45 automatic I carried in Korea only carried seven in the magazine and one down the spout."

"Yeah," I said, "but the .45 shoots real bullets. That there wonder nine is a goddamn cockroach killer, not a man killer."

"What do you mean?" asked Chris. "The nine millimeter will kill you."

"Sure it will—two weeks after you shoot someone. Which is two weeks after you're dead."

"Bullshit."

"Gentlemen," I said. "If the man standing in front of you means to kill you via the handgun he has pointed at you, if he holds it with one hand your odds are much better of living through the day than if he holds it with two. You likewise hold a handgun. Now in my left hand is a nine millimeter cartridge. In my right hand is a .45 automatic cartridge which I am sure you will observe is about twice as large as the nine. Which one would you want your life to depend on?" I looked at them and no one said a word. "Thank you. This concludes our lesson in street survival for today."

"But, Mark," said Michael. "If you ever saw Chris shoot, you'd see that he absolutely needs all the bullets he can fit into the gun." He grinned at Chris. "As for me, I'm Irish. I prefer a big stick to a gun."

Everyone laughed and another round of drinks were poured.

"Hey, Marine, watch this," Chris said.

He slapped the loaded clip into his pistol, jacked the slide back, dropped the clip, pointed the gun up, and pulled the trigger. The hammer wouldn't move.

"Built-in safety. It won't shoot with the clip out."

"Damn," said the Marine.

"So you're saying they made the gun Coastie-proof?" I asked.

That brought some smiles.

"Too bad we have that officer up there. We could burn up some of Uncle Sam's ammo," Chris said downing his shot.

"Now, now, boys," I admonished, "guns and alcohol don't mix."

"Well, I'll tell you, sonny," the Marine said tossing back his last shot, "it probably tastes like shit too but I better get back on deck or my wife will be pissed."

"I second that," the farmer agreed.

Drinks were downed and we all rejoined the women and the shrink topside. I returned my crew to shore.

It had been a fine day. My guests were both excited by our adventures and exhausted. I was quite sure that none of them would ever again sit in a fancy restaurant and order a lobster dinner without considering what effort had been exerted to put that lobster there before them.

I cooked up that catfish, as promised, and served it, hot and succulent, to an excellent-looking young lady from California. She was the dessert.

Chapter 13 - The Windsurfer

L ate September. The day started out warm and beautiful but the afternoon turned cool as autumn afternoons do once the equinox has passed. I didn't care. I love autumn, not only for the cooler weather but because the tourists go away. I had just dropped the last trawl of the day and was about to head in. I knew I was the last boat out and the sun was low in the sky—not much light left to this day. I was three miles outside the Eastern Point Light Buoy or "groaner" as we call it. It makes a sound like someone groaning when it rises on the swell. My buddy Michael Moriarity, "Moe" as we call him, says it sounds a lot like "Moe-e-e-e" and calls it the Moe Buoy.

As I headed back toward the harbor I spotted something strange floating a ways off my port. The shape fit nothing I recognized.

"Oh, what the hell," I muttered and motored over. At five hundred yards I saw movement. Someone was waving. I waved back and went to full throttle.

As the distance between us narrowed I saw the red sail and the board. A wind surfer. How the hell do they get out this far? But I knew the answer even as I was thinking it. It happens sometimes. Inexperienced wind surfers who didn't know how to handle a sail could get caught in a wind gust and shoot far away from land without any control over their board.

Dumbass, I thought.

As I pulled alongside I saw that it was a girl, probably not more than eighteen or nineteen. She clung to the board shaking with cold, her eyes wide with terror. Poor baby. I leaned over the side and lifted her off the board and up onto the boat.

She was trying to say, thank you, but her teeth were chattering and she was shivering too hard to make a sound. She wrapped her arms around me and hugged me hard, clinging tight. Being in the North

Atlantic alone and freezing is a state I am well aware of—it just really sucks.

"Hey, it's okay. I've got you now," I said.

She wore about the tiniest bikini I'd ever seen and her whole body was cold as ice. She was not going to let go.

"Come on," I reassured her. "Let me just grab your stuff and we'll get you into some warm clothes."

She let go reluctantly but her lips were too numb and blue to speak. I leaned over and pulled the board and sail on board. The poor girl was literally shivering too hard to walk. I picked her up and carried her down below where I keep a half dozen changes of clothes. When you get wet as often as most fishermen do, you learn to keep warm, dry clothes in good supply.

"Here," I rummaged through my clothes pulling out a sweatshirt, socks, etc. "You better get out of that wet suit."

When I turned to hand her the clothes she had done exactly as told. She was stark naked—"bolickey" as my Dad used to say—much to my astonishment. She was a great-looking girl, dark-haired and beautifully built with long legs and a tight butt. I started to turn away—honest.

"I'll be up on deck."

"No." She scrambled into the sweatshirt, a pair of my jockey shorts, and pulled on warm socks and a stocking cap. "No. Stay." She looked at me with those big eyes. My sweatshirt barely made it to her thighs. My clothes had never looked so enticing.

"I was so cold," she said stepping closer to me. Much closer. "And so scared. I thought I was going to..."

Her arms were back around me.

"It's okay," I said, "you'll warm up in a few minutes and I'll take you home."

"You're such a gentleman," she whispered, snuggling up against me. She obviously was not a mind reader.

I held her telling myself she just needed to be warmed up but she had a really delicious body, very soft in the right places and very firm in the rest. Before I knew it her mouth was locked onto mine and her tongue was down my throat. She tasted like 100% knock-dead female.

With extreme effort I pulled back.

"It's okay. You don't owe me anything." Honest. I really did say that. I did so.

"What's the matter?" she giggled. She was warming up really fast. "Am I too young? Is that the problem? Are you too old for me?"

I stared at her. Old fuck at twenty-nine. She had clearly recovered from her fear. Her mouth was back on mine and her hands were all over the place.

"Think you can handle a younger girl?" she said when she took a breath.

"I think I can keep up my end," I told her.

"Well," she snaked her hand down the front of my pants, "this is a good start. I need to keep these clothes on for a few more minutes to get warm but you get yours off."

I don't know if she was still in shock, reacting out of gratitude, or dazzled by my sterling good looks, but in a matter of minutes we were both naked, extremely warm, and the cabin was filled with the magnificent fragrance of girl.

She must have been dating Gloucester guys whose idea of foreplay is a kiss on the cheek before ramming it home. One of my fellow lobstermen said once, "Every once in awhile it's nice to take one of the younger girls home and give her the sword right to the hilt!" I timed our movement with the movement of the boat which kept it from ending in a slam-bam-thank-you,-ma'am. Just about the time I was going to run topside and run up Code Flag Alpha ("commercial dive operation in progress, diver is down") the glug, glug of twin wet exhausts grew closer and steadier.

"What's that?" she asked between thrusts.

"That, sweetheart, is a total and complete waste of our tax dollars," I said. Shit. I knew what was coming.

"Marke-e-e."

I recognized the voice immediately. The pricks.

"Marke-e-e-e-e, what are you doing down there?"

"What the hell is that?" she asked.

"My friends," I said with one hard thrust. She yelped.

"What do they want?" she asked between gasps.

"Honey, like all real friends they want to fuck with you whenever the opportunity presents itself and nothing, and I do mean, nothing, is sacred."

"Marke-e-e-e......"

"Marke-e-e-e, we can see the surf board on your deck. We know you've got that girl down there." I really hated those guys.

I got up.

"Where the hell are you going?" she demanded.

"On deck."

"Like that?"

"Certainly not." I picked up the stocking cap and put it on my head. She giggled.

"Well, come back soon and bring that." She pointed.

I walked up the three steps to my pilot house.

"Don't be long," she giggled again.

I stuck my head out of the cabin door where two of the sorriest examples of Coast Guard wasted tax dollars ever, were on the bridge of CG 41 footer. Chris held the 41 footer perfectly still alongside by running the dual engines against each other. Mike and Chris run boats like Gloucester fishermen, the best small boat operators in the world. Michael stood leaning on the rail grinning like the annoying little prick he takes pride in being. Two female crew in pumpkin suits—orange survival suits—were at the rear of the boat.

"Can I help you gentlemen?" I asked.

"Marke-e-e, we're looking for a young lady on a wind surfer the description of which is extremely similar to the one that just happens to be on your deck. Do you know where she is?"

"Well, actually, until you two ugly-assed motherfuckers made your inauspicious and untimely arrival, she was at no time further than eight inches from me."

"Sounds like a boast to me," Seaman-forever Moriarity said.

I stepped out into plain view, my most redeeming feature still at nine o'clock.

"Good God, shit, boy-howdy, I thought you were Irish," Mikey said.

"Black Irish," Chris laughed.

The two girls were pointing, giggling and recoiling in mock horror. Everyone was laughing.

"So, seriously, what are you doing, Markey," Chris asked.

"Playing basketball. What the fuck does it look like I'm doing?"

"So, you have her onboard?"

"Even two mentally challenged representatives of the branch of the worst boat handlers ever to run a boat should know that the sail and board sitting most prominently on my deck would tend to indicate that she is indeed on board. Unless you think I keep that so I can windsurf in my lobster tank in my ample spare time. So doesn't this big, hard patrol boat full of seamen have anything better to do than help me develop some kind of sex problem."

One of the female Coasties called, "It doesn't look like you have a problem to us, sir." They giggled again.

"So, Markey, you are assuring us that she is below."

"Yes, I am."

"And safe?"

I glared at him. "Where the fuck is an Exocet when you need it?"

"What do you mean?" Chris asked.

"The missile, asshole, to blow your sorry ass out of the water."

I glanced at the bottom sounder. "Well, we're in twenty fathoms here. Aren't you Coasties supposed to stay close to shore in the shallow water so you can walk home if your boat sinks?"

Mike hollered laughing, "Why don't you go and be the eighty-ninth Gloucester fishing vessel to accidentally sink this year?"

"Hey, did you guys hear about the new Coast Guard monument?"

Chris sighed. "No, but I'm sure you'll tell us."

"Yeah, it's a statue of a landing craft headed toward an enemy beach and the Coastie driving has an M1 stuck up his ass by a GI to keep him from turning around. Why don't you just go Semper Pardus someplace else, for Christ's sake?"

"Just so you assure us the girl's onboard." Chris retorted.

"Yes, she is. And she'll be a lot better if I go below and get her off."

"Excuse me!" The girl appeared on deck wearing my jockey shorts, which were doing their best to fall off of her, and nothing else. Chris and Mike's eyes about popped wide open.

"Excuse me," she repeated. "Do you mind? I'm trying to get laid here. What's the problem?"

"Ahhh," Mike stammered, "well, it seems like there isn't any force being used here."

"Force?" she stared at him. "Force? I didn't force him to do anything."

"Uhhh, miss," Chris was equally lost for word. "Uh, yes, miss. Just as long you're alright and not here by force."

She threw her hands up in a "helllooo" gesture. "The only force I intend to use will be on my boyfriend if he hesitates when I grab him by the ears. He dove right down on me," she said pointing to me.

"Yes, ma'am." Chris mumbled.

"Boyfriend?" I said.

"Now, why don't you go and guard the coast or whatever it is you people do and let him carry on before I goddamn explode." She grabbed my hand and pulled me toward the cabin door. "You get down here, I'm not anywhere near done with you."

"Sorry, guys," I said. "I better go before she forces me."

Chris and Mike motored off howling with laughter.

Three miles outside the groaner, the Sheep rocked gently up and down on the swells. It was a perfect ending to a day of fishing, or anything else for that matter. I returned her to the dock where her parents were waiting.

"Thank you for rescuing me," she said as I handed her the wind board.

"Thank you for everything."

She turned away.

"Hey," I called.

"What?"

"What's your name?"

"Erin," she grinned, waved, and disappeared into her father's waiting car.

So there it was, the perfect relationship—great sex and no commitment. And I never saw her again.

Chapter 14 - Frenzy

For some reason the day's last trawl seems to be a jinx—something usually goes wrong. I've managed to pull a Humphrey Bogart more than once—in "The Caine Mutiny" he runs over his own tow line with a destroyer. This was a gray day but productive. Lots of bugs in my traps, "bugs" being a lobsterman's term for lobsters.

The last buoy of the last trawl slid down the port side of the boat, up and over, plopping into the water as ten pots glided down to the bottom twenty fathoms below. I jotted down the numbers. It's early, about three o'clock on a Sunday afternoon, three miles off Good Harbor Beach. It's time for the best part of the day, the ride home. Contrary to popular belief, lobstering alone in the North Atlantic consists of a lot more than riding around in your boat looking for whales and watching seagulls fornicate.

Shovel wet snow for fifteen minutes, drive your car for five minutes, stop and shovel wet snow again—keep this cycle up for eight hours and you have a good idea of what it is like to lobster. It's a bit more than an hour at the gym. After lobstering for eight hours it's hard to describe how good it feels to point the boat toward the mouth of the harbor and just drive it. It's mid-afternoon on a Sunday, the wind is in my face. I have a full lobster pool and a three dollar cigar going—everything is copacetic.

A whaling boat chugs in from Jeffrey's Bank, its exhaust following it like a fog bank. It's packed with tourists—we call them "cattle boats". They used to alter course to pass by us and show the folks some real lobster men at work. Problem is that whale boats leave a four to six foot wake at twenty knots. They would blast by us when we were dead in the water trying to haul gear so what the tourists got to actually see was one or two fishermen bracing for the biggest wave of the day with little or no warning. Smash, BOOM! If you didn't have time to swing your bow into them, the wake would knock you flat or, at the very least, send shit flying all over the deck. It was a real pain in the ass. We did try to be nice. We called them on the radio and tried to reason with them. They were very polite and continued blasting right past us at warp speed.

Next we added a personal touch. We tried visiting them on-board their boats and politely explained, in front of the tourists, what was going to happen to their wives and children, houses, cars, and, of course, their boats, if the buzzing continued. They called us and, of course, it was a bluff.

We employed an extended middle finger next, to no avail.

Moving to Death Con Two, some of the more unsavory among us would choose a less than private moment to urinate. This slowed them down and, naturally, some of the boys mooned them. That proved moderately successful but it was a real hassle to drop your rubbers in order to drop your pants. Or so I'm told.

On this particular September afternoon I stopped my boat to check on a buoy that looked like one of mine. One glance at the numbers assured me it wasn't. The ocean had greased out and was flat calm. The intellectually stimulating conversation of my fellow lobstermen had driven me to turn the radio off long ago. After neither seeing nor talking to another individual for eight hours, you can get what I call the "blabbers". The first person lucky enough to see you upon your return gets overwhelmed with eight hours of pent-up conversation. But usually I'm fine with quiet. Silence and solitude allow one to think. I have always gotten along with them just fine.

An inordinately loud and obnoxious sound begins to reverberate from far off. You hear them before you see them—off-shore power boats. Thup, thup, thup. They blast out of the mist guzzling gas and creating waves, usually with stupid names that advertise their owners's sexual insecurities. Far less annoying are the blowboats—sailboats to most people. They drift by all day, quietly, effortlessly, often with scantily clad females stretched out on them, a pleasant diversion from tending lobster gear. They do cause many cuts, banged heads, stubbed toes, and other assorted injuries but we don't complain. "As scarce as a sober blow-boater on a sunny Sunday in August…" That's what the boys say when there aren't a lot of bugs around.

All these boats have one thing in common—they're plea-sure boats. They are here because they want to be and more power to them. They might spend a few hours underway on weekends. Lobsterboats can easily be underway seven to eight hours a day, six or seven days out of the week. In one week a lobster boat spends as much time on the water as most pleasure boats spend in a year.

"Mark, things seem to break down on your boat a lot more than they do on mine."

"Well, tell me, Mr. Toy Boater, don't you think my boat gets a wee bit more wear and tear than yours? I don't just take my boat out for a few hours and blow around. I take it out and max out the engine, hydraulics, the pumps, electrical system, and slam traps all over it."

Peter Benchley, in one of his books, referred to lobster men as curious people who put their traps everywhere—in mooring areas, in the channels, and just about anywhere where they are in the way. Why do lobstermen put their traps in these places? Now, let me think. That's a tough one. I don't know, Peter, could it be because THAT'S WHERE THE FUCKING LOBSTERS ARE? Difficult as it may be to understand, you tend to catch more lob-sters if you set your gear where the bugs are—not where they aren't. In shark-terms it's called "territoriality". The ocean is where livings are made. It's our workplace. It's where we spend most of our day for most of the year.

This has been a good day. The ten lobsters from the last trawl are all new shelled which means they shed their old shell. Their new shells are bright reddish-orange which seems especially brilliant on such a gray day. In the salt-water filled live-well, they make you think of bright red roses on a dull, leaved bush. And the day went well, too. My definition of a "good day" is one in which I can: a.) get the traps hauled up onto the boat, b.) remove an acceptable number of legal-sized lobsters and band them, c.) tend the traps and get them back in the water, while d.) making sure that the lobsterman, which would be me, stays on the boat.

As I stood lighting my cigar with the boat idling so I could enjoy the moment and the quiet, the water surrounding the boat began to bubble. As if someone had thrown a switch the bubbling intensified to a white froth and the churning of the bubbles grew and spread, drowning out all other sounds. Above me seagulls floated, their beaks moved but no sound could be heard above the thundering foam. Suddenly thirteen tons of Novi boat under my feet began to rise up out of the bubbling water. Shocked, in total amazement, I stumbled back into my wheelhouse. What the hell was happening? My mind raced. Could a submarine be surfacing under me? That's crazy, I thought. Maybe some kind of underwater pipe had ruptured.

Tat-tat-tat. Under my feet I heard things, many things, smashing against the fiberglass hull of the Black Sheep. It intensified as the roar from the waters around me increased. It sounded like a machine gun. Tat-tat-tat-tat-tat. Suddenly small fish were shooting upward out of the water as if jet-propelled. In seconds they were airborne and then, just as rapidly plummeted down, smacking all over the cabin and the deck. One whacked me right in the face. The deck was alive with shiny, silvery herring piled so deep I couldn't take a step without squashing one or more. I remember thinking I wouldn't have to worry about finding bait for tomorrow.

The tat-tat-tat was joined by a heavier bang-bang-bang. Not as frequent as the tat-tat-tat but deeper. I could feel the boat recoil from the more solid hits. Just when I thought the noise level had peaked it increased and BA-BOOM! Something smashed into the boat so hard I stumbled, fell to my knees, and almost lost bladder control.

Out of the white, bubbling froth blasted a bluefish. Well, shit, that explained the bangs. Trailing white foam he shot almost straight up six or seven feet looking like an airplane complete with contrails. As he reached his apex and began to fall, a monstrous, streamlined fish rocketed out of the foam. It was dark blue to the point of being black with green-gray iridescence on its upper side and back. Its bottom half was silver. The creature was breathtakingly beautiful with large black fins and smaller yellow-tipped black fins. Flying at three times the speed of the first fish it zeroed in on the bluefish, smashed into it and cut it in half. Spinning, it swallowed the front of the bluefish in a gulp then caught the bottom half as it fell back into the water landing on its side and soaked me in a shower of salt water. With a swish of its magnificent tail it disappeared. I stood in awe.

It was like the opposite of The History Channel, I thought. The sounds were in reverse. The boom-boom tat-tat-tat of the cannons and machine guns fired at the Japanese airplanes here were transposed to the tat-tat-tat boom-boom of the tuna smashing into my hull. Although the sounds were in reverse, they still went on all at once and the boat shook and reverberated from the hits.

E-e-e-e-e-e. From all points of the compass, sky rats arrived. Seagulls were everywhere. Bluefish and herring were slapping their tails all over my deck. The boiling, sudsy water surrounding my boat continued welling up and churning as it took on a pinkish hue from the blood of many ripped up fish. The swish of herring, the splash of bluefish, the thumping of the tuna splashing back into the water were each distinct and yet merged with the shrieks of the gulls to create a spiraling crescendo of auditory mayhem.

The gulls swooped down plucking pieces of fish from the melee. Another bluefish cartwheeled into the air munching on a hapless herring, it's bright blue hue contrasting sharply with the red foam. Below me the ocean seemed to have achieved a rolling boil sending an unearthly shroud of reddish mist fully fifteen feet into the air. The pale autumn sun shone through glowing pink and it seemed the air was full of bright silvery fireflies. All around me herring scales fell twinkling like stars. They covered the boat sticking to everything including me. Another bluefish flew over my rail and smashed into a tote of stickless buoys, knocking them noiselessly to the deck where they scattered among the flapping bodies of bluefish and herring. I glanced at the tachometer to check that the engines were still running. Amid the noise I couldn't hear them but the bounce of the needle reassured me. Bluefish continued to arc out of the reddish haze, some flipping head over tail, in pursuit of the herring that fell like hailstones. Fish guts splattered down onto the deck, the cabin and on me. Streaks of blood slid down the cabin windows coating them so thoroughly it turned the glass into a mirror. I saw my own astonished reflection staring back at me, a bloody streak ran from my temple and down my cheek and neck.

I have heard of feeding frenzies but know that few, even among those of us who live our lives at sea, have seen such a spectacle. A spontaneous frenzy like the one I found myself at the center of reaffirms the oldest law of nature: Everything in nature exists at the expense of something else. Nature is ruthless, unmerciful, relentless, and unforgiving. I got down on my knees and drank in as much as I could. Killing to live is first, foremost and always the rule. It is the law of the jungle—or in this case, the ocean.

A huge bluefish, a good twelve pounder, flashed by me trailing bubbles. It smashed into my rubber Grundys and knocked them off their hook, then flew through the cabin door, flipped and slid down the stairs into the forward cabin. Skidding, it crashed into my bed coming to rest on the mattress. I stared at it shaking my head in disbelief. Actually, the fish looked better than the last girl that had laid there but that was the result of a late night and alcohol was definitely a factor.

SMASH! Another bluefish crashed down among the lobsters on my culling table knocking them all over the place. One unbanded two pounder crunched the head of the blue in its crusher claw. Eyeballs popped right out of the fish's head and rolled across the deck. The tunas had arrived in force and the water churned, making a sound like a strong wind blowing through a row of leafy trees. Tunas were everywhere. One blasted by on his side in pursuit of prey. He zigged and zagged and finally sounded—headed toward the bottom—with a flick of his tail.

I glanced back at my starboard quarter in time to see another tuna arch out of the water chasing an airborne blue. He missed. His second lunge caused him to spin like a cartwheel turning head over tail the length of the Black Sheep before smashing into the water like a spinning saw blade. If I live to be a thousand the sight of that spinning tuna with his big black eye spinning counter-clockwise the entire length of my boat will be with me. I could have touched him.

Four more tuna arched out of the water and splashed down again, sending a wave of water that soaked me and the deck. Only the splash of those huge creatures could be heard over the hiss of the churning water. The deck of the Sheep was so covered with fish, blood, shining scales and guts it looked like the floor of Empire Fish after a twelve-hour work day. In the midst of the chaos a tuna rocketed out of the water on my port side and sailed across my deck to crash into the water on the starboard side. The Sheep has a beam of fourteen feet. Stunned I looked up in time to see four crosses floating above the boat. Just that quick one of the crosses folded its wings back, flipped over and went into a dive falling faster and faster, straight by me. White wings with black tips were folded back sword-like as it knifed into the foam puncturing it with the splashless precision of an Olympic diver. A strange bird resurfaced in seconds with a herring in its long, sharp beak. Throwing its head back, it swallowed the fish whole and gracefully took back to the air. Northern gannets. They circled the boat like floating crosses and dove with perfect accuracy. As they neared the water they adjusted maneuvers slightly like a smart bomb, then scythed into the water streamlined and clean. When they resurfaced it was with a fish every single time. Just passing through on their migratory path they took advantage of the opportunity to feed.

With birds acting like fish and fish acting like birds, I felt the overwhelming compulsion to surrender to the instinctual, primitive phenomenon surrounding me. I needed to be closer to the action and found myself, against all reason, snatching up my eighteen inch steaking knife and jumping onto my trap table. The sensible part of my brain knew this was crazy. But when nature offered an opportunity to shift from observer to participant the urge became irresistible. Play it safe, my civilized brain told me, get down where you won't get hurt. But God had orchestrated this event and this was my church, this was where I came to pray. Bold men may lead shorter lives than cowards but cowards never live at all. Bluefish littered the deck, I could take my pick of those, but a fresh tuna—now that's a delicacy. They whizzed past me as I tried to see in all directions at once.

My breath came in gasps. Trying to see what was coming from my blind side, I sensed movement behind me. As I ducked, another large tuna flashed overhead, so close that the turbulence knocked my hat off. This is dangerous, you could get killed, my civilized self said. Do you have a death wish?

But my primitive self was throbbing with life. The nothing like risking death to make your senses come aliv light, vibrant, pulsing with life. My senses were exaggerats anything I'd ever known before. Another tuna leap missing me by inches. The banging I heard over the my heart thundering.

As I regained my footing, the boat sagged sharply to the right. I didn't see him land and it was far too noisy to hear. I spun around. A massive tuna, easily five hundred pounds, had crashed over the stern onto the deck. Thrashing wildly, desperate to escape, it smashed and pounded the blue fish and herring. Furiously, it struggled to get back to the water then suddenly he stopped. He was a big fish with big, but feeling black eyes. His body gleamed blue-black along the back with shimmering silver undersides. His fins were jet black and the finlets were tipped in gold. Staring down at him I thought he was far too beautiful to occur naturally in the wild. Rather he looked like someone captured him and had him spray-painted.

Before I could recover from my sense of awe, with a gargantuan effort, he launched himself straight up into the air and came crashing down on my trap table, that much closer to the water and freedom. I don't remember moving but suddenly I was standing over him with the steaking knife in my hand. I cocked it back. I hesitated.

The tuna season was open. I was licensed to fish tuna. This fish was way over legal size. I may have to apply some creative license as to how I actually got it on the boat but I'd manage. He looked up at me with those big, black eyes.

Come on. Shove that eighteen inch blade in to the hilt.

A person in his situation pleads for his life but the big fish just looked at me.

Come ON, bambi-boy. What are you waiting for? Plunge that beauty in. In the midst of total pandemonium all I could see was that black, human-like eye. All I could feel was the knife.

Fish were being slaughtered all around me. It's the natural order of things, I told myself. You're higher up on the food chain. STICK HIM!

I felt it behind me too late. I believe he just grazed my right shoulder. I guess a couple of hundred pounds of tunafish at thirty ꞏ forty miles an hour exchanges some serious kinetic energy when ꞏntacts something. It felt like I was hit by lightening. Like a giant ꞏ slammed my shoulder. My knife went flying.

I was unconscious before I hit the table.

Somebody was frying eggs. I heard the sizzle of the eggs in the pan and the snapping and popping of bacon. I could smell them. I lay on my back, head toward the bow, spread eagled. Rain, steady hard drops splattered me and peppered the ocean with the sound that I mistook for breakfast cooking. The diesel purred reassuringly at idle. My eyes stung painfully as I struggled to open them. Everything was black, was I blind? I began to hyperventilate. Having been this route before I caught myself and forced myself to take long, slow, even breaths. Many short breaths lead to panic and death. I had a good teacher, I carry his stocking cap below for luck.

The blackness turned slowly to gray. As my vision cleared I could see the dark clouds overhead. The dim light of the overcast day seeped into sight. With my head banging I managed to sit up on the third try. It was raining, a steady, hard, drenching rain. What was I doing sprawled on my trap table in the pouring rain a few miles off Good Harbor Beach? Could I have fallen and smacked my head?

Disoriented and dazed I felt my way to the cabin. The deck was slick and clean. I couldn't remember hosing it down. I dropped the boat into gear, my head throbbed. Waves broke over the rocks along the shore looking far brighter through the gray gloom and rain. A few miles to my right Brace Cove slid by. Then Eastern Point Lighthouse was just ahead of me. What had happened? The last thing I could recall was writing down the loran coordinates to my last trawl. I ran down Dog Bar Breakwater and took a right with the hammering in my head seeming to grow in intensity.

Michael Moriarity's yacht club passed on my starboard. In the distance Hammond Castle loomed medievally out of the mist. Norman's Woe lay off my stern port a quarter mile or so. Head throbbing I reassured myself that everything was where it had always been. I'd passed this way a thousand times. The Cut Bridge and then the Fisherman's Statue. According to nearly every fishing family in Gloucester one of their distant relatives posed for some part of it. It is, without a doubt, the most posed-for statue in the entire goddamn country. As I passed Ten Pound Island I tried to clear my head. Something happened. But what?

The Paint Factory drifted by on my stern starboard quarter

and then, through the deepening mist, I saw the brilliant blue towers of Our Lady of Good Voyage Church. Between the towers, the statue of Mary stood holding a fishing boat. It was the last thing I remembered.

Flying tunas. Boiling, churning water red and frothy. Tat-tat-tat. Bang. Bang-bang-bang. Gannets screeching down like Stuka Dive bombers, snaking into the water. Ba-boom. Gulls screaming everywhere. Combinations of eye-numbing colors. Bluefish twisting and turning with tunas in close pursuit. Herring flying like swarms of locusts. Gold fins. Flashing and sparkling fireflies, bloody fish entrails and smashed fish parts splattering everywhere. A massive tuna thrashes on my deck. A knife flashes. I woke with a start, breathing hard, my head still banging horribly. I was in my room. In my bed. I shook my head trying to rid it of the lurid dreams and the incessant hammering.

I drove down to my boat. It was tied up as only I would tie it. The lobsters were under the boat in a keeper trap locked with a lock that only I have a key for. The cabin door was locked. All the switches were off. I checked the forward cabin, everything was fine. Sitting on my berth I tried to clear my head. A bad smack on the head can cause severe hallucinations. Maybe I thought, I should find someone to talk to about this. As the hazy dream images formed into actually memories I told myself there was no way that could have happened. I stood trying to rid myself of the impossible images rushing into my mind. Out of reflex I straightened the blanket on the bed and then yanked it back. It was a rather large bluefish. I bet it was a good twelve pounds.

CHAPTER 15 - BLOW DAY

It was my second year of lobster fishing. The wind was banging—it was a blow day. I stood on the dock with several other lobster men swapping lies. They were all a thousand years older than me. I was the F.N.G.. and they were all vastly more experienced than I in the art of lobster fishing. It was June and the lobsters were scarce, as hard to find as an honest lobster dealer.

"It's those goddamn S.C.U.B.A. divers, I tell you," one exclaimed. Lobstermen are like everyone else, when things go wrong something or someone has to be blamed. There has to be a tangible reason for the shortage of lobsters so who else to blame but the people who swim underwater near their traps?

He's sixty-something. He started making a living lobstering about the time I was born. Long before computers he could smell the rain and predict the onslaught of a killer squall. He fished without radar, loran, and depth sounders. He learned long ago not to follow the lobsters but rather to predict where they were going to be, and to have his traps there before them. He learned to tell the hard bottom from the soft and when to have his gear on that magical lobster haven, the boundary between the two. However, what he did not know or understand was scuba diving or, more specifically, water depths and decompression tables.

"Yeah, it's those fucking divers," the rest of the men agreed nodding.

"Excuse me, gentlemen," I interjected. "You are incorrect in that accusation."

"Oh, yeah? And what do you know, Mr. Fucking New Guy. You ain't been lobstering long enough to know your bow from your stern."

There was a choir of chuckles, they all thought it was quite humorous. In my second year of lobstering I pretty much stayed to myself. I tied back their trawls when they set over me and didn't steal. I lost some traps. I didn't take it personally, it was all part of paying dues in the time honored profession of in-shore lobster fishing. What these guys didn't know was that I was a commercial diver before I was a commercial fisherman.

"Where did they get you?" I asked.

"From Brace Cove all the way down to the Lights—where the hard bottom meets the soft."

"Yeah? That would be about twenty fathoms?"

"Yeah. A hundred twenty feet—give or take."

"And you say the divers are robbing you?"

"I haul a hundred for ten keepers. What the hell else could it be?"

"It could be a lot of things, sir," I told him, "but what it isn't, is divers."

I suddenly had the ear of every lobsterman present.

"We all know," I continued, "if you drop gear along the breakwater the divers will hammer you."

All nodded.

"We all know it's the divers."

They nodded again.

"How deep is the water there?"

One guy shrugged. "Ten...twenty feet." The others nodded agreement.

"The average scuba tank is a seventy-two which means it holds that amount of air."

"How can you measure air in inches?" one asked.

I walked carefully, not wanting to look like a smartass and, yes, in my life that is very uncharacteristic. "For the sake of this explanation, let's just say that the seventy-two will allow your average tube-sucker to stay at twenty feet for thirty to sixty minutes depending on the size of the person, how much energy they are exerting, among other things. As you go deeper the air is burned up quicker—say at fifty feet it would be twenty to forty minutes."

"Why do you call them 'tube-suckers'?"

"Because they suck air through a tube from a tank on their back. Tube suckers."

They all snickered.

"So how long could one of them stay at one hundred and twenty feet?" the old guy asked.

"About five minutes." I replied. "Doesn't give 'em much time to rob your traps, does it?"

"No," he agreed nodding, "it doesn't."

"It's really a bitch to open the door and grab the lobsters underwater."

"How would you know?" one asked skeptically.

"By robbing those old wooden crates you guys used to keep down on the back shore when I was a kid."

There was total silence. He gave me a hard look and laughter began to spread among the others. He finally joined the laughter. There is no book on how to be accepted into the in-shore lobster world. Little by little, I wrote my own.

"Well, then, Mark," said the old guy. "If the divers aren't cleaning out the traps where are all the lobsters?"

"Come on, Mr. Black Sheep," another added, "explain it to us. We've only been trying to figure this out since forever. I'm sure you, with your whopping one-year of fishing experience have it all figured out."

They all crowded around to hear the F.N.G.. make a jackass out of himself.

"Gentlemen, this may be my second year of fishing and, of course, you are all much wiser on the subject than I am but I still believe I have some ideas. By the way," I said regarding my inquisitor, "aren't you the guy who believes that traps built indoors won't fish?"

Most of the men laughed while his face flushed bright red.

"Well, that's the way I've always done it," he said turning scarlet.

"I've lived in Gloucester forever," I said, "and there have been no appreciable amount of lobsters landed in June since dinosaurs were screwing on Good Harbor Beach."

They laughed.

"Did the draggers wipe them out?" another man asked with real interest.

"Nope. They wiped out pretty much everything else as we well know and they took seeders by the thousands of pounds, but they couldn't wipe out lobsters even when they put those fucking rolling rock hoppers on and tried to go where the lobsters lived.

For some reason the otter trawl is just not that effective at catching lobsters especially when they are in the rocks like they usually are, thank Christ." I added.

They nodded agreement.

"So, Mr. Black Sheep," my buddy, the old guy said, "where are the lobsters?"

I shrugged. "I figured you guys were catching them all being you're all so experienced, smart, and good-looking."

They chuckled. In truth, if the same doctor had delivered all of these individuals he would have developed chronic arthritis in his shoulder from the repeated slappings of their mothers for having such god-awful, ugly babies.

"You're so bright. Please don't try to tell us you don't have an answer."

"Oh, I think that most lobsters never move far from where they are born, perhaps some migrate to a point but..."

"You mean to say there are a lot of lobsters around right now?"

"Yes," I replied.

"Come on. I hauled four hundred traps for twenty keepers and you tell us there are lots of lobsters around? You made sense about the divers in twenty fathoms but now you talk stupid. Lots of lobsters around? There ain't shit out there?"

His friends nodded in agreement.

"I said there are lobsters on the bottom. They just aren't getting in to your traps."

"Bullshit," several men said in unison.

"You guys figure your traps catch every lobster that gets near them?"

"Of course they do. Are you dense that you think the lobster traps don't work?"

A few men snickered at the F.N.G.. and his opinions.

"Now, who's talking stupid?" I shot at him. "Gentlemen, in August the traps are everywhere knee deep from shore to twenty fathoms. The buoys are so thick that the toy boats have all they can do to get from the groaner to the head of the harbor without wrapping up a buoy line."

"What's you point?"

"Think about it, you dinosaurs. A trap every few feet? If your traps are catching every lobster that comes near them, think about it. What's wrong with this picture?"

"We would have wiped out the entire lobster population in one week," the old timer said, nodding thoughtfully.

"Agreed," I said nodding back to him.

The men considered the logic of that. Lobstermen are notoriously slow to accept new ideas and these guys were in shock.

"Okay, wiseass," one said, "I suppose you can explain how the traps work."

"As a matter of fact, I can, Mr. Have-to-Build-Traps-Outside."

The other guys snickered but paid attention.

"Most of the time the lobster enters the kitchen head, eats from the bait bag and either goes out the same way he came in or exits via the other kitchen head. About one time in ten when the lobster is eating another lobster enters the trap and they both square off, claw to claw. Now, if the last lobster in is bigger or more aggressive than the one eating, the lunching lobster will flip backwards. He either goes out the other kitchen head and you lose him or, if you're lucky, up into the parlor head and you've got him. About one out of ten that enters the trap gets caught."

"Wait a minute," one guy said. "You mean they don't go in claws first?"

"Okay, wise one, why don't you try to push one through claws first. Trust me, it's tail first or nothing."

"Okay, wise guy, you talk like you were there watching, for Christ's sake."

"I was with my friend on the bottom of Brace Cove hour after hour. I burned tank after tank trying to get the competitive edge on you guys. I watched the lobsters walk in and walk out. Like I said, about one in ten got caught."

The old timer considered this. "If our traps catch so few of the lobsters, why do we have good months in the Fall? Do the traps work better then?"

"A good question, sir, and I believe I have an answer. I believe it all has to do with water temperature."

One of the guys snorted derisively. "What the Christ does

water temperature have to do with anything?"

Several of the men grumbled but the old man held up his hand. He studied me intently. "Water temperature?"

"Just suppose," I ventured, "that lobsters don't move around as much when the water is cold and it's cold eight months out of the year."

"What the hell do them not moving around have to do with anything?" asked the outdoor trap-builder.

"Think about it, my I.Q. challenged friend. If Mr. Lobster sits home all day, what chance is there that he will end up within catching range of one of your traps?"

"I guess a lot less than if he is moving around."

"Thank you," I nodded.

The old man thought this over. "That don't make sense. In June, when the water is warming up we never have a decent month but in Fall when the water is cold we have our best months."

"Think a second. Where did you take the water's temperature?"

He nodded pensively. "At the surface."

"Sir, have you ever heard of a thermocline?"

"Nope."

"It's a layer of water that's much colder than the water above it. Trust me, I've spent a lot of time under water and you can sometimes stand on the bottom and from the waist up be warm and from waist down freeze. The change is just that defined."

Another man gave a disgusted snort. "What does this guy know about shit? For Christ's sake he even bought some of those wire traps. Everyone knows what a waste they are. What a moron."

In the mid-Eighties wire traps were rare. Lobstermen are notoriously slow to try something new. Now most wood traps on the East Coast are found in antique stores. The old guy waved everyone silent.

"Go ahead," he said to me, "this is getting interesting."

"When our catches start to increase, where does it start first?"

"In the bushes...where the water is shallowest," he said nodding his head in dawning realization. "Where the water first warms all the way to the bottom?"

I nodded agreement. "We then start to catch them in deeper and deeper water as the water on the bottom heats up."

No one was laughing at me now.

"It doesn't matter what the temperature is on the surface, what matters is the temperature on the bottom." The old man nodded thoughtfully.

"That's it in a nutshell," I said.

There was considerable grumbling and muttering among the others as they drifted off shaking their heads. This was all too new and radical for their way of thinking. I was left alone with my new friend, the old timer.

He studied me. "Did you learn that thermo temperature shit, whatever-the-fuck in college?"

"No, sir. I learned it last winter in the front seat of my Ford pickup."

His eyes widened and he listened with interest.

"It was last February during that real cold snap, the Alberta Clipper. It banged a million everyday for two weeks the wind chill was that outrageous. I couldn't see my boat on the mooring for sea smoke."

"True," he said. "It was worse than fog, couldn't even see across the harbor."

"So naturally, I got a call from my lobster dealer. Nobody was getting out and he was desperate for some lobsters. So, like a fool, I told him I had seventy or so crated up under the boat. The price at that time of the year is going nowhere but up."

He nodded agreement. "You got that right. February, March and well into April it goes right through the roof. Course it don't matter cause there's no goddamned lobsters around."

"That's what I was counting on when I stuck them under there and let them sit for a week," I said grinning. "So I paddled out to the boat and pulled up to the car. I almost shit. Nothing was moving, no noise, nothing. I figured I was out five hundred bucks. I was beyond pissed. I picked up the car and was close to pitching it into the harbor when I thought I might as well take and cook them. I might find a few good ones and at least have dinner. Even though the entire world thinks lobsters have to be alive when you cook them we know that if you keep them real cold they are good for a long time."

He nodded agreement. "Most of the lobster meat in the supermarket comes from the lobsters that died in the dealer's tank. They just cook 'em up and sell the meat for twenty or thirty bucks a pound. Course they won't pay us that for 'em. One dealer even put up a sign that said 'we don't buy dead or weak lobsters.'" He laughed.

"They might not buy them but they sure as hell cook them up and sell them, fucking thieves that they are."

He snorted. "You got that right."

"Anyway," I continued, "I got the tote back to the truck and I noticed they began to move a little. So, brilliant bastard that I am, I put them in the cab of the truck and blasted the heat. I headed over toward the dealer and within a few minutes they were all coming alive with that clicking clatter that they make, they were just fine. Seeing them come back to life like that first hand was how I developed my cold water theory."

"Well, it makes sense to me," he agreed.

"I dragged the tote through the snow and got some in and this asshole goes ballistic like I was trying to add a couple ounces to the weight or something."

"You bust a nut to help him out and he goes ballistic?"

"Are you surprised?"

He shook his head. "What an asshole."

"Go figure," I agreed.

"They've been screwing us so long they figure that's just status quo." He shook his white head again.

"They use that time honored phrase that thieves have used from the beginning of time," I quipped. "One, two, three..."

"'It's just business'," he said along with me and we both busted up laughing.

"Aw, they get us coming and going. They always round down the lobster—101 and a half is always 101 but when they sell bait, that's always rounded up. If the tote weighs seven pounds, they subtract eight. They never want to weigh the lobsters right out of the tank, heaven forbid they should pay for an ounce or two of water. They give us one price for the whole catch, or boat price, then cull it and get more money for two clawed chickens. More for quarters, halves, deuces, jumbos and as much as a dollar over boat price for Chinas." A China lobster is one that has not shed its shell for quite some time. The shell is very thick and the lobsters are so resilient they could survive a long trip, like to China maybe—hence the name.

"Yup," agreed the old guy, "and they pay us the same price for it all."

"Remember last summer when out of the clear blue all the dealers got together and decided to give us a split price, one for two claws and a lesser one for culls?" A cull is a lobster that is anything less than perfect, two claws the same size. "I told everyone it was total bullshit but they all laughed."

"Son," he said, "I wasn't one who laughed."

"Their logic was killing me. If it wasn't for their benefit, why would they do it?"

"It didn't last long," he said.

"The dummies made a mistake. Turned out it really was to our benefit and they went right back to a straight price real fucking quick, didn't they?"

"Well, sir, I figure the lobster dealers are like the casinos in Las Vegas. They will do nothing that isn't to their advantage. Basically, the price is determined every day by the dealers on the East Coast—they just decide it among themselves."

"I hear you," he said. "The ones that do the buying all decide what the price is going to be. Somehow that don't seem right to me."

"Oh, I agree. Sounds like collusion or price fixing if you want my opinion and that's a tad south of legal. But, as you old timers say, 'it's always been that way'," I grinned at him.

He chuckled. "Well, you may be a rookie as a lobsterman, Mark, but you're not totally stupid."

I thanked him.

"I like you," he said studying me. "In one year you've shown some balls and some brains. Most people who buy a boat and a license don't know squat and are out of business in a year. I think you could be the exception. You listen to me and it will make your next twenty years a whole lot easier."

In the next two hours he told me everything he could think of about the world of the inshore lobsterman. Not one single thing is written in any book, nor will it be written here. He told me how to read the sky and the water, how to read the birds and what depth to be in at what part of what month. He taught me all about different types of bait and what worked best for what season and how to bait a trap with the different kinds of baits, how to read the moon and when not to bother fishing, i.e. the full moon

But more importantly than any of that, he taught me how to deal with other lobstermen.

Like he said, many guys have bought boats and licenses. I've seen them come and go over the years. Most of them are lucky if they last a year. To my knowledge no one has ever come to Gloucester with no knowledge of lobstering, bought a boat, license and gear and survived for more than a year. There was one guy who came from the world of commercial diving. He bought the first lobster boat he was ever on when he couldn't even run a boat. He bought a license and some gear and asked someone how to tie the knots and set the gear out. He kept his mouth shut and learned from those who knew much more than he did. He lost thirty percent of his gear the first year. By his third he lost none. He is a rarity in Gloucester. His first boat sank in February and, yes, it really was an accident. He survived and made a living in the North Atlantic for over seventeen years—most of the time alone.

Now lets see if he can write...

Chapter 16 - Pirates of the Maine Coast

I needed lobster traps and I needed them yesterday. I had just brought the Black Sheep back from Nova Scotia and hadn't been able to order them until I was back with the boat. Now the boat sat idle with the mortgage payment due at the end of the month. I tried to order them from a local trap maker.

"Six weeks," he said.

"Good-bye," I said.

I called a trap company in Maine. He said they would deliver three hundred, shrimp heads and all, to my door in five days. I asked how he could do it so quickly.

"Put on two extra shifts," he said.

Friendship doesn't screw around.

On the appointed day he showed up where I stowed my gear. I paid him and he backed up and proceeded to help me move the gear ten yards to where they were to be stored.

Q. When does a lobsterman have a lot of friends?

A. When they want lobsters at boat price or free.

Q. When does a lobsterman have absolutely no friends?

A. Easy. When he has to move gear to or from the boat or gets a delivery of traps.

We stopped for coffee and a smoke. Like so many Maine guys this one was missing a front tooth and seemed to be a little crazy. I asked a simple question.

"How's it going up there in Maine?"

"Well, okay, I guess," he drawled. "'Cept for next week I got to go to prison for six months."

"What the hell did you do?"

"Well, nothin much, really."

"You must have done something."

"Well, about a year ago me and some friends was clammin', y'know."

"So they throw you in jail for clamming in Maine?"

"Well, there was this warden, y'know, and he was really bustin our balls."

"Uh-huh."

"A-yuh. He was a real asshole. He went through every bushel we dug, he did. He always found some small ones, he did. Hell, if you measure a few thousand clams a few small ones are bound to slip through."

"Sounds like lobstering," I said.

"What does the warden do to you if he finds a couple of shorts out of a hundred or so lobsters?"

"The smart ones let it go," I said. "The dumb ones make an issue out of it."

"That's what this guy done. He'd find three or four small clams outta bushel and he'd give us shit every goddamned day. He were a real pain in the ass, he were."

"Sounds like."

"He were just outta warden school, he were."

"So what did you do? Hit him?"

"Naw. Me and my friends grabbed him up and buried him up to his neck in sand."

"They're putting you in prison for that?"

"Well, not 'xactly. We buried him a few feet from the incoming tide, you know. Like the pirates used to do."

"He must have known you were going to dig him out?"

"Well, no. We made like we was leaving. We even got in our trucks and drove off."

"You just left him?" I stared at him.

"Well, no, we sneaked back around behind him real quiet like. He couldn't see us or hear us, don't ya know. He started yellin something terrible. We was pissin ourselves tryin not to make any noise laughin."

"I can imagine."

"A-yuh. Thing was when the tide was a coupla inches from his nose he went real quiet like, he did. His head got kinda limp like. We went to him and his eyes was wide open and his face was white as a dead man's."

"Really? Did he have a heart attack or something?"

"Well, not 'xactly. We dug him up but he was like paralyzed. White as a sheet, he was. I couldn't understand it. We was there all the time."

"Yeah, but he didn't know that."

"Y'know, that's the 'xact same thing the judge said!"

"So... he was psychologically damaged?"

"A-yuh. They say he can't even work no more. So they give us all time in prison, they did."

"No kidding?"

"A-yuh. Imagine that."

I managed to keep control of myself until we finished our work and the guy drove off. Then I pissed myself laughing.

CHAPTER 17 - DRUGS

Someone I knew had overdosed.

The old man's words came back to me—they may have been intellectually lacking but they were eloquent in their own way. Succinctly terse and to the point.

"Ma-AH-k," he said in that heavy New England accent he had, "Blow your damn brains out."

"Huh?" I was kind of taken aback.

"You heard me. If you want to stick a needle in your arm and shoot that poison into yourself, I want you to save your mother and I a lot of unpleasantness. You're of age, you have a key to the gun locker. Just go downstairs and shoot yourself in the head and get it over with quickly."

I didn't do drugs. I hoped he knew that. But they were everywhere and anyone who knew anyone on the waterfront knew where to get anything they wanted—at any time.

He looked me straight in the eye. "A gun to the head or a needle in the arm will both get you to the same place. One just does it a little faster."

Years later. The coke came into the country from South America welded into the leg of a decompression chamber. It was piled high in the middle of the table—I'm talking Al Pacino in Scarface here. Around the table were some draggermen home for a few days before heading back out for weeks at sea. They were joined by some commercial divers back from the Third World after six weeks of diving from off-shore oil rigs. This is how it was then—each brief stay shoreside was an exercise in excess designed to make the next trip out bearable. All were consuming copious quantities of beer, smoking weed, and discussing the pile of white dust in the middle of the table.

I sat close by at another table preferring the company of a barely legal female with an extremely tight ass and bodacious ta-tas, and a good glass of chardonnay to the manly, masculine entertainments at the other table.

A mirror and a razor appeared. The lines they made were six inches long.

"Hey, Mark, you want some of this?"

Having a really nice breast in one hand and a rather luscious nipple in my mouth I mumbled a negative reply.

"Well, slide over here if you change your mind," one of my friends yelled laughing.

Three of them, with the help of brand new, rolled up $100 bills began to snort the lines. One fell face down into the pile of coke and didn't move. The coke was splashed all around like flour in a bakery. Everyone at the table had a white face. I started laughing hysterically at the spectacle. Everyone in the room busted up laughing at the sight of the white-faced men.

Simultaneously two of the others slumped down in their chairs and slid to the floor as if deboned. They lay not moving. What happened next could best be described as controlled panic. I have never been so terrified while laughing at the same time. Two of the coke-faced men dragged the one who had fallen forward onto the table to the floor. Other men were coated in the white death dust that was becoming increasingly airborne with every set of movements. Fingers were pressed to carotid arteries. I found a towel and held it over my mouth and nose. The coke was swirling like a blizzard and I knew I had to try to stay sober.

Thumbs up. Diver talk meaning breathing and pulse stable, victim improving. I couldn't help it. I was laughing so hard I couldn't breathe. They all looked like albinos. The only people in the room not laughing were those who were unconscious. I opened a window and flipped the fan on. Later I was told I blew over ten thousand dollars worth of coke out the window. Once the room was cleared we managed to get the three semi-conscious men to their feet and walk them around. All divers present, myself included, were cross-trained EMTs. Other than being extremely high, everyone was okay.

We had the coke analyzed. South American coke turned

out to be a bit more pure than the boys were used to—like ninety-nine percent. They all came pretty close to dying. I was never really tempted to try coke after that.

Another flashback. An earlier time. I float above the table. Several men are playing cards and drinking beer. Cigarette smoke clouds the room. In front of one of the men is a glass of wine. He looks up. He is me—I look down from above and yet am seated at the table. It is years before I bought the Black Sheep. My eyes shift back and forth from table level to up above.

The players are mostly offshore draggermen. I know all of them but can't remember their names. I grew up with most of them, went to school with others, and still, to this day, I can't attach names to faces. Why can't I remember their names? We played cards and drank. Later in the night the smack came out accompanied by its works—spoon, candle, rubber band, syringe. The game was halted as the boys began to shoot up. The nameless face to my right began it.

They cooked some scag on the spoon pumping it in and out of the needle, leaving the plunger up and the syringe full as he held the rubber strap tightly around his left biceps. In a well-practiced move he plunged the needle into a protruding vein and depressed the plunger. The look of pure bliss came over him—like an orgasm to the tenth degree. He was in total rapture. His eyes rolled back and he nodded forward, head on the table, his entire body quivering in ecstasy.

He managed to slide the works to the man on his right. Another packet of scag. The same needle enters another protruding vein. Another look of rapture came over another face. I watched the dope work its way around the table toward me. I was somewhere between extremely intoxicated and totally wasted when the works and the packet of H appeared in front of me.

"Come on, Mark, ride the horse. You never have. You're a virgin. Take me," the demon goddess heroin hissed. "Come on, Mark, I want you. You think sex is good? Three seconds—maybe five? Put it in me and I'll give you fifteen minutes of pure heaven on earth. What's the matter, are you chicken? All your friends are doing me, don't you want to fuck me too?"

I was wicked shit-faced, crazy drunk. All around the table I'd watched men shoot up and go into an unbelievable state of ecstasy.

"How can anything that makes you feel so good be bad for you?" she hissed in my ear.

She was evil but beautiful and so enticing. She held the works in one hand and the packet of bliss in the other. She had done her work well all around the room. Men were writhing in unimaginable bliss. I just had to find out. How could I not enter this cavern of ultimate pleasure? She had the head of a snake but it was golden-scaled and exquisite. Her body was that of a perfectly shaped and totally nude girl.

"Come on, Mark, try me. Look how happy I made your friends," she hissed. Her voluptuous breasts enthralled me as she motioned around the room. "Just one time can't hurt you." She flicked her long red tongue out of her mouth and licked her lips sensuously.

"S-s-s-s-s-s-s, here, Mark. I'll get it going for you." Slowly she ripped off the top of the square packet. I was paralyzed. Her eyes were deep, dark green and lifeless, her tongue continued to flick out as she poured the white dust onto the spoon. She added some water and held the spoon over the candle flame.

"You're going to have a great ride." Her tongue flicked against my cheek and into my ear. "I promis-s-s-se."

I sat semi-conscious. It was like swimming against a strong current as hard as you could and being pushed back. No matter how hard you tried, the outcome was never in question. I let her wrap the rubber band around my left arm. She slid across the table in front of me and wrapped her long legs around me. Leaning forward she handed me the same syringe that all the others had used. She stroked my arm with delicate fingers as the vein protruded. I positioned the needle.

"One prick," she flicked her ruby tongue along my cheek, along my lips. "One prick, then blis-s-s-s-s-s." She leaned back and spread her legs wide before me. Her hand slithered down over her belly, over the golden pubic mound between her legs.

"Don't you want me, Markey?"

The vein throbbed. Daintily she placed her fingers on the

lips of her labia and held them wide. Tantalizing wetness oozed from her and pooled onto the table.

"Come on," she cooed. "Give it to me, Markey."

She grabbed me and poised the shaft above the dark reservoir of her very existence. And everything slowed down just so slow. She smiled sweetly as she pushed the needle closer. My very being touched the secretions from deep within her.

"S-s-s-s-slide that beauty in and up ins-s-s-s-side me," she cooed, her flickering tongue teased my ear as the needle kissed my vein.

"Take me," she groaned. "S-s-s-stick it in. Pleas-s-s-se, Markey, pleas-s-se, drive it in until it comes-s-s out my mouth."

The needle pierced the flesh and began its entry.

"Jesus, NO! MARK!" A hand knocked mine away from my arm.

"Oh, Markey," she whimpered disappearing before my eyes, "don't you want to go ins-s-s-side me?"

"Not you, Mark, no," the man said. The demon goddess disappeared into the hellish nightmare world she came from. I looked at him blearily. They called him Fingers. I forgot his real name.

"Get the fuck out of here," he said yanking me to my feet. "Just get out!" I stumbled to the door and turned to nod my thanks. Fingers nodded back.

Within a few years every man sitting at that table was dead. It wasn't the heroin, it was AIDs. Fingers, wherever you are, thank you. I can't remember any of the others. Why can't I put names to faces I'll never forget?

CHAPTER 18 - THE TEST

I saw her name in the Gloucester Shipping News obituaries. She was dead at the grand old age of twenty-nine. No cause of death was given which, in these parts, usually means drugs or its close associate AIDs. I knew her briefly but, oh, so intimately, a couple years before. I broke out in a cold sweat. It only took a few hours to confirm my worst fear—she died of AIDs. I had sex with her before H.I.V. even had a name. In polite society they would say I had "unprotected sex". Where I spend most of my day they would say I didn't put a sock on it, or rode her bareback. I've seen more big, strong fishermen die of this slow, insidious killer than I've seen lost at sea.

I have been scared big time, but this was the worst.

We met at a cool little bar called Halibut Point. As I waited for the test results I remembered thinking how much better off I would have been if I had just had the unmatched guinea fish chowder the place is famous for. But, no-o-o-o. Little Markey had to stick his dick in a hype. Like most males, my I.Q. is reduced by 25% with every drink. When the AL^2 factor is interjected, I'd fuck a snake if I could make it stand still long enough.

We went back to her house and, when I stepped on a toy, I asked where her kids were. She said they stayed with her grandmother on Saturday. We ended up in her double bed doing just about everything little boys and girls can do to each other. After a few hours there really wasn't a whole lot we hadn't done.

Something in her house didn't add up. At one point I opened the fridge and thought it strange that there was nothing in it. She was the mother of two little boys, how could her refrigerator have nothing in it? Several times during the night I thought I heard something in the house. Then I noticed the half open door that connected her room with the kids's room. Sick to my stomach I pulled the door open and saw them, two under-sized, under-fed little boys watching with haunted eyes. They had been in the house all along and they had been watching us. I felt like shit. I had never been lower. Scenes from a movie I had recently seen, "The Sailor Who Fell from Grace with the Sea", flashed through my head. Christ, I thought, how does something like this happen?

I found her in the kitchen on the phone. When I heard what she was saying I wanted to hurl.

"... you got to be good to me this time. That last stuff you gave me was some weak shit."

Beautiful. A smack addict. I pushed the button on the phone cutting off her call.

"Hey..." she turned on me, wild with fury.

"Do you know..." My voice was trembling with rage. "Do you know that your boys watched us last night?"

"Who gives a fuck?" she spat at me. She went back to trying to score some smack.

I stood stunned. The smack was much more important than her kids. That was the closest I ever came to pounding out a female. I went looking for the boys.

"Look," I said feeling worse than ever, "you guys saw a lot of stuff last night that you shouldn't have."

They looked at me with their wide open eyes.

"I'm sorry," I said. "I wish you hadn't."

"We didn't watch much," the older of the two said.

Thank Christ. I left.

As I got in my truck it hit me hard. Mark, I thought, there is going to be a day of reckoning for last night. There is a God and you sure as hell have pissed Him off.

It was, without a doubt, the lowest point of my entire life.

I wrestled with that night for years and, now, as I waited for my test results to return, I couldn't escape the thought that my day of reckoning was at hand. I waited for the jury to return with its verdict of "guilty" and the judge's sentence of a slow, nightmarish death. I waited for the sentence of the insidious killer that pretty much wiped out the off-shore fishing industry and so many of my friends. It was not a good time. I thought a lot.

Was this to be my punishment for not knowing that those

kids were watching? Was I to incur the wrath of God for this wrong-doing? I had wondered this for years, was I responsible? I waited day by day and through endless nights. Little by little a change came over me. Was I to die in a horrendous manner for a wrong-doing I was not aware of committing? I really believe that how one conducts oneself in this world effects one's treatment in the next. One day I will be held accountable for my actions but this one? This shit ain't right, Jack.

Finally, after an eternity, the letter arrived in the mail. I stood holding a letter that would tell me whether I would live, or die slowly, without dignity and in pain. It came to me like a thunder-boomer—if it is positive, you have to kill yourself. What the hell? It's non-survivable, you're just going to die slow and in pain, you may as well kill yourself quick and painlessly. What about the stigma of suicide? Your family and friends would understand, fuck everyone else.

So. It's a done deal. How do you want to die?

First choice would be of extreme old age. I would like to be a hundred and ten and have a heart attack on top of a gorgeous, nineteen-year-old beauty queen. A large caliber bullet to the head would do the trick. No, you might flinch and end up a vegetable that needs to be watered, turned toward the sun, and cleaned up after. Maybe you could just stick the barrel of a large bore handgun in your mouth. Hell, Mark, with that mouth of yours it would be hard to miss. Or maybe I could take downers and drink myself to death. Naw. No class. That's how pussies kill themselves, not manly, masculine fishermen.

After Audie Murphy, one of the most decorated soldiers of World War II was a guy who also went on to become an actor. His name was Neville Brand. After being shot and nearly bleeding to death, he said that the last fifteen minutes were ecstasy. That's it, I thought. I'll wait until my buddy, fellow lobsterman and firefighter, Doug MacArthur has ambulance duty. I'll crawl into a body bag, zip it up to my chest and cut my wrists. All the boys would need to do would be zip the bag the rest of the way. I'd make the call at a reasonable hour and have sandwiches and drinks in the fridge waiting for them.

Maybe I'll just stop the truck on the A. Piatt Andrew Bridge coming in to Gloucester. I could climb that suicide-proof fence they put up and jump off, just that easy. Probably kind of tough to do, however, when you're afraid of heights. How about if I run a hose from my exhaust to the cab of my truck. Nope. Classless.

I've only got one chance at this and I want to do it right, goddammit.

So where do you suppose a fisherman goes to read whether he is going to live or die? Easy, he goes to his boat. The boat is where he has almost died a whole bunch of times yet lived through the day.

Nothing bad can happen to me on my boat. Not when I have my baseball cap on backwards. No harm can befall me on the Black Sheep. I am invincible on my boat.

If you really stopped to think about all the ways you can get hurt or killed during the course of a day of lobstering, you flat out wouldn't get on the boat to begin with. Lobster fishing is inherently fraught with danger. Lobstering alone is a crap shoot. If you live through the first close ones, you develop an attitude of invincibility or you get the hell out. It's like fighter pilots. They view their planes as an Iron Eagle, invincible to all the shit flying up from the ground.

So, there I was in the cabin of the Gloucester Fishing Vessel Black Sheep that night.

Well, dummy, open the letter. Your destiny rides in the contents of this envelope. The jury is back and the decision is rendered.

This isn't fair. I don't deserve this.

Life isn't fair, chump, open the letter and deal with it. How many of your friends have you watched waste away an inch at a time.

It would take me all day just to remember them.

So are you going to go quietly into the night?

People who are close to death all the time develop an arrogance, a complacency. I call it an earned arrogance born of experience. In fishing you either get it or you get the hell out. I had an epiphany, I knew what I had to do. I backed the Sheep out of its berth at Beacon Marine Basin into Smith Cove. My path was clear. My best chance was to open the letter at sea. The Sheep has never done me wrong. If I have the shit, I'll just keep going. There's a big old storm coming up the Coast. I'll just steam right the Christ into it. I'll die like a Gloucester fisherman on my boat. Good, fast way to go. My name will go on The Wall at City Hall with five thousand other Gloucester fishermen that have died at sea. My friends, my football coaches, my uncles. I'll die a Gloucesterman—good company to be in.

I swung the boat around and steamed out of the harbor passing the Coast Guard station on the right. The Paint Factory slides by on the left. Past Ten Pound Island and into the outer harbor finally passing the red light at the end of Dog Bar Breakwater and into the North Atlantic. I figured if this was the last time, then I would take it all in with the relish of a man seeing it for the first time. I turned left and headed into the ten foot swells of the nor'easter approaching. The unmuffled straight pipe exhaust of my diesel chugged steadily as the Black Sheep gently rose up the face of the swell. As it reached the crest, the bow would point down slightly and the boat would pick up speed. The prop would pop out of the water as the stern rose and the cavitation of the prop vibrated, reverberating through and accentuated by the fiberglass hull of the boat.

The bow dug into water at the bottom of the wave, slowing the boat and gently pushing me forward against the wheel, as the bow meet the next swell rocked me back as the boat ran into and up the next one. At the crest of the wave, I'd feel a little lighter, then I'd sway back holding the wheel as the boat raced down the back of the wave at almost forty-five degrees. Whoosh - up. Whoosh - down. Just go with the flow. Don't fight it, just go with it. Back and forth. How to run a boat in the shit can't be taught, it must be learned over a period of time. Fishermen call it paying the dues. The only way to learn what we know is to do it. You won't find it any book (except this one).

The full moon came up between the twin stone towers that are the lighthouses of Thacher Island. Wicked blood red, accentuating the bright red of the moon like Mars shining from all that distance away. The bright lunar landscape was astonishingly clear. The rotating beacon of Eastern Point Lighthouses illuminated the cabin of the Black Sheep every few moments as it rotated guiding mariners on their way. The bell buoy sounded its distinctive groan.

The distance from shore increased. On my right a long line of lights floated high in the sky before gently, noiselessly descending toward the bright lights of Boston and their final destination, Logan Airport. It's a good day to die.

I don't pray much. There must be a God, logic dictates it. So what His plan is for me in the afterlife, I have no clue. I held the letter and said a short prayer. I was proud of the prayer I made that night. I still am because I didn't grovel. It went something like this: "Please allow me to conduct myself with dignity this night and if it is true that brave men live in heaven forever and you deem me acceptable, please let me in."

I took a long pull of Diet Coke as the Sheep started up a swell. I opened the letter, moonlight illuminated the words.

"Dear #54182, HIV test results negative."

I was paralyzed. Emotionally drained. I drove the boat into the coming storm for an hour. The ocean intensified and finally, as it turned white, I came about and headed home.

I always loved running a boat in the shit but the run home that night was sheer ecstasy. The high that comes from facing death and not dying is the greatest high of all. People who have faced death have one thing in common—they really love being alive.

CHAPTER 19 - FOG BIRDS

Fog.

There's fog and then there's FOG. If you can see thirty feet you can run a boat in fog. All you need is a loran to tell you exactly where you are and radar as eyes. How difficult is it to run from Point A to Point B while avoiding other boats, breakwaters, and aids to navigation, etc.? It doesn't take a genius.

Lobster fishing in the fog is quite another matter. It requires one to stop between Point A and Point B some twenty to forty times and find a five by eleven inch piece of styrofoam with a three foot stick through it and get it on board; haul the buoy line and get ten traps on board; remove, measure and band the lobsters; re-bait; push the traps around the boat; and set the trawls back exactly where you took them from without dumping them on your fellow lobstermen's trawls which are but a few feet on either side of yours. It's a test. It takes years to learn the currents in order not to set back on someone and still it happens.

If you cross the trawls of your fellow lobsterman who is not fishing on a foggy day but who is well aware that you are, it leads to a certain amount of consternation and ill will. When their trawl comes up all tangled up with yours it can go like this:

"Jerk was fishing in the fog. I wasn't and he shouldn't have been either."

Out comes the knife and—BOOM!—five hundred bucks heads for the bottom.

To avoid this annoying and expensive situation, there are unwritten but commonly agreed upon rules. From Baker's Island to Brace Rock we set back east to west or the reverse, depending upon which buoy you picked up. Two buoys are used on the east end. So you would set off a few yards east of a double buoy and run the trawl due east, or west if it was a single buoy, to avoid a cross. When you pull up to one of your own trawls, the buoy that is most upwind is hauled. That way the wind will just blow you down the trawl and you won't have to use the engine to move the boat. When you fish alone, this frees you up to tend the traps.

When you're in the fog and have a trawl still half in the water you can't move the boat much. The whale boats and toy motor boats that blast out of the fog are enough to make you old. Where is the most dangerous place to be in a stationary boat within thirty miles of Gloucester? Anywhere between the whales and the whale boats.

One day a mile or so southeast of Brace Rock, I lobster-fished in the fog with a visibility of fifty yards or so. As I carefully set back a trawl a sparrow landed on top of one of the traps. Within minutes he was joined by a few others. As the traps slid down the trap table and off of the boat the sparrows would hop to the next trap still on the boat. When the last trap splashed down, they jumped down onto the deck and began feasting on small shrimp and other treats that had fallen out of the traps.

Birds land on the boat all the time. Blown from shore, they usually rest a bit and then head back in. The old-timers say that it's bad luck. When I brought the Sheep back from Nova Scotia I lost electronics about fifty miles out and, although I was reasonably sure I was on course, it was no small reassurance when a crow that had landed on my roof a few hours earlier took off in the very same direction I was headed. Crows are smarter than most people I know. I missed the mouth of Gloucester Harbor by about two miles.

No, birds landing on my boat are a good thing. Glad to have the company. When you spend eight or so hours alone on a boat, anything out of the norm is appreciated. Once a cool little male goldfinch flew into my pilot house and down into my cabin. Fearing he would die in the heat there, I put my baseball cap over him and carried him topside. He died. Mark Williams, Gloucester fisherman, genetic throwback, hunter-killer, and avid duck hunter, was so upset he went home. Go figure.

This day lobstering was to turn, not only like nothing I had ever experienced before, but like nothing I had ever even heard of before.

The fog thickened. It was thicker than I had ever seen it. It was thicker than I had ever even heard anyone claim it was before.

It was thicker than the proverbial pea soup that the old-timers told of. I couldn't make out the stern of the boat twenty feet away.

With the thickening fog came heat. I could barely see the length of my arm and it was like being in a steam bath. Sound was dampened. I couldn't hear the diesel running. The gentle vibration under my feet and the tachometer needle bouncing assured me I still had power. My moustache dripped and my clothes were soaked. Water exited my eyes and poured down my cheeks in torrents that became torments.

Shapes began to appear out of the gray gloom. Noiselessly they began to alight all over the boat. The rustle of feathers against air was dampened but still discernible. All over the boat birds appeared. Birds, birds, everywhere. We're talking Tippi Hedren here. All kinds of birds fluttered down, some in pairs, some landed alone. Only one seagull landed but seagulls aren't really birds—they're mutated rats that can fly.

I've always been a wicked bird watcher. Most hunters are. Early on I met up with a group of official birders. One day I picked a female mallard out of a group of female Canadian blacks. One of the ladies in the group remarked that it was a very quick I.D.

"It's easy," I said. "You get fined if you kill over the limit."

They just looked at me in disgust.

"How could you kill a duck?" one said.

"It's easy, ma'am. You just lead them right and blow them out of the sky. Boy, are they tasty."

I mostly watched birds by myself after that.

Raptors are my favorites. They don't just sit there, they hunt—just like me. And they are at the top of the food chain—just like me. Only humans kill humans in any great number and only raptors kill raptors most of the time. For the most part they have no enemies except man. Raptors have no fear, one sits on a sign three feet from speeding Gloucester drivers—now, that's balls.

The fog continued to thicken and birds dropped out of nowhere onto my boat. Being in a fog this thick is like being in a heavy wet snowfall with no wind. The normal laws of the universe are changed. Sound is dampened and colors seem to stand out more boldly. A male cardinal, as red as a rising Hunter Moon, alighted on the rim of my lobster tank. A purple grackle and several red-winged blackbirds picked through the leavings on my trap table.

Directly above me a kingfisher appeared hovering a few feet over my head and, as only a kingfisher can, floated down vertically to light on my cabin roof. His sword-like bill protruded like a rapier. Tiny flycatchers with their multi-colored patterns of feathers darted and twisted chasing the many insects that can be found on my boat.

In this surreal fog-shrouded state the rules of nature were temporarily adjusted to fit the situation. A large black-backed gull landed above me next to the much smaller kingfisher. He opened his wings menacingly and moved toward the kingfisher. To my complete astonishment the kingfisher exploded forward like a fencer, thrusting his sword-like bill into the bright white chest of the much larger bird with lightening precision. He withdrew so fast, if not for the blood spurting from the chest of the gull, I would have thought my eyes deceived me. The gull collapsed on his back, a blood geyser, rising a full six inches into the air, then slowed and stopped. The big bird rolled off the roof and fell to my feet on the deck. I tossed it unceremoniously overboard. Like most Gloucester fishermen, I really hate seagulls.

I tossed my brother, and fellow gull-hater, the kingfisher, a fresh piece of herring. He didn't touch it. Unlike seagulls he has too much class to eat something he didn't personally catch.

A crow landed next to the ruler of the roof, the kingfisher, and immediately backed away. Crows are many things but stupid is not one of them. In your lifetime, how many dead crows have you seen? Dead seagulls? I rest my case.

My house sits on a tidal marsh in back of Good Harbor Beach. I work on my lobster traps there and watch hawks soar. But one of the most interesting birds to watch is the jet black crows. Throw some food out and seagulls will go into a frenzied feeding attack oblivious to any danger on the ground. Crows hang back watching suspiciously—better hungry than dead. When they spot a food source that the stupid sea-buzzards have missed, they have a set procedure that they follow. First they fly over it several times (air reconnaissance). Next they sit on the houses, trees, wires, wherever, until they have a 360-degree view of the whole area. Then they send down a scout (sneak and peek). I noticed that the first one down is always smaller and more scruffy than the others. I assume they send in the young and dumb first. He struts like the dinosaur he is descended from all around the food. If anything suspicious appears, he is warned by a chorus of caws from his buddies who are keeping watch. Finally they take turns feeding and keeping watch. Not what I would call dumb. So, tell me again, how many dead crows have you seen in your lifetime?

On one winter afternoon the view from the Williams Guest House was panoramic and very tranquil. Enter the crows. Caw, caw, caw! They start a racket, dive-bombing a fox. They forced him to move out of the marsh and take cover in some thickets. A large flock of Canada Geese was forced into flight. A Great Heron swooped up into the air and was joined by cattle egrets. The crows immediately turned a flock of seagulls into a flock of noisemakers. Next they took off after a large, soaring red-tailed hawk and took turns diving on it like ME 109s on a B17. In seconds the crows had disturbed every living thing in and around the marsh. That is what crows do. They are nature's trouble-makers. As another one landed on the rail by my traps, I looked at it's deep coloring—black beak, black feet, black eyes. The phrase should go "black as a crow", not "black as a banker's heart".

It seemed impossible that the fog could get thicker but it did and it brought with it more birds seeking refuge on the Black Sheep. Barn swallows gracefully zig-zag around the deck, inches from disaster, as only swallows can. Something stopped right in front of me and hovered. It was not much bigger than a bumblebee and had a needle-like beak protruding. A hummingbird. It's wings beat a million times a minute and it dropped down vertically and rested on a rail. Long brown tail-feathers I.D.ed a brown thrasher. Sparrows plopped down all over the place. I was afraid to move for fear of stepping on something. Some have yellow spots on their heads, others gold and yellow stripes. Next I was joined by a magnificently colored black-headed Baltimore Oriole with its bright orange chest.

With a flurry of gold—like glitter in the fog—appropriately-named gold finches arrived. Running up and down the side of my cabin was a white-breasted nuthatch. I spotted a bird whose name is the source of a lot of politically incorrect gay jokes, a yellow-bellied sapsucker. Along with the nuthatch, my cabin walls were being scaled by little brown creepers who ran vertically as easily as the other birds on my deck moved horizontally. A bright collage of colors glimmered through the fog—red patches on a downy woodpecker and a common flicker. White breasted tree swallows join barn swallows jigging all over the deck. The barn swallows appeared to be better fliers but it was a close call.

Seldom does nature allow humans to become so closely involved with one of it's phenomenons but on this day I am witness to a wonder. In seventeen years of fishing I have been blessed this way a few times—it's a good life, and usually not boring. Shrouded deep in fog I blended in as I watched, amazed, as more and more birds gathered. I drank in the sight of them as a thirsty man swills water. A couple of mourning doves semi-crashed onto the deck. Clearly they were not designed for carrier landings.

There were birds everywhere—vireos and warblers and through the dense mist I heard the chickadee-dee-dee-ing of the Massachusetts State bird with it's black face and white chest. The black-faced but gloriously brilliant red cardinal was far more handsome than his female counterpart—just like in humans. All the birds were at peace with one another. Even the accipter raptors sat patiently, their navigation systems useless in the fog. On the stern an American kestrel and a large red-tailed hawk waited.

An unmistakable roar blasted through the stillness. A muscle boat—those obnoxious, noisy, obscenities that are nothing but boat wrapped around a monstrous engine with names that make you wonder about the sexual deficiencies of their owners—Big Balls, Testosterone, etc. At better than fifty miles an hour he roared by my port. His wake slammed the Sheep amidship. The birds were not impressed. They fluttered their wings in unison, rose a foot above the Sheep and then settled back down.

Idiot, I thought, give them radar and all they do is drive more stupidly. Go find a breakwater.

As his throbbing noise faded away, the idling of the Sheep's diesel and the lapping of the water against her sides were all I heard. Then there was the quiet rustling of ten thousand feathers and the mournful sound of the groaner off Eastern Point. Everything was still.

Suddenly, there was a soft thud and scratching sounds as something large landed on the stern. Immediately there was a tremendous rustling of feathers and flapping of wings as all the other birds fluttered toward the bow. They rolled past me like a wave at the beach. The smaller of the birds huddled in my cabin, perching everywhere—on my loran and my depth sounder and the hydraulic tank. All sorts of shapes and colors. Even the larger birds, the raptors and my personal hero, the kingfisher, who had taken no shit from a seagull, sought refuge toward the bow of my boat, behind me as though I was all that stood between them and the large shape on the stern.

I inched forward being careful not to step on anyone. As I drew closer, the unmistakable outline of a Great Horned Owl shimmered through the fog. Fully two and a half feet high, his tufted-feather horns protruded from his head like those of a deer. His vicious beak reminded me of a scimitar—and was just as nefarious. Massive talons scraped the boat as he shifted his weight with the rise and fall of the ocean, like nails on a blackboard.

He stared at me—the totally intense yellow of his eyes accenting the wide, black pupils. Everything in his look screamed, Don't mess with me!

He looked capable of carrying off a small child. It was very clear that the Great Horned Owl ruled my boat.

Before my senses could fully absorb the astonishing thing I was at the center of, I felt a breeze. And, as quickly as the fog covered us, it began to lighten and dissipate. Visibility increased and when it reached thirty feet or so the birds's navigational systems kick in, seemingly all at once and they rose at the same time in deafening rustles of feathers and wings, and swirls of colors.

I stood in awe, my senses completely overloaded. In seconds I was alone on the Black Sheep, two miles from land.

I shook my head and walked slowly around my deck unable to believe what had just happened. But affirmation came when my foot slipped in the seagull's blood. Looking down I saw the proof—little white spots everywhere and feathers. Feathers of every size and shape, feathers of every color. I picked them up and saved them as proof that I was not insane.

What would some people pay for an experience such as this? I paid with seventeen years at sea. Money can't buy such things.

CHAPTER 20 - BOB

A hurricane approaching Gloucester is like a big old nor'east snow-storm coming right at us. It is a weather phenomenon, and hence, a media event. It is tracked on radar and well predicted. The T.V. hypes it and has constant updates. The people of Gloucester look forward to both—grocery stores, liquor stores and Blockbuster Video all do a boom-ing business. Kids anticipate a day off from school. Yuppies anticipate a near-death experience. People drive in a manner I call "snow-stupid". Gloucester drivers are the worst drivers in the world and damn proud of it but in the hours preceding the arrival of a snowstorm or hurricane it is safer to skydive without a parachute than to drive in Gloucester. Excite-ment and anticipation fills the air and the storm is all people can talk about. Everyone buys milk.

If the hurricane misses, or if it rains instead of snows—as it does this near the ocean on a regular basis—there is a big let-down. People who have retired to Florida come back to Gloucester because they miss storms and the change of seasons. When it will begin snowing and how much are usually well predicted. When the hurricane will hit, where, and with what wind speed, is known days in advance but it hasn't always been that way.

In the late 1880s a hurricane or nor'easter would show up on the Grand Banks unannounced and about the time some old bastard felt it in his bones, it would be a tad late. They died by the thousands on more than one occasion. Now the only boats out when a hurricane arrives are thrill seeking blow-boaters who, with any luck, are the only ones who die and not the Coasties who go after them. Most fishermen are in pick-up trucks on the back shore watching the surf with everyone else.

Lobstermen, however, have another concern—their gear. We don't take it home, it's still in the water. You could lose everything you own and be put out of business in a matter of hours. I remember Geoff

Thomas watch one of his five potters be thrown up on the road in front of his truck.

"I think maybe I should have put that one in a little deeper water," he cracked.

As a rule of thumb, twenty fathoms (farmers out there, that's one hundred and twenty feet) is safe from all but an act of God. The Blizzard of '78 and the Perfect Storm of '91 were both acts of God. Both of them were dubbed "the storm of the century"—makes you wonder what weather idiot coined that phrase.

The shallower you set your traps, the greater is your risk of losing them. They call fishing shallow a lot of things—fishing in the bushes, fishing in the damp spot—the old guys love to fish tight and see who can fish the tightest like it is some masculinity test. It's tough on the bottom of their boats and they get put out of business on a regular basis which is good for us new guys. Keep fishing in tight, you manly, masculine dopes.

The old wood traps would take off in a blow much easier than the new wire ones. In sixty to one hundred and twenty feet the wire ones will ball up together, making a mess but not getting lost. During the Perfect Storm I lost not a trap in twenty fathoms. Every trawl was all balled up. I simply cut the tangled rope off and replaced it. Sometimes you have enough warning to move your gear to deeper water but usually not. So as a storm approaches it has a different meaning for lobstermen, your guts ball up as you helplessly watch the storm coming right at you on television. You get together with other lobstermen and tell each other what you want to hear.

We tracked Hurricane Bob for a week prior to its arrival. Most of us moved some gear out to deeper water but we still all had some in danger. He blew in and out fast. For all intents and purposes, Bob was a pussy. The key to its impotence was its speed—it blew but not long enough to pound the gear. The Perfect Storm was here for four days and nights beating the shit out of the gear and the town—to say nothing of the boys on the Andrea Gail. A day after Bob passed its only remnants were big old swells rolling in from the northeast, ten to fifteen footers with the same duration between them.

To people who spend their lives at sea, Gloucester fishermen, they were a mild inconvenience. Actually, it is kind of cool to be working gear with nothing but walls of water in view and suddenly shoot straight up twenty feet where you can see, and wave to, a couple of other lobster boats that were hidden from view a few seconds before. To people who merely visit the ocean—sailboaters making their way up to Kennebunkport from Marblehead—the waves were an obstacle causing brutal seasickness.

It was a red sailboat. One is the same as another to me. I guessed that one to be about a forty-footer when I saw it pulling in to the Eastern Point Yacht Club. My buddies, ex-Coasties, Michael Moriarity and Chris Benton, ran the yacht club then and I stopped in for coffee. The boat's owner was a man in his seventies. He and his friend, a former B47 pilot, were introduced to me and we had a good talk about B47s. The former pilot was surprised that I knew as much about B47 as he did. The History Channel is really cool.

Turned out he also owned a bar in Annapolis that I had done some drinking at—not that his bar was distinguished by this. Both men had been on the boat for a week without any news. Since the older man was a face familiar to most anyone who ever watched the news, I figured he'd probably had his fill of news, but I gave them the highlights—Russia had called it quits and Mr. Gorbachev had torn down his wall. We talked about the demise of the fishing industry in Gloucester and I got to verbally lambaste the main culprits, the draggers. I remember winding up with a story of one of the Russian Generals putting all his mobile nukes in one field in plain view of our satellites. We could have gotten them all with one bomb. This was taken as a sure sign of "we quit".

Walter Cronkite considered that and then asked how I'd feel about running his sailboat, the Wyntje, up to Kennebunkport. Fifteen footers are a bit much for most sail boaters. He was scheduled to have dinner there with President Bush (41) and, for some reason, was more interested in my nautical skills than my political analysis. Go figure. He and his buddy and their wives planned to take a limo up and he said that his captain could use a hand with the boat. I agreed and was given a fifty dollar bill for my services. Mr. Cronkite is a very frugal individual.

The trip wouldn't take more than a few hours. The clouds were high and wispy in the early afternoon when we left Gloucester. The wind had shifted to the northwest as it always does after the passing of a cyclonic low in the northern hemisphere. It gave the rollers perfect form blowing almost directly into them.

The Captain and I got her underway. As soon as we got out of the harbor he yelled, "Go ahead." He was laughing.

"Thanks!" Just what I wanted. I went snooping all over the boat.

When I came back up on deck he said, "Did you find it?"

"Absolut," I yelled, "under the seat at the table."

He nodded. "Take over and I'll make us some sandwiches."

At the time, I'd spent five years or so on fishing boats but had never been on a sailboat. The deck was just full of shit to trip over and hit your head on. Unlike a fishing boat where you have to set gear on and off and actually do work, a boat that just blows from Point A to Point B doesn't need to be as functional. The Wyntje was a good sea boat. It took the rollers with ease. My Novi boat with its fourteen foot beam just plows into them, rushing up one side, and running down the backside. The Wyntje sliced into them, hesitated, floated to the top, then glided back down as slick as snot, handling the rollers in elegant fashion.

Nobody has to teach Gloucester fishermen how to run a boat considering the shit we deal with every day. I quartered the waves, which is how people who know how to run a boat, run a boat. The captain arrived back on deck grinning his approval. He could tell I knew my shit—I ran the boat so as not to spill any beer.

We glided up and down, drinking beer, to within a few miles of the mouth of the Kennebunkport River and the Bush Compound. Two Coastie Zodiacs with black M60 machine guns mounted on the back and manned by Coasties dressed in black gave us the once over and waved. One took his position fifty yards ahead and the other off the stern. I glanced at the radar and the Bush Compound was a black spot—radar blackout. A few large Coastie boats floated a mile or so off the beach, bristling with weapons.

We entered the mouth of the river and people lined the bank waving. I guessed everyone knew Walter's boat was coming. The captain started explaining how we were going to land the boat as though it was as difficult as a moon landing. I can land any boat from a rowboat to an aircraft carrier not because I'm such a great boat handler but because I am an experienced Gloucester fisherman, more specifically, a lobsterman. We are the best, single crew, small boat handlers in the world. Is that a boast? Nope, it just is as it is. I know how my boat is going to respond to my actions long before I implement them. When some of the pleasure boats pull up to the dock, hands come running from all points of the compass. It looks like someone is handing out hundred dollar bills at the Welfare office. Gloucester fishermen use the wind currents and the boat's engine, a thousand times more than any pleasure boater. We are not well coordinated, we may not even be particularly smart.

Here's a typical day on a lobster boat. Start the boat. Drive across the harbor for fuel, pull up to the fuel barge and tie off. Drive the boat three miles outside the breakwater and pull up to a five by eleven styrofoam buoy and pick it up with a gaff in two to four footers and a ten to twenty m.p.h. wind. Thirty to forty trawls a day. You do the math. Repetition is all.

As we passed by one of those billion dollar yachts, I saw Walter out on the deck with a familiar looking gentleman, sausage boy Jimmy Dean. Honest, the name of Jimmy Dean's yacht is The Big Bad John. Honest. I swear. I hope the royalties on a best selling book are as good as the royalties on a hit song. Both men yell.

"Ya'all come here," Jimmy Dean hollered motioning. "When you dock Walter's boat, ya'all come on up for a drink."

As we reached the dock blond people ran from The Big Bad John, you guessed it, to help with docking the Wyntje. Hands were everywhere. I managed to keep a straight face—honest. Warped, sordid bastard that I am I figured that anyone, not naming anyone in particular, wouldn't have many problems meeting someone desirable in a bar since—now how can I put this—both boys and girls were on the menu.

As I stepped onto the dock, three nattily attired gentlemen approached the captain and I and took me aside.

"Mr. Williams, Mr. Cronkite informed us that you would like to meet the President."

"I certainly would."

They fixed me with looks that I had been expecting. "Well, we need a little more time. It seems there are some discrepancies in your background file while you were in Louisiana."

Drat. I should have known better than to imagine that sealed files might get past the Secret Service. Oh well.

"Forget it," I said. "I won't be here that long."

They nodded with that you-made-the-right-choice nod. "Very well. Have a pleasant evening, sir."

The captain spent an hour washing down the Wyntje. By the time we got to The Big Bad John, they were in the middle of dinner. Fifty dollars, a couple sandwiches and beer, no meeting with the President, and snotty-assed attitude from the Secret Service—what a day. At least I had a limo waiting to take me back to Gloucester. The captain suggested we go out to dinner at a local restaurant—on Walter.

Over dinner and more than a couple drinks I asked the captain if Walter was a skinflint.

"That's one word for it," he said with a dry laugh.

"So how much longer do you plan to work for him?"

"Actually, I'm finished at the end of the month," he told me.

"And when do you hand in your vouchers?"

"At the end of the month," he grinned. We'd only spent a few hours together but he knew a devious bastard when he saw one.

Walter became a very popular man in that restaurant on that particular evening. He bought most everyone in there a drink or two and even treated some locals to dinner.

Late, and considerably more inebriated, we got back to the boat where Walter waited for us by the limo.

"You know," he said to me, "these things cost a lot of money."

"Oh," I drawled, "I'll just bet you can handle it."

The captain grinned behind Walter's back.

I got in and rolled down the window. "Mr Cronkite, I, and most of the population of Kennebunkport, thank you for dinner."

The captain covered his mouth to keep from laughing.

"Driver," I said, "drive on."

I waved goodbye.

Chapter 21 - White Squall

Most lobstermen quit hauling gear and go tuna fishing in June, July and August when the lobstering sucks.

"I'm going bluna fishing and get rich," we say with a laugh.

Trust me, most of us that go chasing tunas seldom so much as get one, let alone make any appreciable amount of money on them. Of all the boats that exit Gloucester harbor to chase tunas, few ever bring one home. Most just go chumming, "chunking", as it's called. You just motor out to the grounds for daybreak and anchor up. Usually four baited hooks are set at four different depths and the low man on the totem pole—a son, a daughter, or a dumb friend who wants to go fishing with real Gloucester fishermen—gets to cut the herring and throw it overboard. That's what Chief Brody was doing in "Jaws" when the shark pops up and the chief says, "We're gonna need a bigger boat."

The real fishermen drink beer and eat and cook in the sun. How can you tell a Gloucester fisherman who has gone tuna fishing for the summer? Easy, he's got a big, fat belly. Sometimes you hook up the short line tied to the main line and secure it to the boat. It snaps off like a gunshot and the whole deck goes berserk—an example of controlled chaos. By prior arrangement everyone has an assigned task. Someone runs for and casts off the anchor which has a Gloucester ball or bumper attached so it can be retrieved later. All on deck put on cotton gloves and everyone gets a turn fighting the fastest fish in the ocean, the Blue Fin Tuna. It's some exciting. Men screaming to get out of each others' ways, tripping all over each other as often as not. The fish blasting all over the place. Usually getting off if you get it to the surface. Everyone ends up drenched. Finally someone jams a harpoon in it and it's winched aboard and iced down. I've seen small ones, rats, go for three hundred dollars. A big one, full of fat late in the year, they're called "cows", can go for twenty thousand. Few of us ever make a living at it and soon you return to lobstering which is more of a steady income. You can go a month without so much as a nibble or you can catch five in a row. In truth only a small percentage of gunkers ever get a tuna.

Trolling is another method of tuna fishing wherein the bait is dragged behind the boat and a rod and reel is used to boat the fish. Purse seining is yet another. A big old boat with the help of spotter planes approaches a bunch of fish and sets out a smaller boat that surrounds them with a net and the larger boat reels them in. Donny Kangas, who has been tuna fishing longer than forever, says the poor blunas don't have a chance. He said he got sick to his stomach when he saw them and the collateral dolphins being dumped on deck, blood streaming everywhere, dolphins screaming and tunas flopping helplessly.

"It's a massacre," he said dejectedly, almost in tears. Or, as he would say, 'almost getting some water in my eyeballs'. He has a very descriptive way with words.

The last method of tuna fishing is by harpoon.

"'Pooning blunas," Donny called it.

On this day, we floated about thirty feet above his boat in what is appropriately called a 'tuna tower' or crow's nest. The Salty Two was moving at about four knots on Stellwagen Bank, twenty miles off the Eastern Point Light. The sea was calm and there was barely a puff of air. It was hot, way hot, very unusual twenty miles at sea. The sun really beat down and reflected off the water. It was brutal. Both Donny and I had hats, sun gear, white sun smear and white clothes—the uniforms of stick boaters. It was a perfect day for spotting the sickle fin of a tuna which is usually all you see and all you need to see.

There were many other boats about and spotter planes everywhere.

"There's my brother Dana," he said pointing to a stick boat miles away.

"How can you tell it's the Coot from this distance?" I asked.

He laughed. "Because it looks like it has a big water tower over it."

Dana, riding the crow's nest, is somewhere to the right of a good size. It is cool as a cucumber gliding thirty feet above the water for the first few hours but it gets old when you get burnt to shit, your eyes ache, and, at thirty feet in the air, even a small wave knocks you against the rail of the tower. I saw a sickle four hundred yards distant and pointed it out to Donny.

"Good eyeball," he said, "but it's too far."

"How so?"

"Watch."

Simultaneously a black smoke cloud appeared over every boat within two hundred yards of the fin. The roar of each diesel arrived a moment later as every boat went to full throttle and bore down on the hapless fish from all points of the compass. Planes banked toward the tuna, engines straining. More boats seemed to appear out of nowhere, all at top speed. The first boat to draw near the fish slowed. On the front of the boat a man ran out on the pulpit, which extends phallically from all stick boats. He grabbed a harpoon and held it at shoulder level horizontally moving it left or right, guiding his partner who controlled the boat, as he moved it up for more speed, down for less. Long before he was close enough to throw it, the fin disappeared.

"I wonder why the blunas are so touchy," Donny laughed. "Maybe too much pressure."

"Do you think?" I nodded. There must have been fifty boats and half as many planes hanging in the area where the fin had been.

"I wonder why that fish no come up no more," Donny chuckled.

Donny has 'pooned more tunas than the rest of the stick fleet combined. Unfortunately he did most of them twenty years ago when there was not nearly so much pressure on them and you could get a toss at them. Long before the Japanese developed a taste for tuna they sold for pennies on the dollar instead of $20,000 for one fish. Donny was now a dinosaur and he was smart enough to know it.

"I have no chance," he told me. "All these big, fast stick boats have airplanes scouting for them."

In those few weeks I got so I could see six inches of sickle fin from two hundred yards.

After a very fruitless hot and humid day we headed back in. The only highlight of the day had been ringing the metal high flyer with a .45 round from fifty yards.

"Where you learn to shoot?" Donny asked, wide-eyed.

"Louisiana."

"I no want you mad at me," Donny smiled.

We were at range, five and a quarter miles from the beach when we saw it—on shore moving from the northwest, roughly left to right. A dust cloud with large pieces of debris flying upward. It appeared to be carpet bombing as it moved toward us. The sky went to black and the phenomenon turned right.

"Donny," I said. "What the hell is that?"

"Thunder boomers," he said reverently, almost in a whisper. "A white squall."

"Where is it headed?"

He looked me up and down. "Right at my nose," he said solemnly.

"Can we outrun it?" I asked in as calm a voice as I could muster.

"No." He shook his head.

The sky went to all black around us and a blast of cold air assaulted us.

"You ever been through one of these before," I asked.

"Yes, it was bad..." His voice trailed off. Kangas was the proverbial old salt. He has wrung more saltwater from his socks than most of us have ever passed over. He is more Quint in "Jaws" than Robert Shaw ever was. He has almost died at sea so many times it takes some serious shit to get his attention.

The wind continued to pick up.

"How bad?" I asked, not sure I wanted to hear the answer.

His eyes narrowed. "Get the suits."

He was talking about the survival suits that every boat is required to carry. That was not a good sign at all.

BAM! It hit.

Donny's brother Dana, on board his stick boat Coot, was passing in front of Ten Pound Island when he got slammed. He said later his thirty foot boat heeled over so far he thought it was going to capsize. Ten Pound Island is one hundred yards from land, almost considered the inner harbor. The water went all white and eight footers started slamming into us with just about no duration between them. The thunder was so loud it actually hurt your ears and the lightening was bright enough to make you squint. The Salty II heeled over hard as if being pushed by a giant hand, the wind made all the boats staying wires screech. Donny was scream-ing at me as I struggled to get a suit on while bouncing all over the boat. He kept the boat bow into the waves quartering them. I finally got into the suit and he motioned me to take the wheel.

Before Donny was half into his suit, it went to total white-out. I lost the boat and it went abeam to the waves, port-side down. The deck was awash. The Salty II began to sink. Every time a wave smashed the bottom more water rushed aboard and onto the deck. I shut down the throttle and hung onto the wheel. Donny was below me in the deckhouse, half in his suit. He looked at me intently as he struggled into the suit but said not a word about my losing the boat. When someone of Donny's experience gives you a concerned look, what's the situation? Simple, you're about to die.

"Sorry, Donny," I yelled. "I think I just killed us."

He shrugged. I had absolutely no idea what to do.

"Don't do anything," he screamed.

"Fuck this," I screamed.

I jammed the throttle full ahead. Better to do something than just sit there and die, I figured. The boat surged ahead and I went hard over starboard. The Salty stood right up and, by feel, I kept the bow into the waves as the water poured off the deck. Donny pulled his suit on and came up beside me.

"Please do not go abeam to the waves again, thank you very much," he said smiling.

The whiteout intensified as I kept the bow headed into eight footers that crashed into and over his bow.

"You want to take over?" I yelled at him.

"You do just fine," he yelled back.

In thirty seconds I had gone from a very dead goat to sav-ing the day. In a few minutes more the whiteout began to lift. A sailboat passed by, its sail in shreds.

"That was too close," Donny yelled.

I nodded.

"How you know gun it ahead and cut right?" he hollered with a quizzical look.

"Not a clue," I said shrugging.

We both began laughing. I managed to keep the bow into the waves and slowly they began to crash into the boat with less of a bang and more of a duration. The frequency of flashes and accompanying booms began to slow down. It was no longer necessary to yell. Slowly the sky lightened and the storm abated.

Several boats floated by powerless but not in any danger. Sailboats had shredded sails. Two Coast Guard 41s rounded the breakwater flying, blue lights flashing. A much slower 44 followed. They split, headed toward whatever boats were in the most need. Power lines were down all over Gloucester, Eastern Point was impassable. It looked like it had been pounded by artillery for forty-five minutes. Limbs down everywhere, whole trees blocked roads and leaves were plastered across everything. Nature, however, had calmed right back down as though, having shot its load, it was now exhausted and ready for a rest. Gloucester, on the other hand, was a mess.

Back at the dock Donny and I struggled out of the survival suits. Two guys who had spent the squall in the harbor on their sailboat approached me.

"What was it like out there?" one of them inquired eagerly his eyes wide and excited. "We, like, so wished we were out there." He nodded toward his equally wide-eyed buddy.

"It must have been like a religious experience," his buddy added.

I took one step toward them and then stopped myself. I turned toward Donny who nodded and pointed at the water. I turned back to them and pushed both of the wannabes into the harbor. Donny howled. I joined him.

It took us awhile to figure it out but we realized the boat didn't flip because the tower acted as an outrigger and stopped it from going over. The weather men called it a "micro-burst" but in my memory it will always be the white squall.

Chapter 22 - The 10:21 Wave

Lobster fishing is an inherently dangerous endeavor practiced in what is most assuredly a hostile environment. There are few places more hostile than the North Atlantic in Fall and Winter. The five thousand fishermen's names on the Cenotaph at Stacy Boulevard attest to this. Probably the most common way for a fisherman to die is the simplest—you fall overboard and you drown.

Yes, most lobstermen can swim. However, clad in rubber overalls and boots swimming is impossible. You sink like a rock. You have to wear them—sometimes just the bottoms—but if you go over in them, you are going one way—straight down.

I have logged thousands of hours underwater in all kinds of predicaments and I figure I could get out of the boots and clear the rubbers maybe one time in five. Your average lobsterman may as well fall into molten lava. He has no chance. In winter the shock from the cold water can kill you all by itself.

When you get tangled up in someone else's trawl and you lean out to untangle it, you hold onto your boat, not the trawl line. It can slip at any time. The sides of my boat come almost to my waist, I can lean out almost sixty degrees safely. There are lots of ways to die out here—you can be run down by another boat, sink, die in a squall, get strangled by the hauler, shot by another lobsterman, or you can get tangled while setting back a trawl and go over with it. It takes an enormously stupid lobsterman to go over this way. Most of the time, you just fall over. It's just that simple. That thought is in your head every minute all day long. If you take it for granted just for a second, whoops, splash, you're dead and another name gets added to the wall.

Most of my fishing life I fished alone. For a few years I had a crew man, called a stern hook or back man. I was lucky, I had one of the most experienced hooks on the East Coast, Grant "Sandy" Smith. We were not exactly hauling in the bushes or in the damp spots, as they call fishing in tight to the rocks, but the water was shallow, about twenty feet, roughly a hundred yards off of Eastern Point Light.

It was a little past ten in the morning. We had a ten pot trawl half on board but the sixth pot was rocked down—caught on the bottom. I steamed the boat back and forth to no avail. I tried steaming in a full circle clockwise and then counter-clockwise but we were still rocked down. You can't break the ground line with the hauler, I dogged it off on the davit. I had run out of clearing tricks. I looked at Sandy and shook my head. He knew what was coming next and ducked. I gunned the Sheep ahead. The trap would either come free or the ground line would stretch to its limit and break, snapping back like a bull whip. I once saw a lobster man in Maine with a deep scar across his face. I knew what it came from before I even asked.

A wave is nothing more than energy in the water. Every once in awhile one comes along with far more energy in it than the others. Most of us believe that God has a sense of humor and occasionally it seems the hairy-faced son of a bitch can find nothing better to do than fuck with Gloucester fishermen.

Text books call them "rogue waves". Gloucester fishermen call them "freakers". When someone other than the man at the wheel sees one he yells, "Freaker right!" Or "left" or "ahead" or "behind". Without looking the helmsman will spin the wheel in whatever direction the wave is.

The Sheep was sitting parallel to the shore, starboard facing the sea, engine racing but, anchored to the trap, going nowhere. The fucking trap was not about to budge.

"FREAKER RIGHT!" Sandy screamed.

I didn't even look. I knew what was there and, more importantly, I knew what to do. I spun the wheel clockwise. The wave was twenty-five feet high, maybe thirty. Oh shit. The idea is not to take the wave head on but at about a twenty-five percent angle. We call that "quartering". This time it didn't matter, I didn't even come close to get the bow into it. A wall of water loomed up turning white at the top. It was breaking. Oh shit.

What happened next took seconds. It seemed to take an hour. Sandy and I barely had time to trade "oh fuck" looks.

The starboard side of the Sheep shot up and back teetering on its side as if held by the hand of God. The wave smashed into it with a BOOM! The boat twisted as though on a barbecue spit.

Sandy and I grabbed the starboard side to keep from sliding down the deck as eleven tons of Novi boat rose up as if weightless and teetered on its port side, a hair from going over, smashing us both, and trapping us underneath. A very bad way to end the day.

Fish totes full of bait went flying across the deck and smashed into the port side, the herring blasted up all over the place, a coil of rope smacked into the port side and rolled out into the water. Sandy hung from the starboard rail bracing his feet on a hatch cover. I clung to the steering wheel with my feet against the cabin wall as the boat continued to teeter on its side. Knives, rubber bands and the fire extinguisher became missiles and flew about the cabin. The lobster tank broke free and slid across the deck and blew apart when it hit the rail, shooting lobsters all over the place like shrapnel. Most of them flew overboard. Sandy and I exchanged very disgusted looks at their loss.

"Sandy," I called, "I think I've killed us."

"Well maybe," he replied. "But we definitely lost the lobsters."

Water poured over the port side. The boat listed past the point of no-return and started to go over right on top of us. Suddenly, as if a big hand reached out, the boat stopped. The ground line vibrated against the side of the boat as it reached its limit. The boat hovered and then, unbelievably, seemed to be pulled back and smashed down right side up. I thought I was hallucinating. The water on deck was fully two feet high. Both bilge pumps were on and the water gushed out of the four scuppers as the Sheep struggled to stay afloat. I cut the wheel all the way to the right and slammed the throttle forward. The boat steamed in a tight circle clockwise as centrifugal force shot water out of the scuppers like a firehose. The deck was drained in no time. The two bilge pumps finished the job and their red lights blinked out.

The whole incident took but seconds. Sandy dug a cigarette that had managed to stay dry out of his pocket and fired it up with his butane lighter.

"Got an extra one of those?" I asked. And he gave me my first one in ten years.

"It would seem," I said when I regained my senses, "that being rocked down saved us."

"So it would seem." Sandy considered that. "But we lost the lobsters."

"We lost the lobsters, bait, and almost the boat and our lives." I walked over to the line and cut it with one swipe.

"I vote we go home," I said.

"If you think," he replied.

The wave effected every boat out that day. Among Gloucester fishermen, it is known as the 10:21 Wave.

Chapter 23 - A Garand Afternoon

Everything that exists in Nature lives at the expense of something else. Big fish eat little fish. Violence is integral to Nature. You can't work on the ocean and be oblivious to that. Whether it is the storm that moves in faster than you thought possible, the freaker that comes out of nowhere, or the sickening drag on a trawl of lobster pots trying to tear your leg out of the socket and wrench you overboard to a cold and lonely death, violence is a presence that those who work on the water are intimate with. Some men—probably most men—can work with omnipresent violence and never act on it. But a few of us just aren't made that way. Lines get drawn. When lines get crossed, knowingly or otherwise, someone can die.

A rifle sight appears before me and through the wrenching agony I remember the entire incident. In detail.

It took years to come to a head, traps cut out of a trawl—one here, one there. Buoys cut whenever I set a trawl near his. Trawls towed around and around in circles making a mess that took hours to untangle. Sometimes parlor heads were cut out of the trap, sometimes an entire trawl was missing—every nasty thing one lobster man can do to screw with another. I set my trawl across his on purpose to see if he would tie my ground line back or otherwise mess with me. He knew it was a test and tied it back unharmed leaving that one little trace of doubt in my mind.

Weeks and months would pass between incidents. No one act proved his guilt to me, it was an accumulation of acts committed over time. I knew it was him. I never did a thing to him but it went on and on.

It's hard to describe the anger that comes when you pull up to an empty spot on the water where you had left a trawl. You get sick to your stomach as you stare at the water and realize it's been cut and moved. You have no chance to grapple it back—it's gone and you're out five hundred dollars. The money is bad enough but it's more than that. Someone has taken your property, something you have worked on and hand-lifted onto your truck, something you have dragged to and loaded onto your boat, something you have rigged with rope, branded with your name and Social Security number, baited and driven out to sea to catch lobsters with. Something you make money with.

The rage starts in the soles of your feet and flows up the insides of your legs. It builds in the pit of your stomach and roars up, expanding your chest until it blasts out of your mouth in an insane, unintelligible, primeval scream. The first time it happened I thought I was the first lobsterman to take my gaff, pull a nutty, and smash the windows of my boat out of pure rage. Trust me—I wasn't.

The day came when I reached my breaking point.

The way to catch a lobsterman is when he is in the middle of a trawl with gear half onto his boat. He can't run. I pulled up alongside his boat—just a few feet away.

"I'm more than a little tired of you screwing with me, pal," I yelled.

"I don' know what you talkin about," he responded. "You get away from me."

"I fish where the lobsters are, asshole. Deal with it."

He then uttered the phrase shithead guinea lobstermen have hurled at honest lobstermen since Day One. "I'm just tryin to make a livin for my family. You take my lobsters. You stay away from me or I cut another trawl off."

Bingo! An admission of guilt. What a dumbass.

"*Va fan culo,*" he yelled.

"Yeah? Fuck you, too, you dumb guinea. I'll see you on the dock, shit-for-brains, where I'll change you from a greaser into a greasy spot," I hollered back. "Oh, and don't bother looking for those five trawls you have at the head of the harbor. Those fifty traps will be scattered all over the bottom."

"I gonna shoot your ass," he screamed.

"With what? Your mouth?"

Wrong question. He picked up a twelve-gauge side-by-side and pointed it right at my belly. His eyes went black.

Shit, I thought, that's what the old man was trying to tell me when he said, "If you have to do violence on someone, just do it. Don't threaten, don't never give warning, just do."

I tend to get upset when someone points a twelve-gauge shotgun at me. When a twelve is in my hands, it's just a machine. When it's in someone else's hands, pointed at me, said individual meaning to do me extreme ill will, it looks like two 155mm cannon openings, veritable caves, big enough to climb in and go spelunking. The loudest metal-on-metal click in the universe is the hammer dropping on the empty chamber of a firearm that you need to go off now. The second loudest metal-on-metal sound is two hammers being cocked on a twelve-gauge side-by-side pointed at your gut from two yards away by a person with dead, psychotic eyes.

I walked slowly forward and into my cabin, fully expecting to be cut in half at any instant. It was a very long walk. I carefully put the boat in gear and moved away slowly, trying to save as much face as possible.

"Run away, chickenshit," he yelled, "and don't come back." Jumping up and down he screamed, "I guess I show you."

He ran back and forth on his boat cackling that sick laugh of his. It ripped through me like nails.

He made me think of AK47-armed terrorists who storm past an unarmed security guard and onto an airliner full of women, children, unarmed men. They take the plane over then start jumping up and down, kissing each other and yelling "Allah-akbar" or whatever stupid line they use like they have just reached the summit of Mount Suribachi or some such feat instead of capturing an airplane full of civilians. The truth is if a couple of very small United States Marines faxed some foul language to them they'd pee their pants.

Two things you never do to a man of worth are to call him a 'coward' or to laugh at him. He started pointing to his groin and laughing at me. I stopped the boat cold. I just stood there. Maybe you should just quit this shit, I told myself. You sure as hell aren't getting rich at it. Maybe you should sell the boat and do something else. Chickenshit? No. The man had an inordinately large gun and you had no chance. Maybe you should just stay away from him—everyone else does. He has a reputation as being stark, raving mad.

You should let the law handle it—bastion of law and order that you are. Be reasonable, I told myself. Call it a day. And wimp back home like a little whipped puppy? Not fucking likely.

I dropped the boat in gear and headed toward him, that stupid laugh of his banging in my head. I stopped about two hundred yards from him. You had no chance against a shotgun at five yards. None. What did your instructors tell you to do when someone points a gun at you from a few yards away? Get on one knee and plead for your life? There was no shame? The laugh continued raging in my head.

I went over the edge and pulled right up to him again. He raised the double-barrel cannon and aimed it at me.

"Excuse me, sir," I said looking him straight in the eye, "do you plan to be here for another hour or so?"

"What it matter? I never want to see you near me again," he said, gesturing with Big Bertha.

"I'll take that as an affirmative, you fucking moron."

I gunned the boat and his reply was drowned out by my exhaust. His laughing wasn't.

I started going from mad to crazy mad. It built all the way back into the harbor. Cut his traps? Bullshit. Right about Ten Pound Island I made the defining decision of my life.

Are you going to let him get away with all the shit he has done and then threaten you with a gun? Not today, I think.

It weighs close to ten pounds. The bullets it uses are almost three times the size of the .223 that the M16 employs. The 30 caliber bullet it fires leaves the barrel at 3000 fps and will kill anything on the North American continent, most others, too. It's called an M1 Garand after its inventor. Growing up watching war movies it was always the Good Guy's gun. My life-long hero carried it up Omaha Beach on D-Day. I've watched him get machine-gunned on the old newsreel a thousand times. He never fired a shot. He never saw a German. He and his brothers just kept on coming on D-Day, that defining day in American history.

I remember seeing one on the ground after some idiot had gone postal and killed people with it. I remember thinking, how could it do something wrong? It's the good guy's rifle. The walnut hand grip is stronger than most ladders. Drop a Vietnam-era M16 on the ground and the plastic piece of junk will probably break. Drop my hero's rifle from a second story window and it will still work. It shoots eight times as fast as you can pull the trigger. After the last shot, the bolt locks back on top and a metal clip clangs out. The safety is pressed back and another eight round clip is inserted. The bolt blasts forward chambering a round, if you don't move your thumb fast enough, it's really painful. There's even a name for this phenomenon, it's called M1 thumb. This is where the phrase "lock and load" comes from.

That's an M1 Chief Brody fires at the SCUBA tank in the shark's mouth in "Jaws". For a good example of what the bullet from an M1 can do look at the splashes of the water when he misses. It looks like someone throwing marbles in the water. Fast-forward ahead a few years to "Saving Private Ryan". Mr. Spielberg shows you exactly what high velocity bullets hit like. Great show but if he ever kills Tom Hanks again, we should all boycott him.

The M1 developed into the M14 after Korea. It's basically the same rifle but fed by a twenty-shot clip and capable of full automatic fire. It is still considered the best assault weapon ever made. The U.S. military replaced it with a plastic piece of junk, naturally, called the M16 which was a fine weapon as long as it was kept spotlessly clean and wasn't dropped. Probably kind of difficult in the jungle in combat. My brother and his friends who fought there, tell me the M1 was the perfect weapon for the South Vietnamese Army as it wouldn't have broken after they fired it once, dropped it, and ran.

By the time I had the Paint Factory on my right I was in a complete rage. How fucking dare he point a gun at me? I'm one of those guys that if you point a gun at me, you best kill me because all you will do is piss me off. It seemed like the Black Sheep was barely moving. In fact, the throttle was jammed full forward. Well inside the NO WAKE ZONE, my wake rocked several small boats at anchor fishing. Their occupants gestured appropriately. I pulled into an empty slip at Pirates Lane backing down full. It made a loud noise and the heads of people partying on their boats snapped in my direction. They all knew me and my boat. Several got up and secured the Sheep to the dock.

I was in a state. Some people tried to talk to me but I

couldn't hear them. Their mouths moved but I couldn't hear anything coming out. All I could hear was that ancient, primitive scream beginning deep inside me. I walked up the ramp, got in my truck and drove up Pirates Lane. I was struggling to gain control of what was taking me over.

I took a right onto East Main Street. I'd take the long way home, a shore run would cool me off and help me come back from wherever it was I had been pushed to.

Cut my gear off? Laugh? Threaten me with a shotgun, you dumb, stupid guinea fuck! I passed the Beacon Marine Basin where I dock my boat in winter. I was going totally ballistic. I passed the store called Last Stop Variety. The fishermen call it Last Lick Variety because a bunch of females own it—you figure it out. In the next few hours, I now knew, my life was going to be forever changed. As I passed the entrance to Rocky Neck Art Colony I was shaking with rage.

I tried to reason with myself. You can't do this. If you win, you go to jail forever. If you lose, you die. It's the proverbial double negative, either way you're fucked.

I swung down the hill headed from East Gloucester and passed a large, barrel-chested, dark-skinned man surrounded by young, bikini-clad females—the Mayor of Niles Beach, Joe Paynotta. The first man to dive on the Andrea Doria. He waved, I nodded.

You should stop and talk to Joe, I told myself. No. I'm way beyond talk. I turned up the hill and drove past St. Mel's Day School where the nuns beat the shit out of me and taught me to read and write a few centuries ago. Vengeance is mine sayeth the Lord.

"Not today," I said out loud.

You can't break the Fifth Commandment, I tried to reason with myself.

Why the hell not? I've broken just about all the others. Besides there's an old fishermen saying— there is no Law three miles out at sea and no God after that. If there is a Hell, it's where most of my friends are. Probably a lot less boring than the other place.

I ran the Back Shore, one of the most awesome seascapes in the world, as I had a thousand times before. This time it looked different. Either way it went I'd never see it again.

Come back, Mark. Come back.

Everything looked different, like I was seeing it for the first time. The boats, the water so dark and deep and blue. Waves rose up, curling, churning from dark blue to brilliant white foam as they crashed on the rocks with sunlight glancing off of them and shooting everywhere like tracers in a war movie. The lobster buoys, so brightly painted, disappeared in the dark blue and then popped back up again and again. Geoff and Susan hauling gear on the Blivy Fish with the regularity of the flash of the Twin Lights on Thacher Island. It was the most intense ride of my life.

With my chest heaving, I skidded to a halt on the pebble parking lot at 136 Bass Avenue. My father was mowing the lawn with one of those people-powered lawn mowers that are now extinct. I slammed out of my truck and nodded at him in passing. He nodded back.

In the cellar I opened the gun locker and removed my M1. It had two clips on its sling and I dropped another in my t-shirt pocket for some unknown reason. I stopped at the workbench, squeezed grease out of the grease gun, and streaked my face. It's what men do when the world turns black and violence is imminent. The Siox, the Huron, the Commanche, the Cheyenne—war has been declared. Kill or be killed.

I walked back to my truck, loading the M1 as I walked. My father appeared between me and my truck as I slammed the bolt home chambering a round. He lit a cigarette and took a drag . Slowly, deliberately, he looked me up and down.

"I trust you exhausted all means available before the situation degenerated to this level."

"Yes," I hissed.

He shook his head. "You're not getting by me." He took another drag on his cigarette and stared me in the eye.

I stepped in front of him, close with the M1 at sling arms. "'Ma-AH-k, don't you never start no fights...'" I said, using my father's vernacular from years earlier "'... but don't you never run from one either.'"

He studied me as he dragged on his cigarette then he nodded, threw the smoke to the ground and crushed it.

"I did a good job with you," he said. He stood aside.

"Teddy!" my mother yelled from the house, "where is he going looking like that with a gun?"

"I don't know, dear, but I believe war has just been declared."

"Teddy! You can't let him..."

He held his hand up. "Yes, I can."

She went to all quiet.

I got in my truck and started backing out of the driveway when he motioned me to stop.

"Lady Luck is a whore," he said holding out his hand. "You fuck her this day."

I shook it.

"However it turns out..." Suddenly tears filled his eyes. He took his glasses off. "I made you and I'll stand by you. I'm your father and proud."

He went back to mowing the lawn.

When I got out of my truck at Pirates Lane a freight train roared through my head. I slung the rifle over my shoulder and it felt like I was floating down the ramp instead of walking. Two men jumped up and untied the Sheep. They knew who I was. They knew what I did for a living and they showed no fear to the insane-looking man with the painted face and the rifle on his shoulder. In respect I nodded to them as I backed the boat out into the harbor. They know I mean them no harm. I spun the boat and gunned the engine as I headed out of the inner harbor. Even with the throttle fire-walled the Sheep seemed to barely move as I waked the inner harbor. I had wicked tunnel-vision. All I could see was what was in front of the boat.

How can a few hundred years of the Law replace millions of years of genetic programming? I'm the result of a thousand genera-tions of the best DNA passed down. If you try to hurt or kill me, your odds for success are small. This is not bragging—this is fact. My opponent declared this war. He chose the weapons—firearms. Fine. I'll kill him with one.

I am what I am and I am the result of evolution. I am the product of the DNA of the best hunters, of the most violent, the smartest, with the best vision and hearing, the best hand-eye coordination, the best problem solvers, and the luckiest. The ones who procreated with the most women and made the most heirs to pass on their DNA. Many people with my physical attributes end up playing professional sports. Mine was baseball—All-State Pitcher 1970. Unfortunately I wrecked my arm pitching for both the Junior Varsity and the Varsity when I was too dumb to know that one day rest was not enough between games.

My father was a two-time All-State running back at Gloucester High School, a stand out at Boston College, and played in the show. My younger brother played in the NFL as a lineman for eight years. My sister's son Robert Corkum played hockey in the NHL for ten years starting on several different teams. His son, Kelen, is a protege at fourteen. Above average hand-eye coordination runs in my family.

I'm a hunter-killer. I am an educated man, tempered by civilization but only to a point. I have the ability to become a killer. It is said about guns that it is better to have one and not need it than to need it and not have it. It is the same with the ability to use that gun effectively. My hand-eye coordination wasn't always a part of me. I couldn't hit in Little League to save my life, but now it is keen. By the time I was twelve, I knew how to use it. My baseball batting average in high school was over three hundred. At the age of thirty-nine I parred the first hole of golf I ever played. Three hundred and ninety-six holes later I parred another. I tend to walk softly—my nuclear maid Davya says I walk like a ghost. My vision at distance is better than most.

In college, I took an archery course and grouped the first ten arrows in a six inch bull at twenty yards. The instructor didn't believe I didn't practice regularly. Most people see a cute little bunny—I see dinner. Using the materials at hand, I can kill it, gut it, skin it, and cook it. When I hunt with a group I see the quarry first. I know what to look for and how long ago it passed by. The deli workers at Stop'n'Shop wonder why I stand mesmerized in front of the rotisserie chickens sizzling over the fire. For how many millions of years did my ancestors sit staring into fires surrounded by the dark, hungrily awaiting their food? Television represents a nanosecond in time, staring into fires occupied my ancestors' minds for millennia.

I always knew how to look at the terrain and think like the hunted. Where would I be if I was a pheasant, only high grass around? Where do the birds go? What makes those ripples on the water? Three miles off my bow seagulls are congregating, landing and taking off (called working birds) as they feed on small fish coming to the surface. Where do you think the tuna are? It is as important as having good eyesight to know what to look for. I do. No one ever taught me. At times, when harpooning tuna, the hairs on the back of my neck would bristle.

"Fish!" I yelled turning to see three inches of tuna fin knifing across the boat behind us. The guys with me could never believe it.

"You got eyes in the back of your head," Donny Kangas would say.

As the tide recedes from Good Harbor Beach the ducks float down the creek passing a rock that makes a natural blind. I killed them for years with everything from rocks to a 12-gage shotgun, always in the same spot where at low tide the creek bed was all pebbles and free of water. At the age of ten I didn't need anyone to tell me that the rock was perfect for ambushing ducks. I just knew. Years later I watched a man collecting something from my kill area.

"What is that?" I asked.

He held out thin, very sharp triangular stones. "Arrow-heads," he said.

"How do you know?"

"Look." He pointed out the holes drilled in the bases where the shafts had been fitted by generations of Indians. "I've found over five hundred within five yards of this rock."

I wasn't the only one to use that duck blind.

I'm a genetic throwback. A hunter-killer. The culmination of traits passed down from ancestors who survived, procreated, and passed their genes on to me. Only within the last evolutionary moments has man concocted the complex laws we have now. Before the Code of Hammurabi, before the Ten Commandments, there was the law of the jungle and it is millions of years old. On this day it overwhelmed me. I lost the power to resist it.

As I passed Ten Pound Island the rage fed on itself. Like a

landslide it got bigger and bigger and bigger, moving faster and faster. There was no doubt in my mind what I was about to do. As I passed the red light at the tip of Dogbar Breakwater, if judged by the morals, ethics, and laws of the contemporary society I lived in, I was totally and completely insane. I had regressed back millions of years.

It is not about money. This enemy tried to take my food and starve me. I will kill him or him me. The winner lives to pass on his DNA. It's just that simple.

The light of the breakwater grew smaller off my stern. He's a few miles out on Saturday Night Ledge. I knew his boat by its profile long before I could see its color, that's how fishermen tell which boat it is at a great distance. I headed straight at him blind to anything else. As the distance between us narrows, the civilized part of me tries to rear its head in protest, but an old fisherman's saying pushes it back.

"Three miles from land the only law is fisherman's law, beyond three miles there is no law. And there is no God."

When there was five hundred yards between us, it hit me like a punch. This will not be a fair fight. The U.S. Military says, "We do everything we can to ensure that we have the advantage. We do not fight fair. We fight to win."

If he has slugs or 00 buck in that double, his maximum effective range will be a hundred yards, maybe two. If he has bird shot far less. I do have my moments of brilliance, few and far between though they may be. The good thing is they always seem to come under extreme circumstances. A two hundred yard shot for me and the M1 on a man-sized target facing me stationary is a fucking chip shot. I'll stop, stand off and blow him apart before he is any danger to me.

When I was two football fields away he walked to the stern of his boat with the shotgun. He pointed it at me making obscene gestures and dancing around. He laughed at me. He postured and flashed the international sign of ill will. He made it easy.

I went dead in the water and walked out on deck with the M1 slung muzzle up, my right hand on the stock's hand grip behind me, hidden, at this range, from my opponent's view. He continued to dance, taunting me. Everything began to move, oh, so slowly. He raised the shotgun over his head, holding it horizontal, laughing, gesturing. As it has been thousands of times before, the M1 was spun up and into firing position. The safety was pushed forward into firing position. The front blade sight was aligned exactly half-way up in the opening of the rear peep sight bordered by the two protective ears, the target rested directly on top of the front blade.

BLAM!

The stock smacked back against my right shoulder as the rifle discharged. Almost simultaneously the target exploded. It went from solid to a misty red cloud that turned to particles in less than a heartbeat and drifted on a light breeze.

Both of his hands dropped limply at his sides. The target was neutralized. He tumbled forward onto his knees, struggling to lift his arms. They flopped uselessly to his sides and he tried to raise his head. Finally, painfully he raised both arms above him. In each hand he held half of a shotgun.

In an unmistakable gesture of surrender he threw each piece overboard. He began screaming, actually wailing. His head sat nicely on top of my front sight as I floated between sanity and insanity. He rocked back and forth on his knees howling. I tracked his head up and down, always keeping it on top of my front sight. The styrofoam buoy he had nailed on the top of his cabin must have been very old—it exploded into a dust cloud with the next shot. I blew out his windshield. His sounding machine was splashed. The fire extinguisher was holed blowing a cloud of white foam out of the cabin onto the deck sticking to everything, especially the screaming man on his knees. His lobster tank erupted in a fountain of water washing lobsters all over the deck. A tote of herring rocketed off another tote and spilled sending silver fish slithering through the white foam. Finally, the rail of his boat about two feet to his left turned to dust as the clip sprung out of the M1 with a clang. My opponent knelt there covered in white dust, splinters of wood, and bloody herring pieces. I went to sling arms, my breathing returned to normal.

I stood there looking at him, at total peace with myself. My adversary on the other hand was somewhat south of at ease with himself. Still on his knees he slobbered, crying, his head bobbing up and down. I drove up to him. He babbled in Italian to no one. A real tough guy. He looked good in white. His boat looked like it did a somersault, pieces of glass litter the white dust-covered deck, reflecting the sunlight. Herring lay on the deck and white lobsters eerily scampered everywhere leaving trails in the foam. Dipshit kept babbling to himself. Slowly he got to his feet.

"You better put those lobsters back in the water," I told him. "They die kind of fast in the sun, you know."

I drove off. I learned a lot about myself that day. I am a killer when necessary—not a murderer.

I don't believe he ever told anyone about that afternoon and as far as his lobstering habits, he became quite a gentleman. Later, at the height of the season, when the trawls get real close together and everyone gets knifey on the crosses, I would look for his colors and set right beside him. He was such a gentleman. I wonder why?

I was back on my mooring about to jump into my dingy, the Hiryu, when I heard the unmistakable sound of a Coast Guard 41. It pulled right up to me.

"Excuse me, Cap. Did you hear any shooting today?"

I have four good friends. Fifty percent of them were present on the 41, Petty Officer Chris Benton and Seaman Mike Moriarity who, I am told, was one good seaman when he wasn't in the brig or in some other way being punished.

"Nope," I replied, unslinging the M1 and laying it in the dingy.

Chris looked Michel up and down. "Well then, Seaman Moriarity, those reports of gunfire must have been something else, wouldn't you say?"

"Good God, shit boy, howdy, that would be my guess."

"Well then, we can't be wasting the taxpayers dollars on diesel out here investigating bogus reports of what some yuppie, puke blow-boater thought was the sound of gunshots, now can we, Seaman Moriarity?"

"Good God, Jesus Palomino, I should think not!"

One of the other Coasties approached Chris and whispered in his ear.

"When I want you to speak, I will tell you when to and I

will also tell you what to say. Is that clear, you fucking boot?"

The kid nodded and returned to the stern of the 41.

"Well then, we best pooray back to the station. It should be about time for chow. Baked chicken skin and chicken and smashed potatoes, I believe."

"Sounds like a plan," Mike agreed.

Both nodded to me as Chris dropped the boat in gear. "Have a good day, Cap."

I was at my truck with the rifle slung over my shoulder when the cop car pulled up.

"Mark," Officer Leland Ryan said, "did you shoot anyone?"

"Nope," I replied.

"Did you miss?"

"Not exactly."

"Your father was kind of worried. You better go home and tell him he doesn't have to call Senators or anything. See you later."

He drove off.

It was months later at a Christmas Party. I turned around and there was my buddy looking rather pensive. He walked up to me, looked me up and down. Then he just stared at me.

"Were you really trying to kill me?"

I looked him up and down then looked him right in the eye. I extended my right hand. He shook it.

"Merry Christmas," I said.

I turned and walked out the door.

CHAPTER 24 - THE OLD SOLDIER

He pulled out of Rocky Neck right in front of us. He was doing ten, maybe fifteen, miles per hour—half the speed limit. He had New York plates. Of course my hand moved toward the horn.

"Hold it," my friend Michael Moriarity shouted, pointing. "Look at that."

All across the rear window of his station wagon, through stickers and decals, a story was told: 101 Screaming Eagles, sergeant stripes, different colored ribbons, Torch, Overlord, Market Garden, Bastonge. The man is a living piece of history. Michael and I are fair students of history and could interpret the guy's rear window.

Torch: code for the invasion of Africa. Overlord: D-Day code for the invasion of Europe, June the 6th, 1944. He was a decorated sergeant in the 101 Screaming Eagles who parachuted into Normandy on the night of June the 5th to pave the way for the invasion of the next day. They got the job done but suffered horrendous losses. Later he parachuted into Europe in the debacle that became known as the Bridge Too Far. Again they got hammered. He was at Bastogne in the Battle of the Bulge.

He continued on slowly. Mike and I exchanged glances, no words were spoken. Who in the good Christ was I to bang my horn at this guy? He continued on up the hill, pointing and gawking as tourists will do. There were three or four cars behind us and one began honking his horn. Contagiously, the others joined in. I didn't. We drove by retired firefighter and diver Joe Paynotta's house and he waved to us. We waved back. The people behind us continued honking, one succumbed to road rage and leaned out his window screaming, using words not found in Webster's dictionary.

The old soldier pulled into a parking spot at Niles Beach facing the Dogbar Breakwater. In the distance, planes circled over Half Way

Rock off of Nahant waiting to land at Logan Airport. I pulled in next to him. Mr. Road Rage with the New Jersey plates stopped in the street and continued to scream at the guy. Mikey, seldom at a loss for words, got out of my truck and walked over to him.

"The horn blows and so does the driver."

We had a little talk with Mr. New Jersey Tourist about tourists and their interaction with locals, about staying out of their way and just spending their money and then getting the fuck out before they wound up in Gloucester harbor. He got the message.

As we turned back the old soldier, all five foot eight inches of him, was walking toward us.

"You want a piece of me?" he asked looking directly at us.

We both stifled grins and backed up. "No, sir." We explained that we weren't the ones doing the honking.

We stood there with him watching the waves rolling in and talked. We explained how to get a good, cheap lobster dinner in Gloucester—buy it retail and cook it yourself, $6 as opposed to $24.95. About as difficult as boiling an egg.

He told us what it was like to jump out of a C47 over Normandy.

"Like jumping into hell," he said.

I told him if it was my generation on the C47 it would have returned to England with everyone still onboard.

We said our good-byes and he drove off.

I turned to Michael.

"What do you think?"

Michael shook his head. "I think he would have kicked our asses, is what I think."

We both laughed.

CHAPTER 25 - UNACCEPTABLE SIR

It is a good idea to have bait on the boat the day before you fish. It's a pain in the ass to go looking for it on the day you plan to go fishing. When you have it on board, you just come down to the boat, turn it on and go. On this particular day I didn't fish and the forecast for tomorrow was promising. Todd Gross is usually correct. Mich Micheals is less experienced and not quite as accurate but when she turns around to point at the weather map we cut her some slack -- she's that alluring. Pardon the chauvinism but she is a Looker.

On this day I took the Black Sheep across the harbor from Pirate's Lane to FJ Fisheries located in those buildings I knew so well from my youth - back when it was the Empire Fish Company. I looped a line from my davit around the top of a piling and tied it back on the davit like I had done a million times before. I walked through the plant looking for someone to get me some bait. Nostalgic doesn't quite cover my emotions. It has changed some since it was Empire Fish Company, ruled by my father. It will never change in my mind and memory from twenty years ago.

It took about ten minutes to find someone and another ten to load two totes with herring onto a forklift and get back to the Sheep. When I have occasion to walk through these buildings the memories overload me. I can still smell that almost sickeningly sweet smell of whiting and the, oh, so different, smell of the red fish. I remember the work, and the laughter, and the fights.

"I thought your boat was out front," Peter, the Cambodian forklift driver, said, his voice penetrating a storm of memories.

"What?"

"Your boat. I thought you left it out front."

I snapped back to reality. "I did."

Have you ever had your car stolen? You know how you just stand there, stunned, looking at the spot where you left it?

"Now who would......" I mumbled. "Moriarity." Mike Moriarity, my best friend. That chicken legged, carrot-topped, shaggy-faced Mick. He did it. And even if he didn't do it, it's still something he would do. After all, that's what friends are for - to fuck with you.

"There!" Peter shouts breaking through my haze.

"Where?"

"Out in the harbor."

I looked where he was pointing and there was the Black Sheep out in the harbor with a Coast Guard 47 trying to pull up to it. The guy running the 47 must have been a F.N.G. I stood watching as three times they tried to come alongside and failed. One of the traits of a boot boat handler is that they slam the engines back and forth from forward to reverse. It's called panic throttle control. I could hear it from two hundred yards. I yelled across the twenty yard alleyway of water to the Coast Guard Station Gloucester to one of the Coasties standing there and he relayed the message to the 47. They headed toward me.

A good boat handler knows what his boat is going to do before it does and seldom has to resort to slamming the throttles back and forth. He pulled close enough for me to jump on the 47. On our brief ride over to the Sheep my suspicions were confirmed, he was a new boat handler and, worse, an officer. On his second try he got close enough to my boat for me to jump onboard.

As I brought the Sheep in to dock I hollered to a young Coastie on the 47.

"What did you think of that tie up job?"

"Unacceptable, sir," he yelled back.

That just about covered it. Unacceptable, sir.

CHAPTER 26 - HATCH

Since the time when lobsters were three for a nickel and you ran a better than good chance of ending up as Saber-tooth Tiger shit by going outside the cave to get them, lobstermen have been notoriously reluctant to try something new. Basically, they are fucking dinosaurs, cemented in tradition by the old and totally dumb justification that "we have always done it this way, why should we do anything new?" They are always less than receptive to trying a new idea. Creative thought is extremely scarce in the world of Gloucester fishermen. How you get lobster traps on and off of a Gloucester fishing boat was done in a manner that was considered to be the best and easiest. How dare anyone do it differently? Particularly me, the F.N.G.

For decades the first trap up on the starboard side of the boat in a ten pot trawl would be pushed all the way to the port side of the boat, followed by the second, third, etc. each successive trap lining up behind it. After all ten traps were hauled, emptied, re-baited and pushed into position across the deck, they would then be set back in reverse order, the last trap onboard being the first off and taking the rest with it in succession. The Black Sheep is thirty-six feet long and has a fourteen foot beam amidship—port to starboard, for you farmers out there that means crosswise in the middle of the ship. What this means is a guy like me, who fishes alone, could count on pushing traps for miles every day. With the old wood traps in Mass Bay slop it was a test of masculinity. Even when the lighter wire traps came in, it was a bitch.

Some enterprising individual got the idea to cut the stern out of his boat. This was an improvement which made it possible to just haul the trap and drop it on deck without having to run it all over the boat. It cut the trap-pushing distance by about two-thirds. It proved to be a brilliant idea so, naturally, he was dubbed totally fucking insane by his fellow lobstermen. His innovation made the whole day so much easier.

We can't have that. The boys figured a boat with no stern was bad luck and dangerous. Truth was it could be a little disconcerting in a following sea but, all in all, it was such an excellent idea and worked so wonderfully that in a scant decade, the boys started wacking off their sterns, brilliant, creative-thinking bastards that my brother lobstermen are.

Somewhere in all of this I came by an even better idea. I was too dumb to think of it myself, of course. My mechanic Steve Waldron was on the boat one day when I told him I was going to cut the stern out.

"Why not just run a table down the right side?" he said. "Push the first trap hauled all the way down followed by the rest. Then, when you're ready, set them back with the first one going back in first, exactly the opposite of the way you're doing it now."

Waldron is pretty bright for a former fisherman. I put the table on and it worked the balls—cutting down my movement of traps on board by two thirds.

I was, of course, thought to be totally insane by my fellow lobstermen. "Hey, there's that nut who sets his gear off backwards."

Every year or so an empty lobsterboat is found steaming in a Dead Man's Circle, empty. I think what happens is the lobsterman on board was so dumb he forgot to breathe, suffocated, and fell over.

My innovation was going great and I was pretty pleased with my success. One day I pushed the first trap off the table into the water and was running back to the cabin to grab the steering wheel before the boat could go off course. I stepped on the wood hatch.

SMASH! CRACK! BOOM!

I came to in the bilge, straddling a fast spinning shaft inches from my face and, more importantly, my groin. I was groggy and blood ran from my nose, dripping onto the shaft, streaking it red, and spraying off it virtually blinding me. I couldn't use my hands as they were busy holding my face and groin away from the shaft. I couldn't move and was having trouble concentrating. Instead of setting out slow, I had for some reason, set out fast. Naturally. Wood splinters from the shattered hatch were falling on the spinning shaft turning into missiles ricocheting all over the place. I felt a sharp pain in my thigh and vaguely remembered seeing a splinter embedded in it as several others flew by my face. Only moments had passed since God took time out of his very busy day to fuck with me by disintegrating my deck hatch. Then fate stepped in to liven things up.

Still groggy and having a hard time focusing I stuck my head up and out of the hatch in time to see the brilliant yellow ground line between traps number two and three come ripping down the deck right at the bridge of my nose. I came back to my senses and ducked—fast. The rope flashed by knocking my baseball cap off. That scared me. Bad things could happen to me without my cap on backwards. The third trap whizzed by and the ground line to the next trap followed at warp speed. Trailing three traps in the water the line could rip my head off in a heartbeat. The Sheep had a left-handed screw. With the wheel unattended it had swerved to the left so the rope that would ordinarily feed by the hatch on the right came snapping directly over the hatch—of course—naturally.

So there I was, two miles out at sea, on my knees in the bilge of my boat, a fast-spinning shaft inches from my face and crotch, no one at the helm, and ground lines snapping over the open hatch trapping me. They careened by like deadly yellow snakes. As each successive trap went out it added drag to the ground lines whipping by over me. There was nothing to do but stay in the bilge until the whole trawl went out and hope that the boat didn't hit anything.

A lifetime passed as I hunkered down. I noticed that every minute or so the hatch was clear for about ten seconds. I decided to take a chance. I timed it and up I went. Only I was still groggy and the bilge was oily. I shot up, slipped, and slammed back down again. I decided to wait for the last trap to fly by.

I have set back gear while standing in the cabin, I have set on the anchor of a U.S. destroyer, I've set over other lobster gear—a lot. In fact, I've set on, set over, and set in, but that was the first time I set lobster gear over me while lying in the bilge of my boat.

I started to laugh—not light laughter, but the soul clearing kind that you seldom get to do. As I did a whole pile of ground line dropped right down on my head. Great, I thought, it goes from bad to worse just that quick. Each loop was part of the ground line flying out, one loop snapped tight with a sound like a gunshot and flew out of the bilge. With my hands and feet occupied only my head offered something to snag on. It went without saying that the one loop went under my chin, naturally. I tilted my head back just as it snapped tight and out of the bilge. Finally, the last trap slid down the table and off the boat. I got out of the hatch, limped to the cabin, and pulled the splinter out of my leg still laughing.

Of all the ways to die lobstering, that would have been a first. Lobsterman Beheaded While Setting Traps. That would have made the evening news.

Not being totally stupid, I took the next few days off to replace all of my hatches.

Chapter 27 - UFOs

I never looked at the clock when I lobstered. I knew when it was between twelve and two because I just ran out of gas. I would hit that wall that marathoners speak of—it was time for lunch. It wasn't that I was hungry and wanted to eat, it was more like, I can't continue until I eat. It was a matter of necessity rather than convenience.

I bought Chef Boyardee Ravioli by the case. On a moving boat spaghetti was a disaster. Every morning before I started the boat I put a can of ravioli on the manifold. At 180 degrees it would be ready hours later. On a day when I forgot to do that for whatever reason I went home. Cold food just doesn't do it, hot food is that important. The boat might just as well have run out of diesel. Day cancelled. Go home. Eating hot ravioli was like doing speed.

I always opened the can with my four-inch Kershaw lock blade and ate it using the knife. I would knife through each meat-filled square vertically then run it the whole length horizontally. I'd flick it, covered in tomato sauce into my mouth. I did this more often than not with the boat bouncing all over the place. I learned to time the can-to-mouth movement to the rolling of the waves. In all those years I never drew blood. I never thought to bring a fork and a can opener. Go figure.

On this day I was sitting on the stern, knifing the tasty squares home, when I saw it, a U.F.O.—that's Unidentified Floating Object—five hundred yards distant. I don't just motor out on my toy boat for a few days every summer or come out and blow around forty or so hours a year. I spend six to eight hours a day, six days a week most of the year at sea, working. Some say the North Atlantic is a hostile environment. It's my workplace, I call it home and this object doesn't belong here. Any and all animals and birds are easily distinguishable at a distance—I've been watching them for years. I can pick out a seal's head surrounded by fifty lobster buoys two football fields awayas easily as picking out the plain donut in a box of chocolate honey-dipped. Seals twist and turn in all directions, buoys just point in whatever direction the wind or tide points them—they will all point the same way. Terns and Ross Gulls fly differently from seagulls. Cormorants fly differently from gannets and only gannets suddenly plummet from fifty feet and knife into the water chasing fish. Either by profile or characteristic signatures, those creatures that live in the water or pass over it become familiar to those of us who work on the water every day. A shark fin is different from a dolphin's fin. The sickle-shaped fin of a tuna is unmistakable. A minke fish is easy to spot and nothing on earth looks like the fin of an orca.

Even flotsam and jetsam are quite recognizable at distance. Logs, driftwood, overturned dinghies, dead animals, bodies—I've come across just about anything that can float at one time or another. All of these things look different on the water from the way they look on land. It's a different world here and you have to live here in all seasons to appreciate the distinctions. You can tell the profile of any boat that has fished near you even when two different guys fished the same length and type of boat. And, of course, we can tell the Green Police from miles away. I'm sure you can figure that out.

As I sucked the last tomato sauce from the can, I dropped the boat in gear and headed right for the unknown intruder in my world.

It was four to six feet out of the water, cylindrical and black. It moved up and down in three foot swells. The top of it was genuinely bizarre—it seemed to expand and contract as it bobbed through the swells. From three hundred yards it looked like a monster. Since I was, at the time, not at war with anyone and had no known death threats against me, I had left my M1 at home. But it didn't matter. Curiosity had the better of me.

At two hundred feet my brain short-circuited, this thing fit no recognizable profile. I motored closely trying to coerce my eyes into seeing it as individual parts instead of the bizarrely fluttering and bobbing whole I had observed at distance. At fifty yards I pulled up and brought the boat to a halt. The individual parts began to make sense.

It was a dead whale floating vertically in the water with a

bunch of seagulls sitting on its forehead feasting as it bobbed up and down. To maintain balance they would all extend their wings which merged and overlapped, then tuck their wings back in and then repeat the motion as they continued to feed. I shook my head. It made perfect sense but if I hadn't come in close I would have been sure I'd seen a sea monster.

I called the Coast Guard who requested that I stand by.

Yea. Right. I told them to take a right at the mouth of the harbor and it would be the only dead whale being eaten by seagulls.

I spotted another U.F.O. some time after that. This time I was sure I had a sea monster. It looked like Mercury or Pegasus or whatever the god with wings on his head is. Even at twenty-five yards I hadn't a clue what I was looking at. The body was that of a medium sized dog. The face was bright red, had spines protruding where a mouth should have been. Its ears were massive—it reminded me of the Ferengi on Star Trek. An appendage hung from the bottom of its red face moving back and forth like a snake scenting the air. A real genuine sea monster, who the hell was going to believe this. I wished I had a camera. The thing had a seriously bad case of the uglies and made me think of those weird creatures that come from the very bottom of the deepest parts of the ocean, thousands of feet under water. Since it appeared to have no eyes, I assumed the appendage was feelers of some kind. I pulled up within ten yards.

It just sat there bobbing up and down with its feeler snaking back and forth. What do you do at a time like this? Of course you throw something at it. Lacking a suitable missile I settled on a can of ravioli. I launched it. THUMP. It whacked into it sounding like it was an old carpet hanging on a clothesline. Damn. That got its attention. It took off straight at the boat. More specifically, straight at me.

Attaboy, I thought, that's the way to go. Find a new species, smack it with a can of ravioli, and really piss it off so it attacks and eats you. Dumbass. You couldn't just leave the ugly-assed thing alone? Hell, maybe it just doesn't like Italian food. And me with no weapons onboard. As it closed in on me I grabbed the gaff, got into my left-handed batting position, and waited. The boat reverberated when it smashed into its side right below me. That's what can happen when you attack blind.

A seal, dripping blood from its jaws, popped back as it separated from its intended supper, a common sea robin. The sea robin is a large, puffy thing with sharp fins and a long tail with fins that look like wings. A seal, intending to make a meal of the creature, had become impaled on its back. The seal swam off happily no doubt looking for something less spiney to dine on.

I suppose it is strange combinations like the ones I witnessed that are the basis for most of the old legends about sea monsters. After those two encounters I could certainly understand why.

It was one hell of a day.

CHAPTER 28 - LITTLE FEET

For the most part, lobstermen are like the general population. Most are good, some are bad and there's that one percent that could best serve humanity by being cut up into very small pieces and used as lobster bait. In lobstering, as in life, that one percent can make the day really long.

When we went from one-buoy-per-pot to trawls of five to twenty pots with a buoy on each end, the festivities commenced. Most of the year we set so close together that it is virtually impossible not to drop a trawl across one of your brother lobstermen's lines. It's easy to tell when someone has set across you, the hauler talks to you. It hums a little different and hauls just a little slower. It can be a God-awful pain in the ass reaching out of a rocking boat trying to pull someone else's gear off of yours and I would venture to say that this is how most lobstermen die.

Survival Lesson Number One: Lean on the boat, not on the ground line. It slips. Often. Intelligent lobstermen know that if they take the easy way out, merely cutting the offending line, the next time they cross someone and they have a reputation as a a hacker, they will most assuredly be cut. The First Commandment of Lobstering is simple, you get what you give.

So someone crosses you and you pull his line up, what do you do to clear it? There are a couple of ways you can go. The easiest, of course, is to simply cut him. It's easy, safe and saves your back. Bang! He's gone and you're back to fishing. Clearing trawls in this manner has caused more trouble than the Germans in the twentieth century. Why is this a problem? It seems like it shouldn't be—you cut him and he hauls five pots from one buoy, sees that his line is cut and simply goes to the end buoy and hauls in reverse order. It's a little time consuming and aggravating to be sure but he has his gear back regardless. Except it never works that way. If you snip him in two and he has five pots on one buoy you can bet

Murphy's law will be enacted. A whale boat will come along and bang the line. Good-bye buoy, good-bye traps. He'll be out five pots and retribution will ensue. During the summers when toy boats abound it can be brutal and whale boats are merciless. Just look at their sterns when they're at dock. That's right those are lobster buoys dangling back there—each one leaving ten or so traps hanging. Lost trawls can be grappled back but pieces are usually gone. During the height of the whale watching season the course to Jeffries Ledge or Stellwagen Bank or wherever the whales are is totally devoid of lobster buoys. You can see the paths right to the horizon from miles away.

Intelligent lobstermen and those who want to survive will take the offending goundline and pull as much slack in it as possible making a loop which is cut at the top. Once the bitter ends are cleared off of your line you tie them together and—splash!—down he goes. It's a little more work than just hacking—especially if you fish alone—but it saves tempers and everyone's happy.

The preferred type of knot is a slip knot. It's easy for the crosser to untie. I never could get the hang of it. I'd have to track down the guys and have them come haul the trawl before Murphy did his dirty deed. I went to just wrapping the two bitter ends into an overhand knot. It held but was a bitch to untie requiring a screwdriver or a knife. Some of the boys called it an asshole knot, the name derived from the people that tie them. In no time at all that was the only type of knot I got back. Fine, you get what you give.

One day I turned away from the hauler which was hauling the last trap of the trawl and really moving. Smack! I got nailed right across the back with what felt like a bull whip. It was two ten-foot bitter ends left there just for that purpose. You have no idea, after being alone on a boat for eight hours, how startling a whack across the back is. I didn't pee but it was close.

Raucous laughter came from two boats a few hundred yards away—John Simmon's boat Lucky and Donny Kangas's boat Salty Two—messing with the F.N.G.. The extra long bitter ends they had left are called rabbit ears. It makes the knot all but impossible to untie and lets the offending lobsterman know he should set back a bit more carefully next time. In this case they also found the end result to be quite humorous.

Early on in my lobstering days an inordinately large man in a blue boat pulled up and voiced displeasure at the knots I had left in his brand new rope.

"How about I leave a no-knot?" I yelled.

"You're learning," said Geoff Thomas smiling as he motored off in the BlivyFish. He preferred an asshole knot to no-knot.

I got someone up and had a God-awful mess. I cut myself and steamed to my other buoy, hauled it, set it back on the boat in reversed order and tied my own groundline together. Simple. Much easier than wrecking my back pulling slack in his groundline and no way you could drop him. The offending person never knows he was over someone as he has no knot in his groundline. This can be bad if he continues to set back right over you but, none the less, that was what I usually did. (Let me stop right here and make something perfectly clear. If any of my fellow lobstermen just bought this book for the sex scenes but happened to stumble into this part, do NOT think you have license to drop all over me. My patience does have limits. Plus, if you have purchased my book to read, I am lobstering for exercise now. Are you?)

So, you lost some gear, what do you do? Why, hell, that's an easy one. You merely steam over to the closest trawl and cut the son of a bitch off, right? Now what do you have? You have two people screwing with you—the original offender and the innocent one you just cut off. It takes time to figure out who is messing with you. No one incident is enough to prove anything. What you do is you set a trawl across the suspect and get cut in two—not once but many times over a period of months. This and a lot of other things combined together. It can be as simple as his refusal to look you in the eye, there's no way to explain—you just know.

You now have someone who threatens your livelihood. What's your next move?

A. Shoot him in the head. Although somewhat illegal and moderately unethical, this would certainly solve the problem. A high velocity rifle bullet would pass right through him taking all ballistic evidence, to say nothing of most of his brain, with it. There would not even be any need to deep six the rifle. *Success rate for Solution A: 100%*

B.   Calmly pull up to him off shore and explain what will happen to him, his gear, boat, house, family, friends and anyone who has ever so much as smiled at him if the bullshit continues. *Success rate for Solution B: 50%*

C.   Hunt him. Learn his habits. Where does he moor his boat? Where does he leave his truck when he's fishing? How much does he drink and what time does he leave the bar? Does he pay attention to his surroundings? Is he aware or is his head up his ass? Then you take weeks, months to set it up. Catch him alone and simply appear out of nowhere. Tap him on the shoulder and explain the next time you will have a baseball bat. *Success rate for Solution C: 95% (5% immediate street fight)*

D.   Challenge him on the radio to publicly meet you at a specific place and time to discuss the matter. *Success rate for Solution D: Unknown. No one ever showed.*

E.   Make an incident report to the Coast Guard. *Success rate for Solution E: 0%. They take no action.*

F.   Make an incident report with the Green Police (Environmental Police—their uniforms are green). *Success rate for Solution F: 50%* (As I explained to some of the enlisted ones who seem to listen more than officers, my friend Officer Paul Norton, says that's because the rank and file are smarter than the officers, especially sergeants. One lobsterman pointing a finger at another means nothing but ten men pointing at the same guy does. They stop a lot of trouble before it gets out of hand.)

G.   a.) Quit lobstering, sell the boat and go to law school. Not an option.

     b.) Get a real job. That will be the day.

H.   Call the guy on a cell phone and discuss the problem. *Success rate for Solution H: 95% and no one goes to jail.* It only took a hundred years to evolve to this plane.

Over the years I have brought up all kinds of things tangled in my groundline, tree trunks, old fishing nets, wire cable, washing machines, old belts of .50 caliber ammunition, small sailboats, outboard motors, lawn chairs, lawnmowers, TVs, whale backbones, old anchors, torpedoes, bodies. (Q. How do you know the dead body was a lawyer? A. The lobsters haven't touched it—lobsters are very particular about what they eat.)

Sometimes a fifty-five gallon drum would break the surface hung up in my groundline. The first time I pulled one on board was also the last time. The stench that permeated the boat was as thick as fog and, oh, did it stink. It was an odor that, once you have been subjected to it, you never forget. When I smelled it before it was from a floater six months in the water. White goo oozed from the holes in the bottom of the welded-shut drum. I promptly dropped it back overboard.

I got several more up over the years, always welded shut with holes in them. Sometimes holes were in the top of them, sometimes in the bottom. One day out of the blue it hit me—holes in the top probably meant a quick, clean end. Holes in the bottom meant a slow ride down with the drum slowly filling, as its occupant screamed, soiled his pants, imagined the horror. In a rare moment of brilliance I realized that the quick death was, as certain people say, 'just business'. A slow death was reserved for someone they were really pissed at. Either way it was none of my business.

Usually bodies are reported and the boat becomes a crime scene and is tied up for a few days. One of the guys out of Marblehead brought a girl up with a weight belt wrapped around her feet. He, like any of us, wanted the asshole that would throw a girl over to die like that in jail forever or preferably dead. He called it in and stood-by to help as much as he could. Excellent behavior. Goodwin his name was.

One object really got my attention when it came up. The hauler was engaged and turned inboard as I faced back out toward the incoming trap when a torpedo broke the surface. The ground line was snagged on the double propeller and it was swinging toward my boat. A real goddamned World War II era torpedo! I simultaneously stopped the hauler, gunned the Sheep forward, went hard over right on the wheel, and tried not to pee. The torpedo continued to swing toward the boat. Suddenly I felt like I was floating over the boat as the thing banged into the Sheep amidship with a sickening thud. I popped out of my daze and saw that the front third of the device was missing—the warhead. I learn a lot watching The History Channel. I dropped it back.

I think it was Danny Aparo who brought it up a while later. I'll bet it got his attention, too.

Then there was the anchor that came up with half a hitch wrapped around it. It was big and really old. I was ecstatic. The yuppies will pay big bucks for these. But with the anchor came a strange aura that descended on the boat like a thick fog. It was weird and indescribably, like nothing I had ever felt before. I saw flashes of a boat and white water rushing in. Fear. Great fear and screaming men. The sensation of being on a boat in very rough seas and then it passed just that fast. As I tried to get the anchor on board it banged against the hull, turned to dust and filtered down in a cloud disappearing out of sight.

I was still weirded out by the eerie flash I had just had. I went back to hauling my trawl in a kind of daze. There had been a good-sized storm a few days before and the bottom was all churned up. The traps were full of debris. Halfway into this trawl the soles of little shoes started showing up in my parlor heads. No leather, no upper shoes, just the soles. Child sized soles. One trap had ten in it. Someone threw a bunch of children's shoes overboard, I figured.

A second vision—or whatever you want to call it—blasted in front of me. Men screaming, scratching on wood, yelling, praying, pushing against each other. A terrible sense of wanting to be someplace else, of trying to get out, the rush of water, thoughts of families far off, the terrible feeling of being underwater and not breathing. Cold, wide eyes. The inhalation of frigid, salty seawater. Then nothing. It passed in a nano-second. These were not the soles of children's shoes. They were the soles of shoes of men from long ago, from a time when men were smaller and had little feet. This was all that was left from a boat that sank long ago. I was floating over a grave. In a flash I knew they had huddled together as the boat sank. They were all in one place hoping against hope and all that was left of that cluster of poor, doomed men was the little soles of their little shoes. They ended up in my traps as though to remind someone at least that they had once died here.

There were many lobsters in the trawl. I set it back the other way out of respect for the brave little men with the little feet. I went back to the spot and tossed the soles back over, returning the little soles of the long dead to their souls. Soles back to souls.

They wafted back and forth on their way down until they drifted out of sight. Another fishing boat slid up and I told him the story. Things happen at sea that cannot be explained but those of us who spend our time here share this bond. We both stood with our caps off in silent tribute to long-lost brothers. Then we returned to the business of lobstering. Those poor brave little men with the little, little feet.

Chapter 29 - Grapple

In days of old, right after the demise of the dinosaur, traps were fished singly. One trap was connected by a buoy line to one buoy. When a buoy got snipped by the whale boats, toy boats, or your fellow lobsterman, it was gone. Over a period of time the trawl evolved.

Trawls consist of from two to fifty traps running along the bottom connected by a ground line. At each end trap a buoy line with buoy at the surface marks the beginning and end of the trawl. They can be miles long. Mine are two hundred seventy yards from buoy to buoy. Finding something on the bottom that is more than two football fields long is a lot easier than finding one trap.

Using trawls created a different situation—the retrieval of lost gear. For example, if you do something stupid like drop a trawl between the whales and the cattle boats and three or four props, all equipped with rope cutting spurs, slices off both of your buoys your only chance to get the trawl back is by grappling.

It goes something like this: the ground line between your traps is polypropelene. It floats in a loop between the traps up off the bottom. The loran tells you within a few feet exactly where you are. You take out a big old three hooked device called a grapple—we call it a 'hook'—tie a rope to it and drag it along the bottom.

We set the trawls east and west. When I set back a trawl I take the last buoy coordinates. I use the thirteen and twenty-five lines, your first tells you your north and south, the second your east and west. Aren't electronics wonderful? It allows the Gloucester Dragger Fleet the ability to find their way out of the harbor without smashing into the breakwater. Well, a few still manage to smash into it. Lobstermen enjoy laughing at those geniuses.

I brought the boat back to my buoy coordinates and steer a little to the east or west and cut north or south and slowly drift over the trawl to keep the grapple from bouncing on the bottom and missing the trawl. The idea is to hook either between either the first two traps or the buoy line itself, the grapple being designed to hook up a single line of rope. If you hook in the middle of the trawl, it's a bitch to clear it away.

On this day I turned the corner around the breakwater with ace stern man Grant "Sandy" Smith on board for a day of retrievals. I had five trawls down with both buoys either sunk or cut, either way nothing was showing on the surface. Sometimes the tide can pull them under. I checked at low tide and still nothing showed. I had put them on the same course the whale boats were using to get to Jeffries Bank. Fifty traps, ten percent of my gear. A short time before I'd had a conversation with the captain of one of the whale boats.

"But, Mark, we try to steer around the buoys."

"Oh, please, look off your stern." There were no less than six buoys floating off his stern tangled in his prop. "What are those?" I asked. "Fucking basketballs?"

That pretty much ended the conversation. It's not such a great feat to grapple up something that is two hundred and seventy yards long. It is considerably easier to get traps onboard if you put your hook between the first and second trap or, better still, the buoy line.

I pulled up to the first trawl, matched the numbers, did my thing and neatly tossed down the hook and brought up the buoy line. The trawl was set back in no time. I pulled up to trawl number two and proceeded to hook the buoy line again. Sandy watched with an approving nod, suitably impressed.

"How am I doing?" I asked, my head swelling. I hooked the bridle of the first trap on the next one.

"You see that," I gloated, "first trap—I'm just too good." I picked up the buoy line of the next.

"Look! Another buoy line! I'm just the bee's knees! Aren't I just making your day so much easier?"

"You're just the cat's ass," Sandy held his hands up. "Continue, oh great one."

"I don't need buoys to find my gear," I continued. "Think of all the money I'll save."

"Absolutely," he conceded.

"Okay, bring on the next victim of the fucking cattle boats," I yelled.

Stopping the boat on the next set of numbers, pulling a little north, I hurled the hook. It seemed much easier to throw than the last time. It flew effortlessly as though unencumbered by the rope it pulled and that was because it was, in actuality, unencumbered by the rope that it was supposed to be pulling. As it arched up and away it became nauseatingly apparent. I froze as three hundred bucks splashed down and disappeared out of sight. I had forgotten to re-tie it after the last retrieval. I stood, stunned, my stomach went cold and my head dropped forward onto my chest. Shit.

After a moment of complete disgust I looked back at Sandy. He stood emotionless. His face was completely devoid of any emotion or rebuke. I watched him waiting for him to crack but he didn't. He genuinely looked as dejected as I felt.

"I guess I didn't tie it back," I mumbled.

He nodded gravely. "I guess not. It was a good toss though. That sucker really took off. Nice arch to it and I'm sure it was right on the money." There was not the slightest trace of sarcasm in his voice. Not the faintest hint of a snicker. The prick was holding it back and was beginning to puff up from the effort.

"I've had enough for today, Sandy. Let's book."

"Whatever you think," he nodded agreement as he lit up a smoke and sat back on the stern of the boat.

I wanted to be alone. I returned to the cabin, closed the door and dropped the boat in gear. As I headed back in I glanced back at him. He was struggling so hard to hold everything inside he looked like he was going to explode. I stopped the boat, slid the door open and walked back to him.

"If you don't give me some shit, you're going to explode."

He took a long drag on his cigarette. "I am not so small a person that I can laugh at another man's misfortune, no matter how difficult the urge may be," he stated completely straight-faced.

I was nearly speechless. "Sandy, you're a bigger man than I took you for," I nodded to him. "Really. I mean it."

I turned and walked back to the cabin. About halfway

there it began. Hysterical laughter.

"I'm just so good. What the hell, I don't need no buoys. Ha ha ha. Think of all the money I'll save. Ha ha ha. I'm just the bee's knees. I'm just too damn good. Ha ha ha." He was nearly doubled over laughing.

"I hope you die of lung cancer, you cocksucker," I shouted. I slammed the cabin door and dropped the boat in gear.

"Ha ha ha. You really made this day easier for me." He was howling with laughter now. "Ha ha ha."

I drove the boat back home intermittently running out onto the deck to hurl bloody herring at my uproariously laughing stern man.

CHAPTER 30 - DAVID GRANT

The knife is just beyond my reach. From where I lie, desperate to find a way to free myself from the ground line tearing at my leg, I see the face of David Grant, my friend of many years. My friend who gave me the knife that would save my life if only I could reach it.

Dave is six foot four, at least. He lifts weights every day. He starts at daybreak and goes for hours. It shows. His hair is long and his beard is full and bushy. The muscles from his weightlifting protrude noticeably from his two hundred and twenty pound frame. He is always dressed in work clothes. Dave has piercing eyes and makes knives for a living. He has an affinity for firearms and at one time lived with a thousand cats. He looks like the perfect model for a serial killer named Mucho, or something along that line.

Nothing could be further from the truth. He is one of the most ethical and intelligent men I have ever met. Dave is a perfect example of why you should never stereotype anyone. While completely non-violent, he is more than capable of protecting himself if someone were stupid enough to screw with him. Dave speaks slowly and stops frequently to let his listeners speak. He knows he can be intimidating and bends over backwards not to be. He was an artist. For years he painted seascapes, mostly along Gloucester's breattaking back shore, one of the best vistas in the world.

Somewhere along the line his artistic talents drew him elsewhere. He began making nefarious looking Bowie-type knives at his house in West Gloucester. Artists. Go figure. The knives are gorgeous. The blades, some a foot long, are of all shapes with glossy wooden handles inlaid with gold and silver. Viciously sharp some of them look like the knives carried by Klingons on Star Trek. He has given me several of them.

I seldom engage in knife fights and they are a bit heavy to carry.

Also the local constabulary frowns on citizens carrying double bladed Roman Short Swords, even in Gloucester where flipping out a four inch lock blade to sharpen a Keno pencil doesn't get a second glance from bartenders. He deals in folding lock blades, too, which turned out to be good for me. I told him about a close one I had lobster fishing when my sheath knife hung up on a ground line. He declared a jihad to find me the right folding knife. It had to be a folding knife capable of being carried in my right rear pocket, razor sharp, capable of cutting the floating monofilament ground line and lightweight. The problem was it had to be one I could open with one hand.

We went through about a hundred of them from just about every knife maker in existence. First we tried the conventional knives that were made to be opened with one hand with holes in the blade for a thumb or a lever in the handle. Finally we looked at the non-conventional type switchblades but, like Chief Walbourn taught me years ago, they were made like shit besides being moderately illegal.

Finally Dave had an idea. A knife you could grab by the closed blade in your pocket and flick open and lock with one hand on the way out then spin it and grab the grip. It was an all-stainless four inch lock blade Kershaw. It took awhile and a lot of cut fingers, one slashed foot and a busted TV screen, but I got it down. I can pull it out, flip it around and grab the handle just that fast, drunk or sober, or on a rolling boat deck with my life in jeopardy—first time, every time.

Before today it has twice saved my life. Today I just have bad luck.

So why does David Grant's face come flashing back at the end of my life? Knives maybe. But I think it was because of the day he approached me with a troubled look on his face. He walked up to me shaking his head.

"I just don't understand," he said.

"What don't you understand?"

"My partner. The one who sells my knives out west. He took some money that wasn't his. It was mine."

"You mean he stole from you?"

"Well, yeah," Dave said with a frown. "How could anyone

do that ... take something that didn't belong to them?"

"Some people do," I said.

"But I don't understand that."

And he didn't. My friend Dave lives on such an ethical plane that he couldn't understand stealing. I was awed.

CHAPTER 31 - ACROSS

I was over the trauma of my first boat sinking and the swim I took five miles off Gloucester in February. It was time to buy a new boat.

I took the ferry, The Scotia Prince, out of Portland, Maine. It was a good night crossing—plenty of food, drink, gambling and, of course, girls. I arrived in Yarmouth, Nova Scotia about eight in the morning and drove my truck off the ferry. Stopping at the Customs Booth, I produced my driver's license. Naturally, they pulled me over—I always get pulled over, go figure.

The Customs Agent was female, very polite, and not too hard to look at.

"Do you have any guns, sir?" she asked.

"Yes, ma'am, I do. I have several rifles and some pistols," I said in an equally polite tone.

She stepped back and whispered frantically into her hand-held radio. Three male agents appeared, one holding a Hekler-Koch 9mm submachine gun at the ready.

"He has a bunch of guns," she pointed at me her eyes wide and wild.

"Search him," the sergeant said.

"Sir, would you turn around, put both hands on the truck and spread your legs, please?"

I complied smiling. She gave me a good going over and even patted my groin.

"He's clean," she announced.

"Well then, the guns must be in the truck," said the sergeant.

"What guns?" I asked.

"The guns you said you had with you," the girl said.

"I never said I had guns with me."

Her eyes widened. She turned to her sergeant. "He did so."

"What's going on here?" the sergeant asked.

"Beats me," I said.

"He said he had several rifles and some pistols, too," she said gesturing at me.

The sergeant glared at me. "What in hell is going on?"

I shrugged my shoulders, "She asked if I had any guns. I told her the truth, that I have several and she panicked."

"Well? Where are they?" he asked.

"At home in my gun closet."

He rolled his eyes and the others looked at the girl who turned red and tried to make herself as small as possible.

They waved me through.

I drove up the hill and took a right onto the highway. I headed southwest along coastal Nova Scotia. In Spring and Fall, Nova Scotia looks a lot like Gloucester—a whole lot of water and not a lot of people. I wasn't sure where exactly I was headed but I knew that I'd find a boat in Nova Scotia, it was just a matter of finding the right place.

In no time I came on a cove of Novi boats. I pulled in. The tide was high and I could see row after row of boats from the window of my truck. One boat was loading bait and a couple more waited their turn, tied off of the loading boats port-side.

As I watched I noticed something that anyone who was not a fisherman would not. The men on the boat taking on bait, and the ones on the boat tied to it, didn't speak to each other.

Holy shit, I thought, it's just like Gloucester—half the lobstermen don't talk to the other half. Well, it's good to know that Gloucester fishermen are not the only ones too stupid to put aside petty differences for the greater good. I busted up laughing.

I walked out onto the dock to take a closer look at some of the boats. After all, that's what I was here to do, buy a boat. Half the boats were clean, half dirty. As a rule a clean fishing boat is one making money. A dirty one isn't—not always true but a good rule of thumb. I approached one of the dirty ones and all the men on it went to full attention. I was a little taken aback at first and then I noticed the unmistakable fragrance of marijuana. All the men were staring at me. I got it.

"Hi," I said.

None of them moved or spoke.

"Gentlemen," I said, "do I look like, dress like, or sound like a member of the RCMP?"

They seemed to lighten up a bit.

"Perhaps you think they would go through the trouble of getting an undercover person, in a truck with Massachusetts licenses on it, down here to bust you for smoking a freaking j-bar?"

They went back to work. They were trying to run a hydraulics line from below deck up and around the davit to the hauler, using a rope to secure it. In a loud voice, the way Americans always seem to do as though we think it will help someone who doesn't speak English understand us better, I asked what they were doing. In French and broken English the Captain explained. I motioned for him to stop and walked back to my truck thinking, "Have I gone back in time? Have these guys never heard of duct tape, for Christ's sake?"

I showed them how to tape the hose to the davit and the job was done in no time. I tossed the tape to the captain and told him to keep it. For the price of a half-used roll of duct tape I could do no wrong. In no time a bottle of wine along with bread and cheese was produced. I swapped lies with some fellow fishermen.

Despite the fact that their season was six months long up there, and they made a lot of money, they paid most of it in taxes. I took a look at two boats that were for sale and then headed out down the coast.

In twenty miles of highway I stopped at ten harbors filled with boats. Few had boats with For Sale signs on them. My inquiries led to a few possibilities. There were hundreds of boats here but few were for sale. Or so it seemed. I met up with two fishermen from Gloucester who were also looking for boats. They got discouraged after a few days and went home. I checked into a B&B and had a hell of a time with a fine looking chamber-maid who worked there.

After a week a strange metamorphoses happened. As I drove the highways, people would wave me over and tell me of boats that were for sale all over the place. I had come to be known as "the Gloucester fisherman in the black Ford pickup truck look-ing for a boat". Up here word-of-mouth was how business was done. Harbors that previously had only a couple boats for sale suddenly had ten or twenty. As near as I could figure, the individuals I spoke with only told me about their friends' boats for sale but they didn't put signs on them. Go figure.

I finally ended up on an almost-new thirty-six footer with a fourteen foot beam that seemed monstrous to me. It had that classic high bow and the curved sheer that identified it as a second genera-tion Novi boat. Unlike it is with so many boats up here, the car-penter actually owned a miter box and the finish work was pretty good. Cape Sable Island Novis are famous for two things—great sea-worthiness and poor finish work . Her hull had been purchased from one boat builder and finished off by another. It also had a small diesel engine. It was so huge I could have carried my first boat in it.

I was in love.

The owner approached me.

"She's only six months old," he said.

"Okay, then why are you selling it?"

"Can't see over the bow."

I looked at him. He was slight of build and rather short. He stepped behind the wheel and sure enough the little shit could barely see out of the window let alone over the high bow that char-acterizes a classic Novi boat.

"What the hell?" I said trying not to laugh, "did you shrink after you bought it?"

"Naw, I bought it sight unseen."

"So... let me get this straight. You're selling this boat because your view is obstructed?"

"Yea."

I looked out of the window and could see just fine.

"I'll give you $30K American," I said.

"Fifty," he replied, "and not a dollar less."

It was worth forty-five if is was worth a dollar. I told him I would think about it and meet him on the boat the next day.

That night I came by some great intel from my bed-mate. No less than five people had made offers, none for as much as he wanted, and the guy really needed to sell the boat.

I met him on the boat the next day. I was the fifth American to offer much less for his boat than the asking price. As near as I could figure, the boat was worth the 50K he was asking for and all the other fishermen, like me, knew that. But, just like me, they could not afford it. Thirty was all I had and I offered it. He countered with forty. We continued to negotiate and he was a pretty skillful negotiator, changing the subject back and forth between the boat and fishing. He then made what would prove to be his fatal mistake—he suggested we go and get a bottle to help with the discussion.

Nova Scotia is a cool place in most ways. In one, however, they are barbaric and totally uncivilized, we had to drive twenty miles to the nearest liquor store. A totally unsatisfactory situation. As we wound down the beautiful coast, past small, boat-filled harbors every few miles, he talked rapid fire. He talked about everything but the price—women, food, booze, guns, courage under pressure, violence—the six topics men the world over have in common and can talk about for hours.

We pulled up in front of the liquor store.

"What do you want?" he asked.

I gave him one of my father's quotes. "'I have always believed that if you are going to destroy your liver you should at least do it with good stuff.' Whatever you get, make it top shelf."

He nodded.

When he returned he had a liter of Bacardi, a six pack of Cokes and a bag of ice. We drove back to the boat where the negotiations continued. He made the drinks. On my first swig it hit me like a slap—he had made the drinks strong, about half and half. He was going to try to get me drunk and take advantage of me.

Christ, I thought, that only happens in the movies.

He was doomed from the onset. First of all, I only had thirty thousand so there was no point in asking for more. Second, he was about 5'6" and maybe one hundred sixty pounds. I had him by half a foot and a good forty pounds. Third, I was weaned on my father's Bacardi and Cokes—mostly without his permission. I learned to shoot my BB gun at the bat on the empty bottles.

When half the bottle was gone I purposely began to slur my

words. If he wanted to play games, I could play games. I filled out a Bill of Sale for $28K American. Then over the next eight hours one Nova Scotia fisherman tried to out-drink one Gloucester fisherman.

I awoke the next day in my room with the Bill of Sale on the nightstand and the guy's signature on the bottom of it.

I figured there was no way that it was legal and I was half right. It was not legal in the United States. It was, however, quite legal in Canada. I had just bought a $50K boat for $28K. I headed back to Gloucester to secure financing.

By the time I returned with the money I found my buddy trying to get out of the deal. He realized that he had sold the boat for a lot less than it was worth. I had a pile of papers that a lawyer had convinced me I would need to get the boat back into the United States and tried to charge me thousands of dollars for. The boat owner and I found ourselves in front of a Canadian Customs Official who listened attentively to our account of the less-than-sober conditions we were both in when the deal was made. The Bill of Sale, such as it was, consisted of a lined piece of paper ripped out of a notebook.

After examining the document and considering both of our stories, the Customs Official shook his head and informed me of two things. One, the deal was good and all I needed to do was give him a check and the boat was mine. Two, all I needed was one sheet of paper from the pile the lawyer had given me. Lawyers.

I handed over the check and now owned a Cape Sable Island Novi Boat.

The gentleman I bought the boat from turned out to be a good guy. He took me to find a fifty-five gallon drum of diesel to augment the tank on the boat for the two hundred mile trip back across the Gulf of Maine. I had arranged with a couple friends to come up to Nova Scotia and help me bring the boat home. No one in their right mind would run a new boat two hundred miles across open ocean alone. The Customs Inspector told me that if anyone, Canadian or American, stopped me on the way back I was to call him day or night. He assured me he'd take care of it. So much for all the paperwork that the lawyer had assured me I would need.

I waited a week and no one came. I stayed at the same bed & breakfast and had a great time with the maid. I painted the roof and forward deck on the boat for lack of something better to do. I waited and no one came.

I noticed that the boat took on a little too much water through the stuffing box—the point at which the shaft comes into the boat. It needed to be tightened down. The box was located outside the boat, naturally, and there was not a boatyard for a hundred miles, of course. In the time honored tradition of fishermen who don't have a lot of money to spend on boat yards, or "thief yards" as they are known to fishermen, I decided to ground the boat out at low tide.

Just like in Gloucester, there was a wall you could tie the boat up to at high tide and then wait for the tide to go out. After waiting for hours for the water to recede, a wrench and five minutes was all it took to tighten down the stuffing box. I returned the boat to the dock at high tide and waited. No one came. The boat didn't have an automatic bilge pump. I installed one and waited.

Things started getting bad and once that started it went south real fast. A large pile of shit hit the fan—as they call the propeller in Nova Scotia. Warning! Will Robinson! Warning! Danger! Danger! The maid said she was in love with me and wanted to come back home with me. One week of good sex and the poor girl is in love. Foolish female.

It was a Saturday, early afternoon, sunny, and the ocean was as flat as a carpenter's dream. The weather reports said it would be storm free for a week. The boat's tank was full, as was the fifty-five gallon tank. I had food and water onboard and lots of Diet Coke. I had made arrangements to have my truck taken back to the ferry. Without saying goodbye to anyone save the maid, who was unaware that I was doing her the favor of her young life by leaving her behind, I made the decision to leave. Some people should not get married or have relationships. I, unlike most of them, am smart enough to know I am one of them.

I stood in the cabin of the Black Sheep thinking, no, you can't do this. You are out of your mind. Take an unknown boat across two hundred miles of open ocean by yourself? That's not brave, that's just plain stupid. But I wanted to go home. I am an

American. I have been in other countries before and Nova Scotia is cool. It reminds me of America only twenty years earlier. But it didn't matter. After a week or so, you don't want to be between me and the United States.

"You're outta ya fuckin' head," I told myself. "Two hundred miles alone. What are you? A fuckin' thrill-seeker like the goddamn blow-boaters who go into a raging storm to have some type of near death experience? Putting the Coasties at risk when they have to rescue them? Trying to manufacture an adventure before going back to pushing paper around on a desk all day and having bad days and such boring guppy (same as a yuppy only more appropriate, it's a small fish) corporate bullshit. So what's the difference between them and you? ... Easy. They do it for kicks, you do it because you have to. You take a calculated risk to make a living, they take a risk for the sake of taking a risk. What really makes them dipshits is that they put others at risk and that ain't right."

It was a sparkling sunny afternoon. There must have been a hundred brightly colored boats tied up beam to beam in this small harbor in southwestern Nova Scotia. I stood in the cabin of the thirty-six foot Novi boat Black Sheep. Two hundred miles of ocean separated me from Gloucester, Massachusetts. Fuck it. It's like Curly said, "Jeeeeeez, Moe, it's only two inches on the map."

When you turn on a gas engine, it comes to life slowly. When you turn on a diesel engine, it becomes blatantly apparent where the expression "lite off a diesel" comes from—it explodes. Until the oil has had a chance to circulate, metal to metal noise is overwhelming. It blasted into action with a throaty roar that would thrill any monster truck fan. After three years with a 292 gas engine under me, that engine roaring to life exuded power, reliability, and confidence in getting me two hundred miles across the Gulf of Maine to the United States, Gloucester, Massachusetts, and home. I cast off and headed out of the harbor.

Hey, tough guy, are you scared?

Yes. But in the manner of tough guys everywhere going back to the beginning of time, I wouldn't admit it, even to myself. I pulled out of the harbor and put my stern toward Nova Scotia and my bow toward Gloucester. Two hundred fucking miles. Holy shit, off we go. Leaving the black exhaust trail from the straight pipe

I popped the top on one of the first of many Diet Cokes I was to consume in the next thirty-six hours.

About a mile from the head of the harbor a fog bank loomed before me. Naturally. In no time I couldn't see the stern of the boat. Of course. I came to a dead stop.

In the cabin of a thirty-six foot Novi boat at sea, one hundred and ninety-nine miles from home, alone with water dripping down my nose and visibility gone, the real demons came to the surface.

February. Bitterly cold, and five miles off of Eastern Point.

Something tangled in the prop of the Chassea, my thirty foot lobster boat loaded down with traps. Remove the hatch and clear the prop in water so cold fingers become numb and useless in seconds. The hatch that can't be screwed back on without fingers.

Water rushing in. Trying to scramble into the top half of a wet suit. The smell of gas as salt water covers the batteries. The sickening sound of air being forced out as water poured in. The bow rises as the stern settles deeper and deeper into the frigid February waters. Water rushing faster and faster. The lobster tank slides by, crashing into the sinking stern. Fish totes, buoys. The lone occupant hanging onto the davit trying to stay above the freezing water rushing higher and higher. These are the choices: stay aboard and face certain death with the sinking boat or go into the frigid water and swim five miles with a fighting chance to live.

Fire off the last flare. A hundred pounds of lobsters crated up. Set them free—no need for them to starve to death on the bottom. I grabbed the holstered .45 automatic and looped the belt around my neck—five hundred bucks is five hundred bucks. Into the water and push away.

Mark's Rule of Distance From Shore forms instantly: The distance from shore when you are on a boat is multiplied by ten when you are in the water. It looked a million miles away. I began to swim.

Less than a hundred yards from my boat I was shivering uncontrollably, partly from having two hundred feet of water with unknowns in it under me, but mostly from the bitter cold of the water. The wet suit was no more use than an ordinary sweatshirt.

My teeth were chattering so hard I thought they would fall out. I was woefully far from shore when the most interesting phenomenon occurred. I knew I was not going to reach shore. In all probability I was close to dying and I just plain didn't give a rat's ass.

A great calm came over me. I quit swimming and looked up. Great white clouds in the blue of a crystal clear February sky floated by. Black back and herring gulls soared effortlessly. I looked toward shore and saw the flash of Eastern Point Light, light years away. I got weaker and weaker. Slowly I slipped into that unconscious bliss that a man freezing to death succumbs to. A mouthful of water yanked me back into reality. I tried to rally myself.

If you sleep, you die.

I turned toward the Chassea and saw that, even though completely awash, it still floated. I started swimming back toward it. Again I passed out and got a sobering mouthful of water. I was moving in such slow motion I felt like I was dragging a sea anchor. I wasn't going to make it back to the boat. What good would it do me if I did? What the hell? I was only going to freeze to death slowly.

Stick your head under the water and take a deep breath. End it now.

It's easy to die. Much harder to live.

Have you ever been scared? I don't mean mildly apprehensive. I mean asshole-puckering, piss-dripping terrified. Who you are as a person is not defined by a lifetime of behavior but rather by how you act in isolated incidents. These individual moments determine whether you are a person of worth or whether you have the value of a dead dog. I made the decision to stay alive as long as possible. The correct decision is always the tough one. Hours that were minutes passed.

I heard it before I saw it. A boat. I looked East toward Salt Island in a trance, barely able to keep my mouth above the water. By the bow wake, it looked like a thirty foot tuna boat hauling ass. It planed out a klick or so away. My teeth clattered together and I shook like a big, old, long-haired dog coming wet out of a duck blind. The boat got bigger and bigger and bigger. It wasn't a thirty foot tuna boat, it had bright orange stripes vertically on both port and starboard sides. Black smoke streamed up from its stack and there were figures in blazing red jackets all over it. They saw me and were gesturing toward me. My thinking was completely fuddled but even through my muddled thinking I recognized the United States Coast Guard ninety-five foot Cape Higgon. They were coming for me. They were coming to do what they do best, pull freezing Gloucester fishermen out of the North Atlantic in winter. I couldn't begin to explain what it feels like to be in the water five miles from shore, quietly freezing to death and have a boat full of Coasties pull up, every one of them wanting to be the one that pulls you out of the water. I make fun of the Coast Guard all the time—I can, I have two good friends in it. But don't let anyone else do it in my presence.

It pulled up slick as snot. Must have had a GF at the helm.

I was vaguely aware that a cargo net was dropped down in front of me. The whole port side of the Higgon was lined with Coasties screaming for me to grab the net. I could barely hear them. I remember looking at the net and wondering what I was supposed to do with that. What was this monstrous white boat with a big orange stripe on it? With guys all over it? Where was my boat? Why was I shaking so badly?

I remember going into a fog as I grabbed the net. Voices were yelling at me to pull myself up but my arms had no strength left.

"Come on," they yelled. "Come on. Just pull yourself up."

Why? I thought. What's going on here?

Arms appeared under mine—one right, one left. Coasties aren't supposed to leave the boat under any conditions. It can get you thrown out of the Coast Guard. When they came down that net they did it against orders. What were they trying to do? I went under. Everything was cold and dark. I started to breathe in water. But the hands grabbed me again and I was dragged upward out of the water. The voices were yelling louder. I was confused. Arms were under me now, they were completely in the water. They're not allowed to do that, I thought. But they were pushing me up. More hands were reaching down. Yelling. Lots of yelling. There was a rubber Zodiac. Where did that come from? Pushing, pulling. I was no help but they got me into the Zodiac. The skipper, demonstrating why he was the boss, had ordered it launched when he saw what shape I was in.

Somehow they got me onto the Higgon. I was on my back looking up into many sets of eyes. Boy, am I getting old I remember thinking, these guys all look so young. My pistol disappeared and blankets were being wrapped around me. I was shaking so hard I thought my bones would come apart and I would fall to pieces. Then everything was black.

When I awoke I was down below. I was cold but not shaking. A man, older than the rest, I assumed was the captain stood looking down at me.

"Permission to come aboard, sir," I rasped, barely able to speak.

"Granted." He smiled.

I could think again. I looked around at the room full of young faces, male and female.

"Sir?"

"Yes?"

"Don't you sometimes warm people up by having someone lay down beside them?"

He chuckled. "Sometimes. Which one would you prefer?"

"Female," I said. "Your choice."

Everyone laughed though with the girls it was a more nervous laugh.

"He's fine," someone said.

"It appears you are going to survive, Mr. Gloucester Fisherman," the captain said.

I managed to extend my hand. "Thank you."

He shook it. "You're welcome, Mark."

"Who went into the water?"

He nodded toward two young men who stood with blankets over their wet clothes. They had waited to change into something dry until they were sure I was going to be alright.

"Thanks," I said to them.

The captain nodded. "These are the two who, against my express orders, went into the water after you."

"Didn't hear you sir," they chorused.

"Bullshit." He shook his head and then grinned at them. "Now, will you go and put some dry clothes on before you catch pneumonia and die causing me a shitload of paperwork?"

Everyone laughed as they turned and left the room.

I turned my eyes to the captain. "My boat?"

"Sorry." He turned back to me. "It went awash with six seamen and four pumps on it. There seems to be an air-pocket in the bow that is keeping it afloat."

As he said it I heard the rattle of a machine gun going off topside.

"I'm afraid to ask," I groaned.

"Hazard to navigation. I had to sink her. Sorry. Nothing personal."

I started to laugh a faintly hysterical laugh. "Let me get this straight. You shot my boat with a machine gun?"

As though on cue a voice from above yelled, "She's down, sir."

"It would appear you were successful, captain," I said.

He shrugged. "Like I said, nothing personal."

A short time later I waved goodbye to the crew of the Higgon as I was transferred aboard a 41-footer that would ferry me back to Gloucester under the command of my friend Wesley Dittes.

Mine was one of seventy-nine fishing vessels to sink that year. Care to guess which one I can personally guarantee was accidental?

Wesley Dittes went on to become the commandant of Coast Guard Station Gloucester. During his tenure the Coast Guard was ordered to increase their boarding of Gloucester fishing vessels, due in no small part to the number of them that sank that year. A certain group of Gloucester fishermen got really creative, transferring from one boat to another, sinking the first one, and arranging for friends and relatives to show up later at the Coast Guard Station weeping and wringing their hands as though the sinking was an accident. I never got boarded. Some fishermen asked why and I just smiled.

There's a rumor that a Gloucester fishing boat got caught in a storm, a bad one, and one of the Coasties was hesitant to go out. An old chief is said to have set the record straight by telling him, "You have to go out, son. You don't have to come back." They go out after all manner of idiots who take their pleasure boats and sport boats out in hurricanes just for the thrill of it. But they treat Gloucester fishermen as personal. They know we are there to make a living and pulling our sorry asses out of the water is why they exist.

As for the Chassea, she sits in twenty fathoms in the mud. I talked to the insurance people the next day. My lawyer, like all lawyers, told me his advice was my only chance but I told the whole truth anyway. The insurance agent threatened to send a diver down to examine the boat. I told him that I had been a commercial diver before becoming a fisherman and offered to dive it and video the entire boat. They paid immediately.

I headed to Canada to look for a new boat a few months later. I wanted a much bigger boat this time—one that would take a long time to sink. The Black Sheep could carry the Chassea on her deck.

Fog or no, I had a loran and a course set for Thacher's Light two hundred or so miles away with nothing in between—at least according to the charts. I steamed at eight knots on course, the radar showing all clear. With the reassuring roar of the diesel and the swishing of water running down my new boat, I finally shook myself free of the trauma of the events of a few months earlier. Just two hundred miles straight across the Gulf of Maine. What could possibly go wrong?

I thought I heard waves breaking on the beach. Oh, man, and here I was all ready to make such a relaxing run. I checked the radar. All clear.

Another breaker on the beach. I know that sound. I should, for Christ's sake, I live on a beach. Radar clear. What the hell? Use what you have, stupid. Depth sounder—fifty feet. It was two hundred a short time ago. What's going on? What's wrong? Use what you have. Vision dependent on a machine, depth dependent on a machine. Machines make mistakes but my ears don't lie. Waves. Waves mean a shoreline, a shoreline means land. Running into land means disaster.

I looked over the side and the water was lightening up. It was getting shallower. I spun the wheel ninety degrees left to run parallel with whatever was in front of me. The chart says nothing is there, as does the radar. Trust your senses, something is there. Smell. No machine can smell for you. I smell land. Trust yourself over machines.

The fog lifted a scootch and a white beach appeared fifty yards on my right. At a depth of fifteen feet I ran parallel to the waves breaking white on the beach. In about five hundred yards, the water darkened again. Radar clear. The depth sounder showed twenty feet, then thirty, then dropped off to two hundred fathoms just that quick. I turned back onto course for Thacher's Light. The noise of the breakers faded off my stern and the fog cleared. To this day I have no idea what that piece of land was nor why it didn't show on the radar.

About two hours later a spot appeared and grew into a Novi boat almost a carbon copy of mine. Four men were jigging with poles, having spent some time on the water I knew what they were doing and pulled right up to them.

"Ya going where?" the captain said wide-eyed.

After some brief pleasantries and a reaffirmation of my course I was underway again with a three foot long haddock I planned to cook on the small barbecue I had brought. They also tossed me a liter of Bacardi rum, unopened. Fishermen take care of fishermen. I thought, what the hell? Anybody could run a new boat across the Gulf of Maine sober. And I had plenty of Coke to mix with it.

A short time later I stopped dead in the water and brought down the Maple Leaf and raised the Stars and Stripes. The Black Sheep was an American fishing vessel and would fly the appropriate flag. The Maple Leaf flies over my bed to this day.

Eight hours and eighty or so miles later it was time to transfer the diesel from the fifty-five gallon drum to the fuel tank. I had brought a piece of hose for just that express purpose. Unfortunately, the hose I had brought for that express purpose was too short to reach from the top of the fifty-five gallon drum on my deck to my fuel tank. So, with about two gallons of fuel in my tank, one hundred miles at sea with all the fuel I would need to get home on board but unable to use, I took a brief moment for self evaluation. I have little or no patience with other people's stupidity and absolutely none with my own. It sounded something like this:

"You dumb, stupid, illiterate, brain-dead moron!"

I went on for a good ten minutes. Think, stupid, there is another way! Problem: get diesel from Point A to Point B, a mere six feet away.

Glug, glug. Poof. The engine died away. Out of fuel. Beautiful.

There is just something about being at sea, out of sight of land, and have your engine quit, even when you know why, that really gets your attention and just fucks up the moment. It's the loudest quiet I've ever heard. One of the really great things about fishing alone is that you can make a complete fool of yourself without witnesses and then get back to the problem. So, now that little Marky has had his nutty, it's back to reality.

Problem: the hose is too short to reach from an upright fuel drum to the fuel intake hole.

Solution: Put the drum on its side and use a rag as a gasket to keep the fuel from escaping from around the hose which is considerably narrower than the drum hole. The cloth was rigged and the hose inserted. The drum was lowered and secured to keep it from rolling around the deck, never a good thing.

I stood up and surveyed the situation. Way ahead, off my port, I saw a very big boat. Smoke billowed from his stacks as he steamed left to right. He grew bigger and bigger approaching my bow at a small angle. It was a very large container ship with a bow twenty times the height of mine. White water continually churning up in front of the phallic thing jutting from the bow. It looked like a big dick continuously coming off. I looked in all directions. Great, a big ship headed my way and me with no fuel. Fucking perfect.

In order to get the fuel flowing, I knelt taking the hose into my hand to begin the siphoning or draining of the drum into my tank. I began to suck on the length of garden hose, something that was a novel experience for me contrary to the accusations of a few females from Gloucester (mostly the ugly, divorced ones I wasn't interested in). I proved to be pretty inept at this, no doubt from my lack of experience, and couldn't get the fuel moving. Damn. Where was good old Debbie Do-It when I really needed her? That girl could suck a basketball through a garden hose.

I sucked on that hose for all I was worth. Nothing. I took a good sized wave amidship and the barrel rolled a little. Whoosh! I had a mouthful of fuel and swallowed. It was a less than enjoyable experience. I barely got the hose into my filler hole before I went into uncontrollable convulsions throwing up. I hadn't projectile vomited since I was a kid—it really bites. I rolled around on the deck purging my stomach for an eternity. All I could think of were the old war films of guys being rescued from torpedoed ships covered in diesel oil. Still lying on my back, I forced myself to roll onto my stomach in case I passed out so I wouldn't suffocate if I threw up again—a lesson from the Perch long ago.

Damn. The big ship was getting closer. He was the only ship in any direction on this expanse of ocean and he was headed right at me. Really great timing.

Unable to read his name I managed to get to the radio and hail him on the universally monitored Channel Sixteen. No reply. I let loose with a barrage of unpleasantries and shot him the universal sign of ill will. He continued to bear down on me. At about one hundred yards I blasted my air horn, at a combined speed of about sixteen knots, we closed rapidly. He grew bigger and he towered above me. I had no idea who legally had the right of way but having spent countless hours dodging blow boats and other toys outside of Gloucester on Sunday afternoons, I, like all fishermen who survive any amount of time, know the most important rule of running a boat at sea. The rule that has been around since the wind was the only source of power—the rule that supersedes all others—is the rule of gross tonnage. It goes something like this: when two boats approach each other and you're on the smaller boat, in this case, much smaller boat, the smaller boat gets the fuck out of the way of the bigger boat. Simple. I swung the boat hard over to the right to get the Christ out of the way. Almost at the same time his bow swung to the left. The prick was trying to run me down. The captain had taken umbrage with me. Only I could run into a boat in the middle of the ocean and piss someone off enough to run me down in so short a time.

Because his turn radius was a little larger than mine I managed to run all the way down his port and into the prop wash off his stern. I put the Sheep in neutral, walked out on the deck as the Sheep was kicked around vertically, horizontally and laterally by the turbulent water. There is no rhythm whatsoever to this kind of movement and the only people who can keep their footing in it are those fishermen who spend their lives dealing with classic Mass Bay Slop.

I was greeted, high above, by yelling in a language that I did not understand, and very obscene hand and body gestures that I did. I was taken aback and gestured back with my left hand making what is called in Gloucester "a minge" and pointing at my crotch with the index finger of my other hand. I had no idea what flag he was flying and several of the letters of the name on his stern were rusted out. The brown-skinned men high above me continued to gesture as the turbulence slowed and stopped, the boat likewise slowed and stopped about one hundred yards away. Finally it hit me. The remaining letters on the boat spelled "Moronia". An old episode of the Three Stooges came rushing back. I had a Coke and picked up the radio mike. Suddenly my father's words of long ago flashed through my mind.

"Ma-AH-k, with that mouth of yours it is perhaps a good idea that you learn to shoot and shoot well."

I yelled into the mike. "You guys are from Moronia, is that right?"

I got a reply back in broken English. "What you say, America?"

"It must be tough," I said, "when you guys enter a waterfront bar and have to tell everyone that you are from Moronia and are a bunch of Morons. Boy, that's got to suck." I just kept going. "Or when you go to a party and someone yells, 'Look everyone, the Morons are here.' You guys must get in a lot of fights."

A bunch of garbled gibberish crackled over the radio.

"How the hell would one of you introduce the rest of you? 'Hi, I'm Achmed and these are my friends. We're all Morons.'"

The ships' huge prop, which was halfway out of the water began to turn and suck back water towards itself. It was turning counter-clockwise and as the ship began to move backwards it dawned on me that the prick was trying to back over me. I downed the whole Coke and slammed the throttle all the way forward. I headed dead away from him as he gained speed slowly.

Oh Jeesus! I had about a football field on him. It took him some time but, little by little, he began to gain on me to the cheers of the greasy-looking, dark-faced men with those stupid towels wrapped around their heads, standing on the stern far above me.

So, a hundred miles at sea with a very large boat bearing down on me, loaded with a bunch of seriously pissed off men, fully intent on running me down and killing me, things got really bad. Fog rolled in. I calmly screamed into the mike something to the effect of, "Gloucester Fishing Vessel Black Sheep to any vessel—HELP!!!"

I jammed the throttle all the way forward. The loran read nine knots. The big, ugly boat and its very large propeller, half out of the water and spinning, gaining on me—slowly but steadily. I cut left. So did he. I cut right and so did he. He continued to close with the steady "whooch-whooch" of the prop getting louder with every passing second. The noise seemed to reverberate all over the Sheep. At about a football field away his speed topped out and he began to close faster. I checked the radar. Nothing. Right about this time I was trying to control my puckering butt and to not pee. I got on the radio and called them every nasty, vile name I could think of, then called for help again.

Just a scant first down away the whooshing of the prop drowned out my screaming. Water splashed down, drenching the Black Sheep. I was just about to close my eyes when the sound of the monstrous prop stopped. The radio came to life.

"Gloucester Fishing Vessel Black Sheep, this is the U.S. Naval Vessel on your starboard. Do you require assistance?"

As I pulled away from the tanker I looked to my right and sitting there was the sleekest, gray colored U.S. Navy Boat that ever existed. It had all kinds of weird angles on it and looked like it had come from the future. Modern Navy Boats don't look nearly as sleek as the World War II boats, like the Cassin Young docked next to Old Ironsides in Boston Harbor. But I was still glad to see it.

"Hell, yeah," I yelled into the mike. "This big guy is picking on me. He was matching my speed about 200 yards off."

For some reason I could hear what was being said on the bridge of the destroyer—or whatever it was.

"X.O. I cannot abide a bully."

"No, sir, neither can I."

"I'll have general quarters. War alert. No drill."

"Yes, sir."

The clanging of the General Quarter's claxon blasted around the cabin of the Sheep even over my cheers. White-clad Navy guys were running ass-over-elbows all over the boat. Four missiles appeared out of nowhere and into their launchers fore and aft. They were spun to train on the tanker. The rapid-fire cannon located in the middle of the boat turned left and was trained on the freighter. Two Gatling Guns swung into position. The whole port side of the ship was lined with helmeted sailors holding black M16s. I came out on my deck cheering and waving and the sailors were waving back. I picked up the radio mike and yelled into it in a very adult manner.

"Way to go, asshole, you've got the most powerful military force in the world, the U.S. Navy, pissed at you! You are, like, so fucked."

I guess it was out of some type of defiance or a plain death wish but the prop on the freighter began turning again as smoke belched from his stack. The freaking idiot in an old rust tub was actually dumb enough, one hundred miles at sea without the rest of the world as witnesses, to screw with the testosteroned-out Captain of a United States Navy Warship. I poured another Coke and relaxed.

"Captain of what appears to be the Vessel Moronia, cease your rearward movement!"

The reply sounded suspiciously like, "Fuck you, America."

It was just getting better by the moment. I'm far from the brightest bulb on the tree but I could see the next move. The radio lit up.

"X.O., can we have the rapid-fire put a few rounds safely off the stern of that idiot?"

"I should think so, sir."

"Do it."

"Yes, sir, and how many rounds would my captain like fired?"

"What do you think, Number One?"

"Three would probably suffice but five would definitely make a statement. The shells are quite expensive, sir, taxpayer dollars, you know."

"X.O., did I hear that zipper brain tell me to go fuck myself?"

"Yes, Captain. A rather crude attempt but I believe that was his intent."

"Let's spend some tax dollars, Number One. Three inch, five rounds and five rounds only, as close on that prop as you dare without hitting it, Number One."

"Three inch, aye."

Wham. Wham. Wham. Wham, wham. Just off the freighter' stern geysers of water shot fully fifty feet in the air. I was pissing myself laughing as I cheered along with all of the Navy guys. The boys on the freighter were some quiet. It was to no avail. That big old prop kept turning as the freighter moved backward toward me.

"X.O., it would seem this gentleman is not getting the message."

"Yes, Captain, that would seem to be true."

"Well, now, that is just downright unacceptable behavior, wouldn't you say, X.O.?"

"I most certainly would, Captain."

"I'll have five rounds rapid-fire from the five inch over the bridge, if you would, Number One."

"Very good, sir."

Wham. Wham. Wham. Wham, wham. The shells screeched by just above the bridge. I continued to laugh but the moron from Moronia continued to bear down on me.

"Number One, I am beginning to lose my patience and my sense of humor."

"Quite understandable all things considered, Captain."

"Number One, am I perchance acting a bit hastily?"

"Sir, I believe the Captain has exhibited a virtual mountain of patience, sir. You have been a bastion of diplomacy."

"X.O., is that not a foreign-flagged freighter attempting to run over a U.S. flagged vessel?"

"Yes, Captain, I would most whole-heartedly agree with your assessment of the situation."

"Ask the chief if he can knock down his mast with one round."

"Captain, the senior chief said he could knock down his mast on his very worst day while intoxicated."

"Very well, X.O. Tell him to fire when ready. One round, one round alone."

A few seconds later the five-inch fired once and impacted the very base of the mast on top of the bridge. It toppled like a tall tree falling to the deck aft, sending little brown men scattering in all directions screaming. The Navy guys were laughing loudly and whistling. The prop finally stopped and began spinning the other way as the freighter slowly began to move forward away from me. When he was a mile or so away, the Navy boat hailed me.

"Black Sheep, are you okay?"

"Hell, yeah," I screamed into the mike. "Thanks a million!!!"

"We intend to send a Zodiac over to you for a parlay. Is that okay?"

"Hell, yes, and welcome."

"Is there anything we can bring you?"

"Well, yea. Ice, some food and that three inch gun in case I run into any fucking boats from Moronia."

I heard laughing.

"We'll see what we can scare up and be over in about fifteen. Roger."

"I'll be right here, Navy boat."

The gray Zodiac was at my starboard side a short time later. Two officers and two sailors came aboard. We shook hands all around. The officers were the Captain and his Executive Officer.

"You guys want a Bacardi and Coke?"

"Absolutely," the Captain nodded.

I mixed three drinks, one for myself and for each of the officers. The two sailors looked at their captain longingly.

"Are you guys old enough to drink?" he asked them.

"No, sir," they chorused despondently.

"Sir," I spoke up, "am I to understand that these individuals are old enough to fight and die for their country but not old enough to drink?"

The Captain of the Black Sheep had two instant admirers.

"That does seem a bit stupid," said the captain. He nodded toward the huge bottle of rum and the seamen grabbed it and mixed two drinks—which were about 50-50 as I recall.

They produced a bag of ice from the duffle bag they had brought and in no time we all stood on deck with drinks.

"A toast," I said. "To the brave men of Torpedo Squadron 8."

"Here, here," all the sailors chorused. We all drank heartily.

"Sir," said one of the sailors to his captain, "what was Torpedo Squadron 8?"

"Shame on you, son. At the Battle of the Midway they found the Jap Carriers and attacked without fighter cover. It was a suicide attack and all but one pilot died. It is said that one of the Japanese captains said, 'They tell me that these Americans are decadent and poor fighters but these men fought like Samaris. I fear this will be a long war.' Five minutes later the American dive bombers arrived high above with all the Jap fighters at wave height shooting down the torpedo planes. They sank four carriers in a matter of minutes. That was the beginning of the end for the Empire of Japan in the Pacific. You need to read more than Playboy and Penthouse, young man."

More drinks were made and with a Navy warship as a backdrop we had a fine little cocktail party in the middle of the ocean. They even brought some cheese and crackers. I had some fine roast beef sandwiches with lettuce, tomato and mayo that the cook had thrown in for me. Then the captain took me aside. He led me into my cabin in front of my radar.

"Would you look at this radar and tell me what you see?"

I did and saw the blip of the freighter a few miles away and nothing else. Brilliant bastard that I am it became blazingly apparent how the Navy had appeared from nowhere—it didn't show up on the radar!

"I need you to do me a favor, Cap," he said. "I need you not to tell anyone about this for a year or so."

"Done," I replied. And I wouldn't. Like Pop said, if someone does you bad, you do them worse. If someone does you good, you do them better.

After a few more drinks and many more thanks the Navy went on its way, probably looking for more Gloucester fishermen to save. And I headed on my merry way...

I came to and rolled onto my back looking up at the big, old, fluffy white clouds overhead. The wind had picked up and the water was lapping against the hull as I lay on my back in the middle of the Gulf of Maine. I got to my knees and there on the back of the boat a big seagull sat looking at me stupidly like they always do. The smell of vomit and diesel was overpowering as the now-empty barrel rolled back and forth with the rocking of the boat. After a couple of deep breaths, I managed to stand. I felt like I had expelled my entire stomach during my convulsions and was starving. I capped off the fuel tank and ran for the haddock.

It was filleted in no time. I quickly hosed down the deck and fired up the barbecue. Two eighteen inch pieces of pure white haddock were soon on the grill being heated up—the only way to cook fresh fish.

While the fish cooked I returned to the cabin and heated the fuel with a glow plug before trying to fire off the diesel. It wouldn't start. Of course. Naturally. Instead of pulling another nutty, I decided on a more concrete course of action—I mixed a Bacardi and Coke, very light on the Coke. That would either make things better or worse and at that point I didn't much give a shit. I was high on one drink resulting in a much needed attitude adjustment. I cranked the engine again. Nothing. Okay, think. It has plenty of fuel and battery, why won't it start?

I sat at the stern with nothing but water in every direction and ate a perfectly scrumptious, moist, snow-white fish washed down with more Bacardi and Coke as I pondered the situation. Think. It has fuel but it's not getting to the engine. Start at the fuel tank and work toward the engine. I got to the place where the fuel line connected to the engine and undid it. No fuel coming out. Oh, look, dumbbell, a little plunger just to the right. Brilliant mechanic that I am I surmised that it needed to be pumped. On the second push it was pumping fuel into the engine. The engine blasted to life with the first turn of the key.

Suddenly being one hundred miles at sea didn't seem like a big deal. The engine rumbled reassuringly and black smoke trailed from the stack, narrow at first then expanding, shaping into what appeared to be a horizontal tornado trailing back over the stern and beyond. The bow moved up and down in gentle four foot swells. The gulls floated by under drifting clouds and the Coca-Cola flowed. Water was everywhere, as blue as it could be. Dead ahead I saw a freaker approaching, amid the four footers this one was an easy ten, maybe twelve. I grabbed the wheel and quartered into it. The Sheep glided up gently. At the top I slowly rose to my toes from centrifugal force and the Sheep vibrated as the prop cavitated some, spinning on air, leveled out then slid back down the wave slick as snot. A far cry from my last boat. I got myself some boss Novi boat here, I thought. I didn't even spill my Coke.

All through that night I steamed, finally having to stop every hour or so to lie down for fifteen minutes. There is nothing quite like going below on a thirty-six foot Novi boat, trying to relax and wondering every minute if you are going to be run down by another boat. It is hardly conducive to sleep. By dawn I was a walking zombie.

Right about the time I thought I should begin to see land, another fog bank appeared in front of me. Naturally. I leaned forward like we all do as if an extra few inches would help me see land any sooner. As I entered the fog bank droplets began to form on every surface and to drip from my moustache. I had been dead reckoning since I left the Navy. How much had the wind and the current moved the boat when I stopped to nap? I was two hours beyond the time when I thought I should have sighted land. Lack of sleep had turned me into a worrier. The fog bank disappeared behind and still no land. Another cloud of fog appeared ahead out of nowhere. I flipped on the depth sounder. Forty fathoms. The bottom was coming up, a good sign. I figured I had to make land somewhere. I had a lot of cash on me so it didn't matter where I made landfall. I could just parallel the shore going right or left until I found a harbor or another boat to ask directions from. I started passing lobster buoys at thirty fathoms.

Bingo!!! A flashing red light miles away on my right! A three second interval between flashes. No way that was Thacher's Light! The twin lighthouses on Thacher's Island have been used by fishermen from the pre-electronic days of iron men in wooden ships. When you bring your boat around so the two lights are aligned you are on course, what we call "in range", exactly five and a quarter miles from Good Harbor Beach*—where I grew up. I'm headed right at the Williams Guest House. Home. Not bad for dead reckoning.

In minutes I turned left and ran down the Back Shore about five hundred yards off the rocks. A man standing near the building that is now owned by the Elks, dressed in a blue shirt and pants, waved at me. I waved back. My father. Only eight in the morning, Empire Fish Plant was a catastrophe that day you can be sure.

I steamed by a few boats lobstering. They looked at me wide-eyed, stopped work and waved. I turned right after the break-water. The scent of land was erotic after two days at sea. Even car exhaust smelled good. I put the Black Sheep on my mooring off of Pirates Lane and shut down the engine. The silence was bliss. I walked up into the parking lot of the North Shore Arts Association and past a pickup truck sitting there. The lobsterman sitting in it had not spoken to me ever, cranky old shit that he was.

"You bring that boat back yourself?"

"Yes."

"Trouble? You're way overdue."

"Stopped for drinks," I replied.

He smiled, tipped his hat, nodded his head and drove off.

The Customs Official showed up. He passed the Black Sheep from the lot sans inspection—I have friends everywhere. A bunch of them were pulling into the lot at that moment, laughing.

* *The description of "in range" was written for this book by Geoff Thomas, captain of F/V BlivyFish who passed away March 9, 2005.*

Afternoon of the Dolphin, Part 2

I've got nothing left.

I put up a good fight but I never really had a chance. The pain from the rope cinching my right leg is horrendous. Below the knot my leg and foot are grossly swollen and bloody. Blood flows across the deck. The pain fills my entire body causing me to scream as each wave crests shooting the boat up. I've lost. I just want to die. I'm losing my grip on the stern, I can barely manage to stay on the boat and am growing weaker by the second. I stare at the knife—so near and yet so far away. Time just slows down, oh so slow. But the mind—it keeps on racing.

I've taken calculated risks most every day of my adult life. Sometimes under water, sometimes surrounded by her or in a boat sitting on her. It's got nothing to do with brave, I just chose to work in professions where extraordinary situations could and did occur. I've always survived. I had a real good teacher. My father. He taught me from the time I was a lad to pause, think, to not panic when the shit contacts the fan. Mostly I was just lucky. Death has always been around me. She's always been there, oh, so close waiting for one mistake. She's beguiling, erotic and so enticing. The North Atlantic—death—she can turn on you in a heartbeat. She's a heartless bitch and loves to kill men any way she can.

I've never really faced her, death. I jigged and she missed. I jagged and she took someone else. She missed again and again. So many of my friends died of AIDs but, like the poor marksman she is, she just kept missing me. It wasn't bravery or a staunch belief in a superior being... or clean living. Please. It was just plain dumb luck. It was just that simple. Luck is all.

I've turned the corner around Dogbar Breakwater and into the North Atlantic in the late Fall and early Winter again and again. I'd enter the graveyard and try, with respect, to remember the thousands of Gloucester men who have fished here before me and died. During the

Civil War it was safer to be on the battlefield at Gettysburg than it was to be a Gloucester man at sea. Fishermen were classified 4F during World War II—most served anyway. Day after day, year after year, I spend the day in white water that most people wouldn't even pass through, let alone spend the day in. I fished mostly by myself, never acknowledging, never admitting, that the ocean I made my living on could kill me at any time in a myriad of different ways, no matter how close it came to cancelling my ticket. That's how you handle a dangerous situation. It's simple—it's just not going to happen to me. Someone else will die.

The real Gloucester men died by the thousands. These were my Grandfather's generation. Boat after boat went down with all hands, simply disappearing from the face of the earth. Did they keep returning to the sea out of bravery? Nope. Eternal optimism, that advanced human trait, has allowed normal men to take incredible risks since the first of us brought back food to the cave. They and all their brothers truly believed that the other guy was the one who would end up being squeezed out of the butt of a Sabre-toothed Tiger. Random chance. Most fishermen are tough guys and revel in risk taking—I'm no different than most. It's always going to be the other guy who dies.

This time random chance has gotten around to me. There are no odds left for me. The pain is unbearable, my strength is nearly gone. I manage to stay in the boat as something courses through my brain—that small, insignificant, minor influencing factor in all of human history... is there a God?

I was little when I asked my father that question. He lowered his glasses and took a knee in front of me.

"I once listened to an atheist explain that there was no God," he told me. "He said that long ago a bunch of chemicals had somehow been combined and started the evolutionary path that led to the creation of man. You understand that?"

I nodded.

"Well, then my question to him would be, where exactly did the chemicals come from? Nothing comes from nothing," he said raising his hands. "You understand?"

I nodded again. It was the most simplistic yet logical explanation for the existence of a Being or Intelligence way beyond human ability that I ever heard. It's totally devoid of any religious bullshit. Short, to the point, and extremely difficult to argue against. It's what I call a reverse explanation. It's not how can God exist but rather how can He not exist.

I listened to some guy call the creation of man "spontaneous generation". He claimed it was like the maggots that appear in piles of horseshit spontaneously, out of nowhere. The dummy used this as an analogy to how man just appeared out of nowhere without a God. He never mentioned the flies who laid their eggs in the crap.

He laughed. "I have known some people who act like they were created in a pile of shit." He laughed again.

Nothing comes from nothing—that explanation of creation is well and good. Something beyond us had to get it all started.

Myself, I never had a problem that there was a power far above my ability to understand it. I have, on occasion, taken issue with many of those purporting to be His earthly representative. I have no use for the Jesus-people who use the words "God" and "Jesus" every third word like soldiers use the word "fuck". I have no use for the people who O.D. on the Lord. Every one of them I have met has turned out to be a hypocrite and I really hate hypocrites.

But a long time ago, when I was young and dumb, I actually saw Him. Yeah, that's right. I saw God. Of course, I didn't know it at the time but it was definitely Him—the apparition of God on Earth in human form.

Toward the end of summer lifeguards everywhere have spent too many days in the sun. After a week long stretch of sunshine we would do rain dances or call up people who seed clouds—anything to get a rainy day. It was finally a cloudy day on Wingaersheek Beach. There were four of us guards on duty. Only a few people were on the beach. Three of us played poker and the fourth guard patrolled the beach paying special attention to those parts hidden from the guard shack by the rocks.

The tide was out and, with the gradual incline of the beach, it was ten times as big at low tide as it was at high. Wingaersheek is one big beach at low tide. The current from the Annisquam River scoured out a pool behind one of the largest rocks. The pool was a good thirty feet in diameter and dropped off gradually to about six feet in the middle. It was there that I was to see God.

I had just drawn a third queen to the two I already had when we heard yelling. We were all up and looking for its source. The roving guard emerged from behind another rock at a dead run, headed toward the tidal pool, blasting on his whistle, dropping his white safari hat and hurling his red jacket high in the air—all signs that something was terribly wrong.

Hats and jackets were airborne in a heartbeat. Three of us headed right at the pool. I was ahead of the other two, about twenty yards from the pool, when the rover hit the water. As I closed on the pool I could see an unrecognizable object seeming to float in the middle. I slid to a halt at the edge and there He was—God. All that was visible of Him were His hands and arms. He was holding his little sister above the water's surface. He was totally submerged—drowning. Even though he was about to die he still held his baby sister above the water. I hit the water swimming, head up, eyes locked on the victim as I'd been taught. Just as Guard #1 reached her, the arms collapsed. The girl fell into the water, screaming. Guard #1 grabbed her as the arms disappeared from sight. He pointed down as he treaded water holding the girl. I grabbed her brother on the first dive. As I surfaced with him the two reinforcements arrived. We swam the boy to the beach. He was breathing on his own before we had him out of the water. He said his sister stepped in over her head and began drowning and he went after her. The catch was, he couldn't swim a stroke but nothing was going to hurt his baby sister, he told me. All he could do was stand on the bottom and hold his sister out of the water. He had no idea we were on the way. Four lifeguards were awed by his audacity.

In three years as a commercial diver and almost twenty as a Gloucester fisherman, it is not that I have never seen such a display of selflessness and courage. It is that I've never heard of one without wondering if maybe God appears on earth from time to time and manifests Himself in this manner to show us that He really does exist. All it takes is some brilliant bastard like myself, who only took twenty years to figure out exactly what it was he witnessed that day and pass it on. Maybe it's just that simple. It don't take religion, it don't take education, it don't take philosophy or a strong belief in the hereafter. It sure don't take using the word "God" five times in every sentence. Maybe it just takes the good luck to be a witness to, or the courage to be a part of, someone willing to die to save someone else. Someone willing to "lay down his life for his brother". Perhaps every time one of these instances occurs the human race takes a little step farther on the evolutionary plane to wherever we are supposed to be evolving to.

Oh, what the hell. I'm not far from finding out about dying myself.

Her job was to watch people die. She said she was a cancer nurse—Kathy, I think her name was. Her job was to tell people they had terminal cancer, that there was no mistake in the diagnosis, and they were going to die. Cheery work I'd say. Kathy, like most nurses, was paid about a third of what she was worth. Nurses put up with blood, guts, death, psychological damage and egotistical, demagogic doctors. Doctors deal in life and death with their actions seldom being questioned—no wonder they get a little weird. Kathy would enter the room and tell the person in it that he or she was going to die. She really felt for them at first but over time her self-defense mechanisms kicked in. She would enter the room with a sullen face, give them the bad news, reassure them there was no mistake—they were, in fact, going to die—cry with them for a time, close the door on exiting and return to the nurse's station. There she could laugh with her friends as if nothing had happened. She developed quite the mechanical self-protection. What choice did she have? That was one mentally tough female.

Many times she was at their bedside when they died. Sometimes she was the only one in the room. She said that she could feel some sort of life force leave the room when they passed. She talked, as if awed, by the unseen, soundless, but very real physical entity that departed the room as each person died—a force, a soul, if you will. Maybe there is a life force in everyone and when the body dies, maybe it passes to another person. Or to heaven. Or to hell. Maybe I'll find out soon enough.

It is the middle of the afternoon a few miles off Good Harbor Beach where I grew up. Where I lived most of life. I am about to die in full view of it. It begins to rain and I am losing strength. I don't want to die. Please, God! I don't want to die! The waves intensify and I am screaming. Screaming for help. Please, someone save me! I scream for my mother and my father. Oh God, please save me... I know I am groveling. I have become the thing I hate most—a groveling hypocrite. It is a terrible thing to behold. But there is one inevitable truth when you know it is over, there is no John Wayne. John Wayne exited the stern of the Black Sheep. Big tears run down my face as I scream and lose control of my bladder. Adrenaline pumps through me and I grasp the stern and then just as quickly lose my grasp. Mark Williams, coward. Mark Williams, Gloucester fisherman. Mark Williams whose name is going on that wall in City Hall. I gasp, sobbing, the will to live is so strong. My mind flashes to the walls in Gloucester's City Hall where the thousands of names are written. Mine will be there, too, right below Sully and the boys from the Andrea Gail.

I met Sully once. He was drunk in a bar called Halibut Point. He had just hit shore after a trip. Sully was a happy drunk, just kind of wandering around swilling a big old draft and bumping into people good naturedly. I didn't know him, I turned my back to him and he smacked into me. I spilled most of my beer all over my chest and his beer slopped onto my back. I turned around and we squared off. The bar went quiet as we eyed each other up and down and the tension grew. All movement ceased. Hostilities were eminent. Sully cracked a smile from ear to ear. He took what was left of my beer and, reaching up, poured it over his own head. The nhe poured his own on himself as well. I laughed. He stuck his hand out and I shook it. Noise slowly returned to the bar as he ordered two more beers.

Instead of two fishermen engaging in close-quarter hand-to-hand, we drank and talked and smoked cigarettes and tried to screw every female within reach. As I recall, we were both successful, at any rate it was an improvement over beating the shit out of each other. Haven't we evolved? From preferring to settle differences with violence to drinking, talking, and getting laid.

Sully died a short time later. Weather-nuked by the Perfect Storm.

It starts in the very tips of my toes. It feels like high voltage electricity as it surges up my legs and encompasses my whole body. It reverberates through my entire existence and I get high. The highest of highs. The mother of all highs. From somewhere in the D.N.A. that's been passed on to me for millions of years the will to survive surges. I force myself to breathe long and slow, striving for that rush of adrenaline that gives me the strength for one more try at the knife. In between great breaths of air I hear screaming. Is that me screaming? I am screaming at the Almighty.

"I'm not dying today, you hairy faced prick! I'm not going quietly into the night or any of that shit. If you want me, dick-face, you're going to have to do better than this! You want me? You come down here and get me!"

Insane actions are understandable in insane situations. I began smacking my head on the stern of the boat. I went totally berserk blotting out everything but the knife. I saw nothing but the knife. I didn't see the birds or the hear the rumble of the diesel. The knife is life. You reach the knife, you live. You don't, you're a dead man. It's just that simple.

My head started bobbing up and down again. This time I am not groveling. Quite the opposite. I begin laughing.

You grubbling, pussy-assed baby, are you going to cry some more? Is your little chinny going to bob up and down? Maybe you can shit your pants this time, are you going to call for your mommy again? Well, pussy, are you? Are you a Gloucester fisherman or not?

Yes, I fucking AM!

I blasted out and away from the stern, removing my hands from the lip to which I have clung for over an hour. Holding on has kept me alive but now it is all or nothing. But my efforts land me inches short of the knife. With my chest heaving and scream-ing for all I am worth I stretch my arm as far as I can. In wicked slow motion my index and middle finger strain across the deck just touching it. The knife moves ever so slightly when—WHAM! I am slammed backward straight into the stern. The drag of the line blasts me upright and, as if fired from a cannon, I am yanked up and then slammed down across the stern, every bit of breath knocked out of me. I gasp. In three monstrous breaths, I fill my lungs. Suddenly, violently, I am catapulted out of the boat. I fly over the stern and into the water hitting it feet first. My traps drag me down five feet where I suddenly stop and hover. The cloud of bubbles from my catastrophic entry into the water clear and I can see the prop of the Sheep turning counterclockwise above me. The next trap hits the water and I am dragged lower still facing my boat above me. Again I am hanging, waiting for the next trap to leave the boat. For the briefest of moments I stare at the rudder. Curious, I just changed the zincs and they're half gone already.

Yank! I am being drawn down farther, slowly. I look down into the darkness and fight the urge to kick for the surface. I am aware that any movement, particularly one that is a strain, will hasten my end and I have vowed to stay alive as long as possible. As bad as it is I'm not quitting yet.

The bottom of the Sheep gets smaller. I look up at it moving away. I figure it is the last thing I will see on this earth. I fight the impulse to breathe. For someone who has spent thousands of hours under water, it's simple. It's the opposite of being on the surface where to breathe is to live. Underwater to breathe is to die. As poor as my chances are of all the lobstermen I know, I have the best chance of surviving this.

As the trawl line sinks deeper the traps to my left and to my right move downward faster dragging me with them. JUST FUCKING LOVELY! My own traps dragging me alone underwater in the darkness—all of man's greatest fears coming together. The water turns from light blue to dark blue to a brownish black. I pinch my nose and clear my ears as if a pair of blown eardrums are my biggest problem.

The cold of the water eases the pain in my torn and bleeding leg but I am nearing the bottom. I hold my hands out as though pleading, someone help me! A gentle thumping begins in the middle of my head. I look at the trap on my left, my mind racing. I pull on the groundline but there is no slack. Same with the trap on my right, no good. That trap has landed upside down. I never thought of that—that must be why in a trawl of loaded pots one comes up empty. They don't fish when they land upside down. After fifteen years of fishing you finally figured it out, Mark. Great timing—real useful now. Way to go, Mark old boy.

Having passed through thermoclines the water is very cold. The thumping in my head is pounding now. Think, boy, think. Don't give in yet. My eyes ache as the pounding intensifies. I hit the bottom and mud mushrooms up around me. The nylon rope holds taut. I lunge toward the surface but it snaps me back and I boomerang down among the rocks. Breathe, my mind screams, just end it.

No!

It's over. Everybody goes some time. I'm dead. Just breathe and get it over.

No! I'm no quitter.

He's there. In twenty fathoms of water he's there in front of me in his blue uniform with T-E-D written over the pocket. He's been dead for years but now he's there smiling at me. Tapping his temple.

He mouths the word, "Think."

I stare at him and he glances down at my feet. I follow his gaze. There among the rocks at the bottom is a glitter. Glass. A bottle. A wine bottle—how appropriate. Adrenaline pumps through me and I lunge for it. One last chance at life. I grab it and smash it against a rock.

No, motherfucker, it ain't over until it's over and I'm not dead yet. I hack maniacally at the rope around my leg. The old man stands there smiling, pumping his fist. I slash at the rope cinched around my leg with total abandon, mindless to the inky dark clouds of my blood blooming around me. I can't even feel the glass cutting my leg. I'm on fire from the inside out. The pain is a thousand times worse than any case of the bends I ever had but I have a chance. Jesus, help me. Anyone, help me. I can't hold on any longer. My head is exploding, I'm burning up from the inside. I bend my legs and push off from the bottom. I've got to get out of here! One last crazy, futile try for the surface. I hurtle upward but the line yanks me back. Then, just as suddenly, it parts. As if by magic I'm free.

It's as if a dam above my ankle bursts and life flows back into my foot. But there is very little life left in me. Suddenly I am back in the creek in back of Good Harbor Beach in front of my house.

The water was over my head. I was little and couldn't swim. I was located exactly where my father had thrown me, that's how one learned to swim at 136 Bass Avenue. Our house borders on water at high tide. It was a good idea for small boys to know how to swim.

"Swim!" he bellowed. My head popped up out of the water.

"Reach your hands out, cup the water, and pull it to you." I did as told.

"Good! Now kick your feet. Excellent! You're swimming! Way to go!"

Now, over a hundred feet under the water, his voice roars at me from so long ago.

I point my head upward at the light and kick for all I am worth. Unfortunately, I'm worth very little. Voices seem to be shouting at me in some type of English I can barely understand. More voices. More yelling—in Italian, in Portuguese, in English that I recognize. Voices all different but all with the same message, "Swim! Live! Make the surface!"

Fishermen, thousands of them, urging me on. I have no life force left, my arms are limp at my sides and I can't kick. I'm burning up from the inside out. My head is banging long past unbearable. I'm dead and have been for minutes now, just too damn stubborn to give in to the urge to breathe. It's dark and I am alone far below the surface. It's so easy to just let go. It's so easy to give up and, ever so gently take in that clear, cold water—flowing into my mouth just like cool autumn New England air. It slides down my throat, salty, but like soft chocolate ice cream on a hot August afternoon.

Instead of filling my stomach it fills my lungs. The crispy coolness spreads out through my whole body, cooling it, cooling the fire raging through me. Turning it to ice. It rolls down my legs and out my arms. It extinguishes the fire and stops the banging in my head. It takes the hurt away. The salty, comforting chocolate eases all the pain and soothes me. The cold water filling me becomes my best friend. It is like the aftermath of an orgasm making me drowsy and gently, ever so gently, I slip downward into sleep.

It's so easy to die underwater.

I know. I did it—I just let go.

SMASH!

It hits me right under the sternum. It drives in and up knocking every bit of water out of my lungs. My eyes snap open. With pain and shock I am jolted back to life. Grayish blue shapes swish all around me. They move in close surrounding me. As the salt water erupts from my lungs, I gasp and there is air. There is oxygen! Right in front of my face, a bubble of oxygen has formed around me and I inhale instinctively. Even as I am bent in half from the pain of the blow my lungs are coming back to life as they fill with air.

That punch to the gut... I stumbled backward to a chair falling into it making the gurgling sounds you make trying to suck air fruitlessly into lungs devoid of air. Where did that punch come from?

It was the last time my father hit me. The gray shapes swirl around bumping against me, warm and insistent. A soft eye appears before me, looking at me, seeming to urge me upward. A baby eye . . . a baby dolphin eye looking right into mine.

When he played college football the only black man my father ever knew would miss key blocks resulting in Pop getting decked in the backfield. Hence, all black people were no good. I've known people on both sides of the color spectrum whose prejudices have been formed in this manner. And, on both sides of the color spectrum, I have found them in this manner of thinking to be too stupid to waste time talking to. Even extremely intelligent people can, in some instances, arrive at a conclusion that is totally stupid through flawed logic.

There are dolphins all around me. With them a mother and her baby. It was the mother dolphin that hit me. She smashed her snout into my solar plexus purging me of salt water.

Pop's granddaughter had just married a black Army captain and they pulled into the parking lot of 136 Bass Avenue. Aware of his views and always the unrepentant wise-ass I merely asked if he wanted me to get him a gun so he could shoot the blighter.

As the mother dolphin glides by me I feel the bubble of air touch my face and I breathe it in. I come alive.

When everyone came inside I was still incapable of speech. I managed a faint wave as I sat gurgling on the couch. My father was never a bigot after that day. A black man had become family and he changed just that quick. In my whole life I have never seen anyone do a one-eighty like that.

I grab her dorsal fin and she moves toward the light slowly. My grip is weak but she senses it and moves carefully. The baby swims ahead of her and keeps looking back as if encouraging me on. There are dolphins all around us. Dolphins with those big, soft, life-filled eyes. Tails swishing up and down gliding up with me and, as if sensing my state, they parallel in front of me exhaling air bubbles around me. It is surreal. I feel some strength returning as Mama Dolphin pulls me upward and the water turns from black to blue.

Williams folklore has it that as my niece and her new husband pulled away from our parking lot a certain Italian neighbor approached the old man and asked, "Was that a black man your granddaughter married?"

"It could have been a lot worse," my father is rumored to have retorted looking his neighbor up and down. "She could have married a guinea!" He laughed and walked away.

The water goes from dark to light. Just a few short feet of the surface, still more dead than alive, I begin to breathe water again. I let go of the Mama Dolphin and swim with everything I have. I come out of the water to my waist puking up water, exhaling and trying to suck in great gulps of air into lungs half full of water. One of Doug MacArthur's big old double-east buoys bobs in front of me and I grab it. I am literally breathing with two lungs half full of water. I spit up saltwater for what seems like hours, fighting the panic that comes when you can't take a full breath and clinging to the buoy.

As my body fills with air enough life force returns to my oxygen starved body and I manage to turn around. The Sheep is about twenty yards away, snagged on a buoy line, stern to the wind, motor stalled. I have a moment of exhilaration but it is fleeting. There is no way for me to climb back on board.

A year ago I fell out into the water climbing onboard the Sheep from the dingy. The dingy took off in the wind. I couldn't even come close to climbing back in the boat—it was just too damn high. And I was one hundred percent at the time. Now I am half dead.

Then, while I was in the water vainly trying to get back in the boat, the Coast Guard showed up in the forty-one. Thank Christ neither Chris or Moe was on duty. As they pulled up, five pairs of eyes intently studied the fully-clothed man hanging off the lobster boat.

"I've fallen and I can't get up," I quipped, mimicking a popular television commercial. I held my arms up.

They had me back on board in a jiffy. I had threatened to blow their boat up with them on it if they told either Chris or Moe and off they went. They ratted me out, of course.

I slowly swim toward the boat, dazed and unable to lift my arms out of the water. I barely make headway. Dolphins are swishing all around me on the surface. Some swim on their sides with one eye out of the water as though watching my progress. Suddenly there is a chorus of squeaking and just that quick I am alone. Weird.

I see the triangular fin first just above the gray shape directly in front of me. Moving toward me. Just beautiful. Blood from my torn and mangled leg trails through the water. Just what I need, a shark. Lovely.

It begins circling me, looking at me with those black, lifeless eyes. A shark. For Christ's sake, will this day never end? One way or the other? He isn't alone. I can feel another one smack into my leg, testing as sharks do.

Dumbass. The way I'm bleeding you'd think the son of a bitch would just chow down. I thought these things were eating machines, that they could distinguish food from other things miles off, sense a drop of blood in thousands of gallons of sea water and all that shit. It's bad enough to get eaten by a shark but by retarded sharks? Give me a break! That's insulting.

Hey, what happened to Mark?

He was ripped apart and eaten by brain dead sharks.

That's really got to suck.

I move in slow motion fully expecting to be ripped apart at any moment. I make the Sheep and grab onto the wood trim, a one by three inch trim that runs from the stern almost to the bow about two feet above the water line. I've made S.C.U.B.A. jumps off the boat for years when it was moored and I needed to clear a fouled prop. I'd lower a line over to tie my tank and weight belt to. With fins on it sometimes took two or three times to flip high enough to get over the rail of the boat. Now, in my present shape, sans fins, I have no chance. I'm dead again.

I cling to the trim by my fingertips as I get colder every

second. The hairs on the back of my neck stand up. I manage to turn and there is this big old shark making a run on me. I give up. What does it matter? At least getting eaten by a shark is faster than freezing to death. I've already come close to that. No thanks.

He is closing and I see his lower jaw pivot forward. At the same time my right foot rests on something solid. So does my left. I stiffen my legs automatically. I am propelled upward and just that fast the shark smashes into the side of the boat teeth scratching against the fiberglass like fingernails dragged down a blackboard before it falls away. That has to be the dumbest shark I've ever heard of. Leave it to me to run into a bunch of retarded sharks. Maybe they ate a bunch of tunas and swordfish with real high mercury levels.

Faster and faster I am rising up out of the water until I fly over the side of the Sheep, over the railing and onto the deck in a somersault, smacking my head and landing on my back. I struggle to sit up but pass out falling back and smacking my head again.

I dream of dolphins. Of it being cold and black and of not being able to breathe. I drifted up and up, the black turning to dark blue and breathing water and dying and grey shapes and a smash in the stomach. Dolphins. Dolphins everywhere and eyes, life-filled eyes. A resolve not to breathe an d not to die and swishing tails and bubbles. Bubbles or life-saving air and breathing underwater without a helmet on and no mouthpiece just bubbles and gliding up always holding onto a dolphin. Holding on for my life. And the dark blue turning lighter and smashing up out of the liquid medium and into the air and light and life and the Sheep waiting for me and the retarded sharks smashing into the Sheep and an express ride up, up and down and darkness again.

I wake up with a boat under me. Face up I struggle to sit up but slump back down on my back. High up, so high, billowing white clouds wafted by. Billowy and fluffy, twisting, oh, so white, and turning back on themselves like the froth of waves breaking on the beach. Gulls glide far below them. I can't hear anything and it feels as though with the loss of my hearing, my sight is magnified to the tenth degree.

I sit up groggily and a gull lands with a scratching thump on the cabin roof.

The wind is as noisy as thunder and it creates waves that hiss like eggs frying in oil. Thump, thump. The waves sound like a man kicking, as they bang into the Sheep. The screeching of the gull on my roof and of others floating over me is overpowering. My hearing is back.

I stand up and all my senses are alive like never before. Miles away on Good Harbor Beach I can almost see the faces of the people walking there. My brain begins slowly to focus on things and it hits me. It flows through me and to all parts of me like blood.

I AM ALIVE!

Above the sound of the gulls and the waves I hear another sound—dolphins clicking and squeaking. I stumble to the rail and, holding it, lean over. A short distance away two baby dolphins are being circled counter-clockwise by mature dolphins like Indians around a wagon train. Sharks are swimming outside the circle of dolphins. Whenever one of the sharks peels off and tries to penetrate the circle to get closer to a screaming baby one of the dolphins smashes into it. My head is spinning from my landing on the Black Sheep. Two dolphins peel off after a shark and leave a hole in the defense. A Mako slips through and bores down on the babies. There is no dolphin with an angle on the shark. The help-less dolphins begin to jump out of the water as if in frustration.

I black out. The next thing I remember is looking at the front blade half way up in the rear peep sight and the shark's left eye is perched on top of the blade and I track, my right index finger snaps the safety forward inside the trigger guard, and then pull the trigger back and the stock smashes into my right shoulder. The water around the shark's head turns white and erupts twenty feet into the air cascading down all over me. The shark continues on, passing out of the bullet churned water into the clear, trailing a stream of blood from a hole directly between his eyes. He continues on through inertia. Nothing on him moves. He's stone dead. He begins to nose down headed for the bottom, the stream of blood emanating from the thirty caliber hole in its head begins to thin but expands quickly, tornado shaped, behind the fish following it as it picks up speed on its way down.

All of the dolphins, as if on cue, stop cold and stick their heads out of the water looking at me with those kind eyes, gently turning their heads to the left and right. They talk back and forth for a moment, nodding their heads to one another and pointing their snouts at the boat and me. I swear they all nod at once. It is as if they collectively decided on a course of action.

They all go heads down and tail up and disappear. In just a few seconds a big old shark fin appears at the stern of the boat. Every time he tries to sound, the muffled thump, thump, thump of dolphins smacking into his belly and keeping him on the surface emanates like far off drums in an old Tarzan movie. One by one they begin driving sharks down the right side of the boat. The first one is a ten footer. He tries to sound but the dolphins smash into his belly keeping him on the surface. They control the shark easily—they are much faster and can maneuver more quickly. When he is parallel to me I raise the rifle, yell "clear" and, amazingly, all the dolphins disappeared with flicks of their tails. It's another easy head shot and another shark headed toward the bottom leaving a trail of blood.

I kill shark after shark as the dolphins herd them by me. Twice the empty clip springs from the M1 and is replaced. Finally there are no more sharks left and the deck is littered with golden 30 caliber casings rolling back and forth as the water gently moves the boat.

The misty rain that had been falling all day stops and the boat is surrounded by phins, talking to one another and nodding their heads. I stood on the trap table holding the M1 and it hit me again like a hammer—I'm alive and I shouldn't be! Oh how I shouldn't be. I begin dancing around with the rifle for a partner.

The sky fills up with big old dark clouds and it starts raining. I continue dancing around on the trap table. The phins start jumping all over the place in a celebration of life. I took such joy in just breathing great, deep breaths in and out. What a goof it was just to be able to breathe.

BA-BOOM! Thunder boomers start banging off so loud they hurt my ears. The sky lights up and goes back to dark and lights up again with another smashing blast. The wind blows as the water goes to white and the boat rocks. The noise is overpowering. The bolts were shooting over—some close—but the dolphins and I continue our celebration.

I am so high, flying. I've been as close to the other side as a person can go. There was nothing artificial about it. What I experienced is simply the highest state that exists anywhere on the planet. As suddenly as they began, the boomers turn off and the rain ceases. A ray of sunlight shoots through a hole in the black cloud cover and beams down like a searchlight right onto the boat illuminating the Sheep and the dolphins in the water surrounding her. A rainbow appears with a brilliant collage of colors. Everything is magical and surreal. Three of the dolphins slide by the boat on their tails as only dolphins can, three more fly over the boat silhouetted against the sky. A second, smaller rainbow appears in their splash as they re-enter the water and just as suddenly disappears. The mother and baby dolphin are there with their heads just above the water watching me. I sank down on one knee overwhelmed and awed, totally at peace with myself and with nature. I feel in some sort of union with the life force of all beings. I had been close to that before but never this close.

I lean over the side and reach out to the Mama dolphin and her baby. They let me touch them then flip backwards and disappear. I stay on my knees until the rainbow is gone. The dolphins squeak and leap and move away off into the water, schooled together, the Mama and baby among them.

Kneeling, dazed, overwhelmed, I stay motionless until the buzzing in my head reminds me that my body is addicted to nicotine. In all the excitement I have forgotten that. I rise and walk to the cabin to strip a Marlboro out of the pack. I inhale down to my shoes. It is the best smoke I have ever tasted or ever will again.

The ride home is a joy at the end of any day of lobstering. On this day the ride home is orgasmic. I keep reminding myself, "You're alive, you're alive." I keep shaking my head as though to clear it. Could this last hour really have happened?

As I round Dog Bar Breakwater with its blinking red light I see the statue of the Man at the Wheel on Stacey Boulevard facing out to sea. Beyond him on the hill are the towers of City Hall. I know exactly what I have to do. I have some thanks to give and I know where I have to go to do it. I have stops to make.

The Liquor Locker is first—for a bottle of Bacardi, a quart

of Coke and a bag of ice.

My father's grave is next.

I make two rum and Cokes—one for him and one for me—and drink both. I think of a year or so before his life came to an end. He was walking down a hospital corridor with my mother when he stopped and said to her in total sincerity, "I was fine until you made me stop drinking."

He died a short time later. Parkinson's Disease is not a good death.

If he hadn't been hard on me, the crabs would be eating my guts out right now.

The wind bangs northwest as it has since the beginning of time after the passing of a low. It rustles the leaves not fallen in early autumn. It blows dry, clean, and chilly. The rustling sound blends with the cars passing above. High above it blows thick white clouds fast making them thin out, stretching them almost transparent with white smoke rising.

A large plane is visible not making a sound. How the hell can those things fly, they're so heavy? I dumped rum over the ice in my glass, added a splash of Coke, and took a good slug. All in all it had been one hell of a day. The robins are running everywhere, stopping suddenly and straightening up like a statue before shooting forward again, spear-like, pulling their heads back, and swallowing a worm whole as only robins can do.

A crow screams by, its wings squeaking with every up and down movement, feathers rustling, with a mockingbird, one fourth its size, in hot pursuit. The crow looks at me with wide, frightened eyes, scared shitless by the relentless pursuit of its much smaller adversary. If I know anything about birds, that crow earned the ill will of Mr. Mockingbird as well as this pursuit.

I really like mockingbirds. They take no shit from anyone. Like me. Below the clouds, above the trees a large-winged hawk floats. Two more crows appear, one above, one below the hawk. They twist and turn and try to get on his six as if they had machine guns to shoot him down with like ME109s and B17s sixty years ago. I gaze at his tombstone long and hard.

"Thanks, Pop," is the most eloquent thing I can muster.

On the way out of Calvary I pass by Buddy Muniz, then

Mark S. Williams

Duke Leland Ryan and his wife. I nod.

"Goodbye, Duke and Gert," I say to my father's good friends.

I have other people to thank. Lots of them.

Gloucester is the pizza capital of the civilized world. I stop at Delaney's just as they are about to close for the day and pick up a linguica, pepper, and mushroom pizza to take with me. Not surprisingly I am ravenous and no food ever tasted better.

I drive to City Hall.

I was born in Gloucester and grew up here. Like most people, I take my heritage for granted just like we take the incredible seascapes for granted. You see them every day. But from this day forward that is changed. As I climb the steps of City Hall I know that I will always be acutely aware of those fishermen who have gone before me.

I enter City Hall with my bag of goodies—pizza, rum, Coke, ice—turn left and climb the stairs. And there they are. The names. Over five thousand of them stenciled in the walls rise to the top of the stairwell all around me. It is overpowering. All those men, all those lives, lost at sea since 1716. Their names, year after year, throughout Gloucester's history. A worse mortality rate than Pennsylvania mining towns. Almost as many as in some of the European towns wiped out by the Germans in the Holocaust. Men who fished. Men who died fishing. I am awed.

It isn't the few losses of my generation, though they are enough, nor even of my father's generation. It is the men of my grandfather's generation. In the 1800s they died by the thousands, sometimes a hundred or more in one night. This from a town with a population seldom above 25,000.

Real Gloucestermen moved by sail, not engine. What a display of audacity these guys put on.

I put down my package and walk to the last column. There they are, name after name, one to a line. There it is—the empty space on the wall where my name would have gone. I shudder and stare. I know the name that would have been the one above mine. Not well, but well enough. Small town.

My breathing is long and deep. I splash rum into a glass

and stand there drinking. I fire up a smoke. I roll up a piece of perfect pizza. I stare at the names towering over me as I eat and drink and smoke. Nothing ever tasted so good.

A hand taps my shoulder. It's the janitor. Drinking and smoking are not condoned in City Hall but I ignore him.

I don't know how long he is gone. I am too busy taking long, deep, glorious breaths of air as the shock and horror of the day gradually subside. I'm alive. I'm not on the wall. I can't believe it.

Two of Gloucester's Finest arrive. They stand looking at me intently. One approaches me and I turn to him. He looks into my face and then says quietly, "Close the door on your way out. It locks automatically."

I stare up at the walls and then I begin. I start with the first name, "1716, Jeremiah Allen..."

I read it out loud and continue to the next. All night I read the names. I eat and drink and smoke and breathe. And read name after name of those fishermen who did not come back.

I leave at first light. I close and lock the front door of City Hall. Dawn is breaking over the harbor.

I fished half a dozen years after The Afternoon of the Dolphins. On a Spring day I stood in my yard getting ready to load some gear in my truck to take to the boat. I was ready to start fishing again after a long winter. I had received a letter from the bank telling me my boat loan was paid off. Brilliant financial bastard that I am I thought I had two more years left to pay on it. And it was a lot. Unlike most lobstermen I had no wife or ex-wives, and no children to support. I was the only one I had to support financially. Just like that I had an extra two grand a month to screw with.

My back, like most lobstermen's, is a mess. My left shoulder is shot from a case of the bends a long time ago and my right isn't much better from playing baseball when I was too young and dumb to know I needed to rest more than two days between games when pitching both Varsity and Junior Varsity during high school.

Sometimes if I do anything physical first thing in the morning my right shoulder will pain me to tears, particularly after shoveling snow. I sit in my pickup truck and dream of a time long ago when I blazed base-balls by batter after batter. And just as quickly the pain ceases.

I had money saved, I could easily take a year off. What would I do? That's a tough one—nothing. Sit on the beach, read a lot. Whatever. Maybe try writing.

Fate is fickle. In rolls a Bronco and out pops a yuppie puke right on cue.

"Those traps can't make you much money in the yard, can they?" he said with his perfect dumb, stupid, yuppie puke look and annoying droning New York accent, and that goddamn pathetic New York freaking Yankee baseball cap. That no doubt made him a Yankees fan which was reason enough to screw with the guy.

"That's very funny. Would you like to tell me which of my shit-head friends set you up to get smacked by me or are you going to keep me guessing."

"N-n-no," he stammered. "I want to rent your traps."

"Yea? For what?"

"Well, uh, we're making a movie from the book 'The Perfect Storm' and we need a lot of traps for the set."

"Very funny." I took a step toward him and he whipped out a Warner Brothers picture I.D.

"I will rent them for three months. We pick them up and bring them back. Money up front, all in writing."

I nodded.

I took it as a sign from God. That's something I've learned. I rented him my traps. And I made a vow: from this day forward, from where the sun rises, I will lobster no more forever.

ACKNOWLEDGEMENTS

The Author wishes to thank the following for their contribution to making this book possible: Michael Moriarity, Christopher Benton, J.P. and Allison Williamson, David Grant, Harrison Golden, and Susan Thomas.

This book was edited, copy edited, and designed—excellently—by Kathleen Valentine.

Mark S. Williams
Gloucester, Massachusetts
May 2006

Printed in the United States
56011LVS00003B/280-306